Childhood Autism & Structural Therapy

Alan J. Ward, Ph.D

Childhood Autism & Structural Therapy

SELECTED PAPERS ON EARLY CHILDHOOD AUTISM

with contributions by
H. Allen Handford, M.D.
Virginia M. Leith

Nelson-Hall
nh Chicago

LIBRARY OF CONGRESS CATALOGING IN PUBLICATION DATA
Ward, Alan J   1936–
    Childhood autism & structural therapy.

    Includes index.
    1. Autism—Addresses, essays, lectures.   2. Child
psychotherapy—Addresses, essays, lectures.   I. Handford, H. Allen, joint author.   II. Leith, Virginia M.,
joint author.   III. Title.   IV. Title: Structural
therapy. [DNLM: 1. Autism, Early infantile—Collected
works.   2. Milieu therapy—Collected works.   WM203
W256c]
RJ506.A9W37   618.9′28′982   76-23171
ISBN   0-911012-56-7

Contents

Preface

The problem of *early infantile autism* as a diagnostic entity and treatment enigma was first brought to my attention in 1964. Prior to this time, my activity had been that of a clinical researcher who had specialized in trying to understand the development and improve the treatment of both adult and adolescent schizophrenic people. My research and clinical experience in this area led me to the opinion that such pioneers as Frieda Fromm-Reichman, John Rosen, Harold Searles, Sandor Ferecenzi, and Paul Federn were on the right track with their emphasis upon active intervention in their therapeutic approach to these seriously disturbed people. This approach was in opposition to the more common "blank screen" or passive approach to psychotherapy. Thus, my own therapeutic activity was directed towards developing and refining a therapeutic approach that combined the components of a selectively active, intrusive, and sensitive psychodynamically oriented approach.

A turning point in my experience as a clinical researcher was my exposure to the stimulating ideas and clinical skill of Dr. Austin DesLauriers, during my two-year U.S.P.H. Post Doctoral Fellowship at the Psychosomatic and Psychiatric Research Institute at Michael Reese Hospital in Chicago. Early infantile autism was revealed to me in all of its complexity and reminded me of maps from the Middle Ages that were often dominated by large blank areas labeled "Terra Incognita," or carrying such arcane warnings as "Here there be tygers!" As both a clinician and a researcher, I found it impossible to resist the lure of such a collection of unanswered questions as those represented by the concept of early infantile autism.

My clinical and research curiosity led me to explore the possibility of engaging in some long-term research in this fascinating area. As there seemed to be a fair number of anecdotal or individual out-patient case reports present in the literature, I decided to take some hypotheses from my work with schizophrenic patients, in combination with ideas stimulated by my exposure and interaction with Dr. DesLauriers and his staff, and use these as a basis for an intensive, longitudinal investigation of early infantile autism on an in-patient basis. I sought out a residential treatment setting to allow as much possible control of extraneous variables, at the same time hoping that such a setting would provide as "pure culture" a population of autistic children as possible.

In September of 1966, I was fortunate to become aware of a new state hospital, located in a suburb of Philadelphia, Pennsylvania, and devoted entirely to the care of emotionally disturbed children. Not only was the Eastern State School and Hospital responsive to my area of interest, but they were actively searching for someone to program for their large population of autistic children. This happy coincidence of interest and need led to my joining their staff; meeting my colleague and co-director of the Autistic Children's Treatment, Training, and Research Service (ACTTRS), Dr. H. Allen Handford, as well as Miss Virginia Leith, speech therapist; and meeting the many fine staff members who were most helpful and responsive to a young and enthusiastic researcher with strange ideas about how to work with these "hopeless" children.

My first meeting with Dr. Handford found him on his hands and knees repairing a wooden jungle gym in the middle of a dayroom. I found this both encouraging and emblematic of another person who shared my strong interest in truly working with these children; he was to prove readily responsive to setting up the total milieu of structural therapy that I had come to investigate.

It is not possible to list all the staff that enabled me to spend the next eight years researching and treating the children that are called autistic by mental health professionals. A total team was developed which included psychologists, psychiatrists, social workers, psychiatric nurses, volunteers, child care workers, a pediatrician, a neurologist, educators, speech therapists, and trainees of various disciplines. We all worked as a team, investigated many blind alleys, made many errors, had our own internal team conflicts, and at the same time learned a great deal that resulted in our seeing positive growth and development in children who had been given up as hopeless. This living area changed from a shunned area that staff had previously felt was a "punishment tour" assignment, to an exciting atmosphere that attracted many young enthusiastic people who were willing to work with the idea that perhaps there actually was hope for these children.

My position as Research and Treatment Director for this venture gave me the opportunity to record and attempt to analyze, with the help of many team members, many fascinating clinical phenomena. I had the privilege of training and collaborating with the team in the active individual and milieu treatment of these children; and as a team we had the opportunity to share our experiences with many laymen and professionals in the Philadelphia area, through presentations at local, regional, national, and international professional meetings, and through publications in the professional literature. Many team members were kept so busy by our exhausting endeavor (often requiring twenty-four-hour availability), that I was not able to get them to document their valuable experiences, insights, and clinical work. This is especially true of the vital areas of child care workers, psychiatric social workers, and psychiatric nurses. The child care workers and nurses were with the children twenty-four hours a day; while the social workers were flooded with individual, group, family, and couples counseling and casework, as well as with other agencies. Indeed, discharge time approached for these children who no one had ever thought would leave the hospital save for lifelong institutionalization.

Thus, this book is not a complete report of all the valuable work that was done by the treatment team of ACTTRS. Rather, it is an attempt to share some of the high points of the work that has been carried out over the last eight years. Many of the early papers contain thoughts about the parents of autistic children that were current at the time this research began, but which are no longer held by the team. I invite you to read these papers slowly, argue with them, search the succeeding papers to see if we attempted to answer your questions, and to await the completion of all of the papers prior to reaching your decision as to the details of our final position on this most complex area of childhood psychopathology. I hope the information proves helpful to all families, researchers, therapists, and others who are interested and concerned with the autistic child.

I hope also that your completion of this material will allow you to share a part of the sense of gratification that I feel after the completion of ten years of research and treatment in this very difficult yet fascinating area.

Acknowledgments

I am pleased to acknowledge permission obtained for the publication of the following from the journals in which they appeared:

"Early Infantile Autism: Diagnosis, Etiology, and Treatment." *Psychological Bulletin.* 73: 350–62.

"Structural Therapy: A Developmental Approach to the Treatment of Early Infantile Autism." *Schizophrenia.* 1: 243–48.

"An Application of Structural Therapy to the Residential Treatment of Early Infantile Autism." *Schizophrenia.* 2: 92–102.

"Childhood Psychopathology: A Natural Experiment in Etiology." *Journal of the American Academy of Child Psychiatry.* 13: 153–65.

"The Joint Treatment of an Autistic Child by Clinical Psychology and Speech Therapy." *International Journal of Child Psychotherapy.* 2: 451–71.

THE PROBLEM

Early Infantile Autism: Diagnosis, Etiology, and Treatment*

The syndrome of early infantile autism (EIA) has stimulated much clinical and research interest in the last two decades, but the nature of its diagnosis and treatment remains in dispute. The syndrome was first distinguished and labeled in the seminal article published by Kanner in 1943. The present paper is restricted to studies subsequent to Kanner's, which have specifically attempted to deal with either autistic children or the cause of early infantile autism.

Since Kanner's initial labeling of the syndrome, there has been a wide spectrum of opinion as to the necessary criteria for its diagnosis. This spectrum includes a range within the work of Kanner himself. The initial article (Kanner, 1943) listed 12 diagnostic features which he felt to be characteristic of early infantile autism:

1. The autistic child is always aloof (as opposed to a withdrawal from established contact).
2. The autistic child looks normal, alert, and expressive.
3. Motor coordination seems normal with quick, skillful movements.
4. The child avoids eye contact and lacks visual or auditory responses to others; thus, the child appears to be deaf and blind to people.
5. There is no physical reaching out from infancy.

*Reprinted with permission from *Psychological Bulletin* 73 (May 1970): 350–62.

6. The child does not initiate sounds or gestures (e.g., waving "bye-bye").
7. There is a failure to use speech for purposes of communication.
8. The child has a marked facility with objects (in contrast to his response to people and to language).
9. Psychometric performance indicates that cognitive potentialities are masked by the basic disorder. The appeal of form boards and pegboards yielded evidence of normal or superior performance.
10. There is an obsessive desire to maintain sameness.
11. Bedwetting, thumbsucking, nailbiting, and masturbation are rarely associated with early infantile autism.
12. The rate of occurrence is less than 1% in the general population.

However, the latest article by Kanner (Kanner & Eisenberg, 1956) on this topic indicated that the major diagnostic characteristics of early infantile autism now are:

1. The lack of object relations.
2. The maintenance of sameness via stereotypic behavior.

Kanner's extended research on this syndrome revealed that all except these two major characteristics could be found in other types of childhood psychopathology.

DIFFERENTIAL DIAGNOSIS

Many theorists have felt it important to distinguish between childhood schizophrenia and early infantile autism. The differential diagnosis between the two is especially difficult since both types of children have poor object relations, poor contact with reality, and poor body images. However, although Kanner (1943) included early infantile autism under the diagnostic rubric of childhood psychosis, it appears clear that an essential difference between early infantile autism and childhood schizophrenia is that the former may be viewed as a development arrest or fixation, and the latter as a problem due to profound regression. Kanner himself stated that the object-relatedness of the EIA child differs from that of the schizophrenic child, in that there is "from the start an extreme autistic aloneness . . . [Kanner, 1943, p. 242]," whereas the schizophrenic child displays a "withdrawal" from previously formed relationships.

Although both EIA children and schizophrenic children display poor reality contact, the schizophrenic child manifests this deficit via an extremely vivid and distorted fantasy life, delusions, hallucinations, etc., while the EIA child displays a narrow focus of attention upon stereotypic physical activity (rocking, twiddling, slapping, screwing, rolling, etc.) to the exclusion of the rest of the external world. Thus, although both categories of children do display poor reality contact, schizophrenia appears to result from distraction due to a complex internal fantasy life, while early infantile autism appears to stem from an extremely barren fantasy life, combined with a focus upon an extremely restricted aspect of the external environment. This restricted focus may be viewed as the foundation for Kanner's stereotypic maintenance of sameness, one of the two diagnostic characteristics of early infantile autism (Kanner & Eisenberg, 1956).

Moreover, the area of body image illustrates both a similarity and, at the same time, a difference between EIA children and schizophrenic children. Discussions of the problems of body image in schizophrenic children repeatedly emphasize the fact that these children experience the percepts of images of others as "blurring," "fusing," or "melting" (Despert, 1968; Mahler, 1968). The confusion experienced by these children has to do with *complete* images of themselves and others. On the other hand, EIA children have consistently been described as failing to experience either themselves or others as whole bodies. Instead, the EIA children have been noted for their lack of awareness of pain, for relating only to a part of another person's body (Kanner, 1943) if forced to relate, and, in general, for giving every evidence of failing to have achieved a complete body image for themselves or anyone else. Thus, it seems that the superficial similarity, in respect to body image, between childhood schizophrenia and early infantile autism, masks a qualitative difference, in that the former has a far better developed body image. The differential diagnosis between these two diagnostic categories is important for both theoretical and practical reasons in regard to treatment strategies and the use of therapeutic treatment time.

Rimland (1964) pointed out the following differences from childhood schizophrenia:

1. Presence of the syndrome from the beginning of life.
2. The lack of physical responsiveness.
3. Autistic aloneness.
4. Preservation of sameness.
5. Unusual capabilities in memory, music, and mechanical performance.
6. Good physical health and motor performance.

The first three of Rimland's differential diagnostic characteristics may be subsumed under the heading of lack of object relations, as all three focus upon the child's lack of awareness and responsiveness to human beings. His next two differential characteristics deal with the EIA child's tendency to order the world into repetitive patterns, while the last point emphasizes the fact that the child must be free of any neurological, organic, or developmental impairment. Thus, in summary, it may be seen that Rimland's list of diagnostic characteristics is very similar to that presented by Kanner (1943) and Kanner and Eisenberg (1956), but where Rimland required that the syndrome be present "from birth," Kanner's criteria require only that the "detachment" be present "no later than the first year of life [Kanner & Eisenberg, 1956, p. 557]."

The above point, time of onset of pathology, is the sole feature used by Reiser (1963) to distinguish "infantile psychosis" (EIA) from childhood schizophrenia, by means of the *difference* in the time of onset of pathology. He felt that the diagnostic category of childhood schizophrenia included both those children whose disordered behavior appeared after an initial period of normal development, and those cases where the pathology became evident past the age of 5 years. Thus, Reiser apparently agrees with Rimland's (1964) requirement that early infantile autism is a syndrome which must be present from birth, rather than allowing the year of "normal" development described by Kanner (1943).

Mahler's (1952, 1968) differentiation between autistic psychosis (early infantile autism) and symbiotic psychosis was based on the failure of the infantile ego, in autistic psychosis, to emotionally perceive the mother as the first representative of the outside world and reality. The failure of the EIA child to use the mother as the first representative of reality is seen as resulting in the distinctive features described by Mahler (1968):

1. An obsessive desire for the maintenance of sameness.
2. Lack of the *use* of speech for communication.
3. A stereotyped preoccupation with a few inanimate objects or action patterns toward which the EIA child shows the only signs of emotional attachment.

Thus, Mahler's (1952, 1968) differential diagnostic criteria may also be divided into the categories of (a) lack of object relations, and (b) the EIA child's tendency to order the world into repetitive patterns, in the same manner as the criteria of Kanner (1943), Kanner and Eisenberg (1956), and Rimland (1964).

Starr (1954) described early infantile autism as a deficiency disease characterized by an inadequate, unstimulating, and excessively diluted mother-infant relationship. This diagnostic criterion focuses basically upon the characteristic of lack of object relations.

Anthony (1958) accepted the existence of childhood psychosis as a "basis for the investigation of autistic behavior," and he delineated two basic patterns of development. The first pattern is characterized by an "early onset with little or no upheaval." The second pattern is seen as containing a,

> period of normal development, followed by an episode of great turbulence subsiding into a withdrawn, regressed, and rigid period, and finally a phase of partial recovery at a lower level of functioning [Anthony, 1958, p. 213].

These two patterns are labeled as primary and secondary autism. Subsequent investigation revealed that the cases of primary autism were children who were "grossly understimulated" for any number of reasons, while the cases of secondary autism were "grossly overstimulated" with a major involvement of "gross cerebral disease." Anthony identified primary autism with the syndrome of early infantile autism as described by Kanner (1943), and ascribed the psychosis to the failure of the child to develop a self-protective ego barrier, due to a combination of a constitutionally "thick" barrier and an insensitive and unresponsive mother. Anthony agreed with Mahler (1952), Starr (1954), and Norman (1954) as to the etiologic importance of an unstimulating mother-infant relationship. Anthony dealt with the conflict of time of onset of pathology as a diagnostic criterion by agreeing that the syndrome of early infantile autism is present from birth, but he also suggested that gross cerebral disease or "profound regression" after an initial period of normal development (childhood schizophrenia) could result in a behavioral picture that was at least superficially identical with that of EIA or primary autism. However, Anthony does appear to agree with the majority of theorists in viewing early infantile autism and childhood schizophrenia as being on a continuum of pathology, with EIA being at the lowest extremity.

The Barrier Hypothesis (Bergman & Escalona, 1949; Freud, 1955) played a great role in Anthony's conceptualizations about early infantile autism, and he used the concept to explain the development or lack of development of a protective ego barrier.

Lack of object relations, the major diagnostic characteristic that Anthony (1958) focuses upon, is felt to stem from the presence of a "constitutionally abnormal" stimulus barrier that makes it difficult for the child to respond to stimuli from the external world. These conceptualizations are based upon the Barrier Hypothesis (Freud, 1955) which stated that "interposed between every organism and its environment (internal and external) is a stimulus barrier [Freud, 1955, p. 58]." It is hypothesized that the primary or constitutional barrier must be supplemented by a maternal barrier, which is eventually replaced by an autonomous ego barrier modelled upon it, but more selective in its operation. Anthony used this Barrier Hypothesis to explain the development of object relations and reality contact in a manner very similar to Mahler's (1952, 1968) description of the movement from "normal Autism" to "normal symbiosis" via acknowledgment of the mother as the first representative of reality. Both the Barrier Hypothesis and Mahler's description of ego development emphasize the vital role of the mothering figure to the child's development of good object relations and reality contact.

Anthony's (1958) theoretical position vis-a-vis early infantile autism is very similar to that taken in a recent paper by Ornitz and Ritvo (1968). This later study views early infantile autism, "certain cases of childhood schizophrenia," the atypical child, symbiotic psychosis, and children with unusual sensitivities, as variants of a unitary disease. This unitary disease is felt to be delineated by subclusters of symptoms which are labeled as:

1. Disturbances of perception.
2. Disturbances of motor behavior.
3. Disturbances of relating.
4. Disturbances of language.
5. Disturbances of developmental rate and sequence.

The disturbances of perception are felt to be "fundamental" to the other aspects of the postulated disease, and to be manifested by early developmental failure to distinguish between self and environment, to imitate, and to modulate sensory input. Ornitz and Ritvo described early infantile autism as a "behavioral syndrome," and interpreted the symptomatology as being expressive of "underlying pathophysiology rather than being purposeful in the intrapsychic life of the child [Ornitz & Ritvo, 1968, p. 77]." Thus, these authors eschew any concept of a unitary syndrome of early infantile autism, and view EIA, certain cases of childhood schizophrenia, the atypical child, symbiotic psychosis, and children with unusual sensitivities, as the behavioral manifestations of various types of organic and developmental malfunctions that are caused by a breakdown of homeostatic regulation of sensory input. This breakdown results in a condition of perceptual inconstancy. Thus, Ornitz and Ritvo (1968) view all the above types of childhood psychopathology in the same way in which Anthony (1958) defined his concept of secondary autism.

Kanner's papers (Kanner, 1943; Kanner & Eisenberg, 1956; Kanner & Lesser, 1958) defined the syndrome of early infantile autism as a type of "psychotic illness heretofore undescribed" which should be differentiated from childhood schizophrenia "by virtue of detachment present no later than the first year of life, and from oligophrenia by the evidence of good intellectual potentialities [Kanner & Eisenberg, 1956, p. 557]."

Garcia and Sarvis (1964) "believe that autism is most usefully thought of as a reaction to an overwhelming inner or outer assault at a vulnerable developmental stage," and feel that a "basic paranoid attitude is the core of the autistic reaction [1964, p. 530]." Their study involved a series of "over 100 autistic children," but did not discover or propose any differential diagnostic characteristics. Instead, almost all types of "atypical" children seemed to be included under the category of EIA by these authors. No differences were seen among children whose etiology for their autistic behavior ranged from psychodynamic conflicts, to environmental conditions, to organic insult, to development and/or perceptual problems.

Green and Schecter (1957) used the term autistic to connote the inadequate interpersonal relatedness of the child which is felt to be demonstrated by the child's "lack of successful, meaningful, verbal communication, in spite of demonstrated linguistic and physiological capacity [Green & Schecter, 1957, p. 629]." This study involved blind children whose parents were described as interfering with and smothering their need for investigation and discovery of the outside world. This fact, in combination with the authors' description of the phenomenon of "shared autism" between parent and child, raises serious questions as to whether these children are similar to other children who have been placed under the rubric of EIA. Instead, the outstanding feature of this study seems to consist of a report on the deleterious effect of the "smothering symbiotic attitude of the mother" upon the development and functioning of perceptually handicapped children. These children appear to have been as "overwhelmed" as those reported in the previous study (Garcia & Sarvis, 1964), and more likely to meet the criteria for the category of secondary autism (Anthony, 1958) and/or symbiotic psychosis (Mahler, 1952, 1968), than the category of early infantile autism.

Polan and Spencer (1959) presented five case histories of early infantile autism and suggested that the

> primary symptom of Early Infantile Autism is a lack of integration pervading all the behavior of the organism and manifesting itself in the distorted language, in the lack of social responsiveness, and in the lack of adaptability to environmental change [Polan & Spencer, 1959, p. 198].

Thus, the diagnostic characteristics focused upon by Polan and Spencer may be subsumed under the headings of lack of object relations, and the attempt to maintain sameness in the environment, similar to those headings offered by earlier theorists (Kanner, 1943; Kanner & Eisenberg, 1956; Mahler, 1952, 1968; Ornitz & Ritvo, 1968), although nothing is stated in regard to the question of time of onset of pathology.

Gordon (1961) described the "typical autist" as a "good placid baby" who showed little interest in his new world, and showed a lack of response to the human voice. Gordon saw the autistic child as losing earlier acquired training and his speech as deteriorating to echolalia, or disappearing completely. Also, Gordon reported a compulsion to keep objects in the mouth, a preference for strong acrid, or bitter flavors, and an intense need for rhythmic motion. Thus, this diagnostic description and Anthony's (1958) definition of secondary autism both describe the loss of previously acquired capacities.

An overall evaluation of the literature indicates a great deal of confusion as to those features vital to a differential diagnosis. However, this evaluation does indicate that there are at least two groups of children who are often labeled as being cases of early infantile autism. The first group, described by Anthony (1958) as primary autism, is seen as being grossly understimulated, and as having a "thick" ego protective barrier. The features of a lack of environmental stimulation or a thick ego protective barrier are also seen as important differential diagnostic characteristics for this group by Mahler (1952), Norman (1949), and Starr (1954). This type of dichotomy is in opposition to the position taken by Garcia and Sarvis (1964) and Ornitz and Ritvo (1968), as both sets of authors appear to view EIA as a behavioral syndrome, regardless of the etiology of the autistic behavior.

The second group, which Anthony (1958) has labeled as secondary autism, has been characterized by a "thin" or defective ego barrier, gross overstimulation, a normal period of development followed by regression (Anthony, 1958; Gordon, 1961; Reiser, 1963), and major involvement of gross cerebral disease (Anthony, 1958).

The other studies referred to above (Green & Schecter, 1957; Kanner, 1943; Kanner & Eisenberg, 1956; Kanner & Lesser, 1958; Rimland, 1964) all seem to refer to cases of primary autism, whereas Polan and Spencer (1959) appear to be discussing cases of secondary autism which have a number of organic factors present. Thus, it appears quite likely that there is an overlap of behavioral symptomatology between the groups of primary autism and secondary autism. This hypothesis is supported by a recent study (Ward & Handford, 1968)[1] which indicated that many features used by theorists for differential diagnosis of EIA failed to discriminate among groups of EIA subjects, retarded subjects, brain-damaged subjects, and schizophrenic subjects. The only features found by Ward and Handford (1968, see note 1) which differentiated early infantile autism from the other diagnostic categories were:

1. Lack of organic dysfunction.
2. Maintenance of sameness via stereotypic behavior.

This current evaluation indicates that the syndrome of early infantile autism is actually made up of at least two basic diagnostic types of children. One group consists of children who are lacking in object relations, demand maintenance of sameness in the environment, are physically healthy, and in whom the syndrome of early infantile autism has been present from birth. Anthony (1958) reported a great deal of psychopathology present in the families of these psychogenic autistic children.

The second group of children may be labeled as organic autistic—children who have histories of difficult prenatal and perinatal development, followed by numerous types of developmental and perceptual problems. These children are often reported to have had a period of normal development followed by regression. The families of this group of children are reported to manifest much less psychopathology than the families of the psychogenic autistic children (Anthony, 1958).

This evaluation is congruent with the findings of Goldfarb (1961), who found that the diagnostic category of childhood schizophrenia actually contained a group of organic schizophrenics as well as psychogenic schizophrenics. The differences in the presence of organic factors, and the pathology of the families (Anthony, 1958) revealed in cases of early in-

1. Ward, A. J., & Handford, H. A. Early Infantile Autism: syndrome, symptom, or wastebasket? Paper presented at the meeting of the Midwest Psychological Association, Chicago, May 2, 1968.

fantile autism, seem parallel to those of Goldfarb for cases of childhood schizophrenia.

The consensus of the literature evaluated by this study suggests that the EIA child may be differentiated by the following criteria:

1. Lack of object relations from birth.
2. Lack of use of speech for communication.
3. Maintenance of sameness via stereotypic behavior.
4. Lack of neurologic or developmental dysfunction.

ETIOLOGY

Kanner (1943) ascribed the etiology of early infantile autism to an "emotional deprivation" resulting from the "refrigeration" of the parents. These parents were all from the academic and professional communities, and their family life was characterized by obsessive meticulousness and intellectualization. Kanner felt that the lack of emotional spontaneity and warmth of these parents played a large role in the development of early infantile autism, and referred to the syndrome of "hospitalism" as an example of the biological effects which could result from a "total psychobiological disorder" (Kanner & Lesser, 1958).

Garcia and Sarvis (1964) take the position that "autism is most usefully thought of as a reaction to an overwhelming inner or outer assault at a vulnerable developmental stage [p. 530]." Their study reports a number of etiological variables gathered from a study of over 100 autistic children. These variables were broken down into the following categories:

1. Family characteristics specifically promoting autism.
2. Family psychodynamics enabling autism.
3. Circumstances (situations over which family has no control, such as father being drafted).
4. Assaults on the child, including maximum developmental insult and over- or under-reactivity of the perceptual apparatus.

All of the above etiological variables have to do with the amount of stimulation given to the child and/or the condition of the perceptual apparatus for handling this stimulation.

Green and Schecter (1957) take more of a psychodynamic etiologic point of view than Garcia and Sarvis, but it is exactly the opposite position to that taken by Kanner (1943; Kanner & Eisenberg, 1956; Kanner & Lesser, 1958). Whereas Kanner views the etiology of early infantile autism as intimately determined by the "emotional coldness" of the parents, Green and Schecter speculate that the "child's need for investigation, communication, and contact with the outer world [is] frustrated by [the] smothering, symbiotic attitude of the mother [p. 642]." These authors go on to suggest that "autism is a severe and encrusted defense against unsatisfactory relatedness, and that this defense masquerades as the total psychosis [p. 644]." Thus, these authors postulate that early infantile autism stems from too much intrusion by the mother figure, rather than too little. In addition, Green and Schecter seem to feel that the condition of the perceptual apparatus plays a relatively minor role in the etiology of EIA. This position is highlighted when the authors state that "even in cases where there is a primary constitutional deficit," this merely acts as the "trigger for the vicious circle of anxious parental over-responsiveness [p. 645]."

An article by Polan and Spencer (1959) did not take an explicit position in regard to etiology, but did present a "Check List of Symptoms of Early Infantile Autism." This check list broke down symptoms into the following groups:

1. Language distortion.
2. Social withdrawal.
3. Activities' lack of integration.
4. Obsessiveness and nervousness.
5. Family characteristics.

Observation of the above symptom clusters indicates that they examine both the functioning of the perceptual apparatus, as well as psychogenic factors related to deviant styles of interpersonal relatedness. All cases reported in this study were slow to develop as far as the normal milestones of development—the infants talked late, and were essentially passive. The slow development of these subjects raises the question of whether their central nervous system suffered any damage. Also, the passivity of these subjects agrees with Gordon's (1961) description of the typical autist, but not with the picture given by Kanner of an active, intelligent child who refuses to acknowledge people.

A case history presented by Lewis and Van Ferney (1960) suggests the etiological importance of both emotional isolation and a temporary insult to the perceptual apparatus within the first six months of life.

Another case history presented by Loomis (1960) implicitly emphasized the etiological importance of both minimal brain damage and a home situation which does not demand that the child deal with reality.

The papers of both Anthony (1958) and Ornitz and Ritvo (1968) emphasize the etiological importance of a defective perceptual apparatus which often makes its presence known via a heightened awareness of sensory stimuli, heightened sensitivity, and irritability resulting in fearfulness and/or intolerance of various stimuli and experiences, or nonresponsiveness to various types of stimuli. This defective apparatus presents a distorted or unusual picture of reality to the child, and increases the difficulty of development of object relations and good reality contact. Anthony (1958) described this problem in his definition of the development of secondary autism, and Ornitz and Ritvo (1968) felt that problems of perceptual integration are the cause of the majority of cases of early infantile autism and other types of childhood psychosis. However, a basic difference in etiological conception is that Ornitz and Ritvo ascribe the development of EIA to an unknown "basic disease" which is manifested by a breakdown of homeostatic regulation of sensory input. This breakdown of homeostatic regulation is felt to result in a condition of perceptual inconstancy which then creates the behavioral manifestations labeled as early infantile autism.

Although Anthony (1958) acknowledged the importance of defective perceptual apparatus in the etiology of early infantile autism, he also attempted to understand the development and functioning of the autistic child from a psychoanalytic point of view. His investigation of early infantile autism revealed that the parents of primary cases of EIA have many more difficulties in interpersonal relationships than the parents of cases of secondary autism. The cases of secondary autism indicated the presence of organic factors, and the majority of this group were found within the working class, while the majority of the cases of primary autism came from the professional classes and were low in the presence of organic factors. Finally, the parents of the secondary cases of early infantile autism were found to be better adjusted, warmer, more accepting, and less critical than the parents of primary EIA cases. Investigation revealed that the latter had displayed a "lack of sensitivity and responsiveness over and above the 'thick skin' of the child [Anthony, 1958, p. 218]."

In summary, it seems that the following questions are relevant to the attainment of a greater understanding of the etiology of early infantile autism:

1. What is the role of defective perceptual apparatus in the development of early infantile autism?

2. Is there a particular level of or type of stimulation which promotes the development of early infantile autism?
3. Is there a particular type of parent or of parental behavior which promotes the development of early infantile autism?
4. Is some particular combination of the above factors necessary to the development of early infantile autism, or is it a unitary phenomenon that occurs on a random basis regardless of all these factors?

TREATMENT

Evaluation of a representative sample of the literature on the treatment of early infantile autism reveals a general feeling of futility. This feeling is exemplified by such statements as "psychotherapy in general seems to be of little avail [Kanner & Eisenberg, 1956, p. 560]," "treatment has little, if any effect on the progress of the patient [p. 560]," and "none of the varieties of psychiatric treatment employed had any noticeable effect [Polan & Spencer, 1959, p. 198]," and "no form of psychiatric treatment has been known to alter the course of autism [Rimland, 1964, p. 17]."

Some clinicians have attempted to modify the behavior of autistic children by the use of classical and instrumental conditioning techniques (Ferster & DeMyer, 1961; Gewirtz, 1961; Lovaas, Berberich, Perloff, & Schaeffer, 1966). Evaluation of the results obtained by these methods reveals a slow rate of symptom change.

This slow rate of symptom change is exemplified by Lovaas's report that 90,000 conditioning trials with oral reinforcement were needed to develop two words in the speech of an autistic child. Lovaas attempted to use learning theory principles to establish and modify the speech behavior of EIA children. Four steps were developed to establish imitation. First, the child was reinforced for all vocalization by a spoonful of food or by fondling. Inattentive, self-destructive, or noisy behavior which interfered with training was accompanied by a 5-second removal of all positive reinforcers, or by a mild punishment including a loud stern "No," or a slap on the hand. When the child reached a level of about one verbal response every 5 seconds, and was visually fixating on the adult's mouth more than 50% of the time, the second step of the program, involving the acquisition of a temporal discrimination by the child, was begun. The adult emitted a vocal response on an average of every tenth second, and the child was reinforced only if he vocalized within 6 seconds after the adult's vocalization. The third step was begun when the frequency of the child's vocal responses with the 6-second interval had tripled its initial level. The third step required that the child match the adult's verbalization before receiving reinforcement. The fourth step was a repetition of Step 3, but with a new sound which had not been presented before. This program was conducted several days a week, for periods of from 2 to 7 hours per day. Lovaas himself stated: "One of the disadvantages of the program, . . . lies in the large amount of time which is consumed in accomplishing its ends [Lovaas, 1966, p. 145]."

Bettelheim (1967) made the point that this type of behavioral change does not appear to have affected the basic psychosis. This assertion appears tenable, in light of the fact that the focus of this treatment approach is upon the aberrant behavior of the child, rather than upon the features of poor object relations, poor reality testing, or poor body image which are seen as being diagnostic of childhood psychosis. In addition, the lack of rigorous diagnostic criteria raises serious question as to the type of child involved in treatment by Lovaas. Although the behavioral modification approach does set firm limits and is very intrusive, little or no emphasis is put upon making this a pleasant experience for the child. This fact raises further questions as to the type of expectation produced in the child by such an approach. Finally, the lack of any outcome studies on those children involved in the behavioral modification programs leaves many unanswered questions as to the effectiveness of behavior modification as a treatment approach to early infantile autism.

The only approach which seems to have shown some partial effectiveness in promoting "human" responsiveness in cases of early infantile autism involves the presence of a warm, firm, spontaneous, and flexible human being. Several studies (Lewis & Van Ferney, 1960; Polan & Spencer, 1959; Schopler, 1962; Zaslow, 1967[2]) report significant behavioral change and increased responsiveness to people, following brief periods of play therapy. The EIA children were found to respond to "persistent verbal and physical stimulation [Lewis & Van Ferney, 1960, p. 11]." These authors felt that their success at attaining a change in the "autistic behavior" of a child diagnosed as displaying early infantile autism at 6

---

2. Zaslow, R. W. A psychogenic theory of the etiology of infantile autism and implications for treatment. Paper presented at the meeting of the California State Psychological Association, San Diego, California, January 1967.

months, at least raised the question of the importance of providing a "warm relationship in the treatment." However, the validity of this inference is thrown into some question by the early developmental history of the authors' subject. This child had casts placed on both feet at the age of 3 months, and contracted otitis media at the age of 6 months, which resulted in an 8-day hospitalization. These two factors suggest that the child would be most accurately labeled as either a case of secondary autism (Anthony, 1958), or the type of autistic child referred to by Garcia and Sarvis (1964) or Ornitz and Ritvo (1968) that arrives at autistic behavior via a number of external environmental and developmental problems rather than via internal predilection present from birth. The use of casts at such early age has been shown to have a deleterious effect upon normal ego development (Friedman, Handford, & Settlage, 1964),[3] and an inner ear infection at such an early age would seem likely to have a distorting effect upon the perception and integration of auditory stimuli. Thus, the most that can be asserted about this study is that one case of secondary autism has been shown to be responsive to a treatment regimen involving persistent verbal and physical stimulation.

Polan and Spencer (1959) reported that brief periods of play therapy with four cases of essentially secondary autism (Anthony, 1958) or organic autism produced positive therapeutic responses, although no basic changes in the autistic behavior were noted.

Schopler (1962) developed a treatment approach which relied, to a significant degree, upon bodily manipulations. The rationale for this focus of the treatment arose from Schopler's feeling that "some conception of body image is vital to an understanding of childhood schizophrenia or primary disorders of childhood [Schopler, 1962, p. 191]." He saw the body image of the child as being flexible and "subject to constant revision by various stimuli [Schopler, 1962, p. 193]." It was further hypothesized that the body image attained flexibility and adaptability from the stimulation gained through physical interaction with the environment. The preceding conceptions led Schopler to hypothesize that a lack of physical handling or stimulation caused a basic distortion in the development and integration of the body image. Data from a study

---

3. Friedman, C. J., Handford, H. A., & Settlage, C. Child psychologic development: The adverse effects of physical restraint. Paper presented at the meeting of the Regional American Psychiatric Association, Philadelphia, April 1964.

by Wapner (1961) [4] was used to suggest that bodily contact would "articulate and correct some distorted bodily feelings [Schopler, 1962, p.
197]." This theoretical point of view assumed that the EIA child's defense functioned on more of a sensory level; hence, the concentration
upon physical interaction.

Schopler (1962) used the above treatment approach with one EIA
child for 30 sessions on a 3 session per week frequency level. The therapist sought an "optimum adaptational situation [Schopler, 1962, p.
194]" between himself and the child, with an emphasis upon what was hap-
pening in the immediate present. More attention and analysis were given
to the reactions of the therapist than to those of the child. The therapist
initiated body contact by holding the child, and attempted to turn this
interaction into "a simple and pleasurable body game." Schopler observed that this procedure seemed to help the child define his own bodily
limits more clearly, and made it easier for him to distinguish himself
from objects in the environment. The outstanding features of this treatment approach are again the emphasis upon an "intensive" therapeutic
involvement, with the medium of therapeutic interaction being physical
rather than verbal. Schopler delineates the tentative nature of his findings, and suggests appropriate future research.

Zaslow (1967, see note 2) proposed a "rage reduction technique"
as a therapeutic model for body interaction in the treatment of autistic
children. This technique emphasized attainment of "tactile-kinesthetic
mastery" in a manner that replicated the mother-infant holding position.
The basic holding position of this technique was a horizontal one, in
which the head and legs of the EIA child were cradled in the arms of the
therapist. Whispering in the child's ear and playful kissing of the face
from ear to lips were used to stimulate smiling. The therapist attempted
to gain "dominance" over the child's bodily actions, and to redirect his
behavior towards more meaningful affective contact. This goal was due
to Zaslow's feeling that early infantile autism is the most extreme example of the use of motoric resistance to express rage, and that "rage barriers maintain the condition of infantile autism [Zaslow, 1967, p. 11;
see note 2]." Zaslow felt that the effect of these procedures made the
child more responsive to human control and socialization. The tactile-
kinesthetic modality is focused upon due to a feeling that it is the most
fundamental level in the development of basic trust.

4. Wapner, S. Body image and pathological states. Unpublished symposium,
   Veterans' Administration Hospital, Houston, Texas, 1961.

Two features are outstanding about this treatment approach; the most outstanding is the introduction of an intensive physical interaction between the therapist and the EIA child. This position is similar to that of Schopler (1962), and is in marked contrast to the negative position taken by Freud (1954) on this type of intensive therapeutic involvement. The second feature of this study is the emphasis placed upon dominance and "control" of the EIA child. It would seem that this emphasis would lead to a direct power struggle between the therapist and child, unless some provision were made for a gamelike approach such as the one suggested by Schopler (1962). Also, one wonders how attractive relating to people would appear to the EIA child after constant involvement in a physical dominance struggle.

Garcia and Sarvis (1964) felt that the "necessary attitude on the part of the therapist must be one of open-mindedness," and indicated that the therapist "should always remain the representative of reality [Garcia & Sarvis, 1964, p. 534]." Loomis (1960) talked of the "need to be awfully patient, ingenious and stable," and at the same time to "introduce tremendous flexibility and adaptability into our relationships with them [Loomis, 1960, p. 48]." Thus, both Garcia and Sarvis (1964) and Loomis (1960) attempted to deal with the treatment problem of the EIA child by offering stability and freedom at the same time. This is in contradistinction to the freedom of the psychoanalytic approach or the rigid "stability" of the treatment approaches proposed by Lovaas (1966) and Zaslow (1967, see note 2).

Polan and Spencer (1959) emphasized the importance of a "warm, human relationship," and of trying to "help these children come alive," by being "real for them," while O'Gorman (1967) talked of the importance of "stimulation" and an emphasis on teaching the patient "how to live." Again, both of these studies emphasized the two-part treatment approach involving a warm stimulating human relationship in combination with a reality-based structure of demand and expectation with it.

Waal (1955) described a treatment approach with one case that began by emphasizing "acceptance, empathy, anxiety-reducing fondling, and soothing [Waal, 1955, p. 443]." This approach then progressed to body stimulation and manipulation, which included "stroking and hugging" the patient as well as "really massaging this [his] stiff parts [Waal, 1955, p. 443]." The patient showed marked progress during this treatment. The author emphasized that the bodily stimulation and manipulation must be done "provokingly" in combination with interpretations as to the child's feelings. "Uninvolved objectivity and acceptance" and "truthfulness and warmth coupled with detachment" are labeled as requirements for the therapists. Waal felt that this technique resulted in a "bodily maturation and a break in the autistic withdrawal," but emphasized the importance of the "working through of the fantasy production and symbolic material on a verbalized level [Waal, 1955, p. 444]." Thus, this treatment approach emphasized an increased level of stimulation provided by a warm, firm person who helped the child to gain an understanding and control of the new feelings which had been aroused.

Bettelheim (1967) claimed to have obtained good results from intensive, analytically oriented psychotherapy with autistic children. A "good outcome" of treatment of early infantile autism of 42% was reported, in contrast to the good outcome of 5% reported by Eisenberg (1956). In addition, Bettelheim reported a "poor outcome" of only 20%, as compared to the poor outcome of 73% reported by Eisenberg. However, Bettelheim did agree on the prognostic significance of the child's "willingness to speak" before the age of 5, although he reported a "meaningful improvement" in 57% of nonspeaking children, as compared to 3% by Eisenberg (1956). In regard to the question of the treatability of early infantile autism, the meaningfulness of Bettelheim's findings is very unclear, due to his failure to make a clear distinction among the diagnostic categories of early infantile autism, symbiotic psychosis, and childhood schizophrenia. Bettelheim made a passing acknowledgment of the categories of primary autism and secondary autism, but did not deal with them in a definite manner in the setting up of treatment strategies. Thus, it may be said that Bettelheim uses the term autistic in a very broad and undifferentiated manner.

Although it is clear that Bettelheim's outcome figures do relate to the treatment of severely ego-disturbed children, it appears doubtful that they can be specifically applied to the syndrome of early infantile autism. However, Bettelheim's treatment approach concurs with those which emphasize the importance of warm human contact, but differs in its emphasis upon a complete freedom of behavior of the child. All of the previous treatment approaches mentioned have emphasized the importance of setting limits or reality boundaries, in addition to requiring the involvement of a warm, spontaneous human being.

Thus, this restricted perusal of the literature has failed to reveal any report of a well-controlled treatment program for the syndrome of early infantile autism that has attempted to deal with the problems of diagnosis, etiology, and treatment. All of the studies examined are open to severe question as to their rigor and clarity in one of these three areas.

As O'Gorman (1967) pointed out, one major reason that the treatment of early infantile autism has proved so difficult is the lack of clarity as to its etiology. Also, O'Gorman (1967) agreed with many other theorists when he labeled "early diagnosis and early treatment ... prime concerns [p. 113]."

Thus, the available repertoire of therapeutic techniques found to be capable of attaining even limited progress with cases of early infantile autism is very small. However, the majority of cases which have reported some therapeutic progress have involved the therapist's use of a very active, intrusive, and pleasant approach, focusing upon increased physical stimulation in a pleasant but structured setting. Only the approaches described by Lovaas (1966a, 1966b) and Bettelheim (1967) disagree with this pattern.

DISCUSSION

The preceding review of the literature has suggested the following thoughts as to the etiology and function of the syndrome of early infantile autism. It seems that psychogenic early infantile autism may be viewed as more a deviant style of ego development that has resulted in the formation of what may be labeled as a behavioral ego, rather than a fragmentary body ego or body image. It is postulated that the behavioral ego is made up of those repetitive, stereotypic activities that the EIA child uses to control his environment. This level of functioning includes such activities as repetitive self-punitive behavior, the taking apart or assembling of mechanical toys or fixtures, the repetition of phrases or television commercials—anything which involves the use of the same set of complex behaviors to avoid the acknowledgment of outer reality.

It seems as if something has caused the EIA child to stop at the point of having experienced only a very small portion of the world around him. Within this small area of experience, the EIA child carries on the same activities of exploration, stimulation, and relaxation that occur in the infinitely larger area of experience available to the healthier child. These behaviors should be labeled as a type of ego function, because they seem to be the means by which the child achieves his desires, experiences, and stimulation. The EIA child guards these behaviors with the same care that the normal child guards his body. Interruption of these behavior sequences is responded to with a great deal of negative and fearful affect, whereas physical injury often elicits no observable affective response, and, many times, is completely ignored.

The behavioral ego is viewed as being representative of a successful adaptive position. This theoretical position is similar to one taken in a recent paper (Ruttenberg, 1968, p. 7) [5] in regard to the function of EIA, which described it as "the lowest level that allows for long-term adaptation and survival [Ruttenberg, 1968, p. 7; see note 5]." The EIA child has usually been quite successful in controlling his parents, attaining his desires without speaking, and in being the sole source of novelty and variation in his environment. He has succeeded in reducing reality to dimensions which he can comfortably handle.

Examination of the question of the etiology of early infantile autism leads to the hypothesis of a lack of novelty, and a lack of patterned stimulation in the environment in the child's early developmental history. The lack of an experience of a varied and stimulating patterned environment may have one of at least three basic causes. First, the child may have an abnormally high stimulus barrier due to some organic problem. Thus, he would not be aware of many stimuli in his environment, and would be thrown completely upon his own resources.

Second, the child may be hypersensitive to external stimuli due to some organic problem (Bergman & Escalona, 1949), and may attempt to withdraw from the painful impingement of external stimuli upon his faulty stimulus barrier. This reaction can result in a withdrawal from the world, which again leaves the child dependent upon his own scanty integrative resources.

Finally, the home environment may be so nonnurturent, unstimulating, and unpatterned (unpredictable) that the child has no recourse but to develop whatever patterns of behaviors he can organize by himself. This last category appears to contain those children for whom Kanner (1943) originally labeled the syndrome of early infantile autism. The lack of stimulation may result from either the physical absence or the psychological absence of a mothering figure.

This review suggests that early infantile autism is a syndrome that develops due to a lack of varying, novel, patterned stimulation in the child's early developmental history. Early infantile autism is viewed as

5. Ruttenberg, B. A. A classification of the childhood psychoses. Paper presented at the meeting of the American Association of Psychiatric Clinics for Children, New York, November 8, 1968.

a deviant style of ego development that has resulted in the formation of a behavioral ego. The behavioral ego is seen as being made up of those repetitive, stereotyped activities that the EIA child uses to maintain sameness in the environment. The intention and capacity to maintain sameness in the environment seems to be the major feature that delineates early infantile autism from childhood schizophrenia (Ward & Handford, 1968; see note 1).

Thus, the schizophrenic child is viewed as having no consistent, organized way of handling the world, due to his fragmentary body ego, while the EIA child has found a very consistent way of handling the world via his behavioral ego. It is hypothesized that the repetitive, stereotypic activities of the EIA child provide the novelty and variation in patterned stimulation which the child has been unable to gain from the world around him. The EIA child is seen as being totally deficient in body ego, with all the cathexis or emotional investment being directed towards the behavioral ego. The EIA child guards his stereotypic behavior in the same manner as healthier children guard their physical bodies.

REFERENCES

ANTHONY, E. J. An experimental approach to the psychopathology of childhood. *British Journal of Medical Psychology*, 1958, 31: 211–223.

BERGMAN, P. & ESCALONA, S. K. Unusual sensitivities in very young children. *Psychoanalytic study of the child*. New York: International University Press, 1949.

BETTELHEIM, B. *The empty fortress*. New York: Free Press, 1967.

DESPERT, J. L. *Schizophrenia in children*. New York: Robert Brunner Inc., 1968.

EISENBERG, L. The autistic child in adolescence. *American Journal of Psychiatry*, 1956, 112: 607–612.

FERSTER, C. B. & DEMYER, M. K. The development of performances in autistic children in an automatically controlled environment. *Journal of Chronic Diseases*, 1961, 13: 312–345.

FREUD, A. The widening scope of indication for psychoanalysis. *Journal of the American Psychoanalytic Association*, 1954, 2: 607–620.

FREUD, S. Beyond the pleasure principle. In J. Strachey (Ed.), *The standard edition of the complete psychological works of Sigmund Freud*. Vol. 18. London: Hogarth, 1955. (Originally published 1920.)

GARCIA, B. & SARVIS, M. A. Evaluation and treatment planning for autistic children. *Archives of General Psychiatry*, 1964, 10, 530–541.

GEWIRTZ, J. L. A learning analysis of the effects of normal stimulation, privation, and deprivation on the acquisition of social motivation and attachment. In B. M. Foss (Ed.), *Determinants of infant behavior.* New York: Wiley, 1961.

GOLDFARB, W. *Childhood schizophrenia.* Cambridge: Harvard University Press, 1961.

GORDON, F. F. The world of the autistic child. *Virginia Medical Monthly,* 1961, 88, 469–471.

GREEN, M. R. & SCHECTER, D. E. Autism and symbiotic disorders in three blind children. *Psychiatric Quarterly,* 1957, 31, 628–646.

KANNER, L. Autistic disturbances of affective contact. *Nervous Child,* 1943, 2, 217–240.

KANNER, L. & EISENBERG, L. Early infantile autism: childhood schizophrenia symposium. *American Journal of Orthopsychiatry,* 1956, 26: 556–564.

KANNER, L. & LESSER, L. Early infantile autism. *Pediatric Clinics of North America,* 1958, 5 (3): 711–730.

LEWIS, R. & VAN FERNEY, S. Early recognition of infantile autism. *Journal of Pediatrics,* 1960, 56: 510–512.

LOOMIS, E. A. Autistic and symbiotic syndromes in children. *Monograph of the Society for Research on Child Development,* 1960, 25 (3): 39–48.

LOVAAS, O. I. A program for the establishment of speech in psychotic children. In J. K. Wing (Ed.), *Early childhood autism.* London: Pergamon Press, 1966. (a)

LOVAAS, O. I., BERBRICH, J. P., PERLOFF, B. F. & SCHAEFFER, B. Acquisition of imitative speech by schizophrenic children. *Science,* 1966, 151: 705–707. (b)

MAHLER, M. S. On child psychosis and schizophrenia: autistic and symbiotic infantile psychoses. *Psychoanalytic study of the child.* New York: International University Press, 1952, 7: 286–305.

MAHLER, M. S. *On human symbiosis and the vicissitudes of individuation.* Vol. 1. New York: International University Press, 1968.

NORMAN, E. Reality relationships of schizophrenic children. *British Journal of Medical Psychology,* 1954, 27: 126–141.

O'GORMAN, G. *The nature of childhood autism.* London: Butterworth, 1967.

ORNITZ, E. M. & RITVO, E. R. Neurophysiologic mechanisms underlying perceptual inconstancy in autistic and schizophrenic children. *Archives of General Psychiatry,* 1968, 19: 22–26.

POLAN, C. C. & SPENCER, B. L. Check list of symptoms of autism in early life. *West Virginia Medical Journal,* 1959, 55: 198–204.

REISER, D. Psychoses of infancy and early childhood as manifested by children with atypical development. *New England Journal of Medicine,* 1963, pp. 790–798 (Part I); pp. 844–850 (Part II).

RIMLAND, B. *Infantile autism.* New York: Appleton, 1964.

SCHOPLER, E. The development of body image and symbol formation through bodily contact with an autistic child. *Journal of Child Psychology and Psychiatry,* 1962, 3: 191–202.

STARR, P. H. Psychoses in children: their origin and structure. *Psychoanalytic Quarterly*, 1954, 23: 544–565.

WAAL, N. A. A special technique of psychotherapy with an autistic child. In G. Caplan (Ed.), *Emotional problems of early childhood*. New York: Basic Books, 1955.

2

Early Infantile Autism: Syndrome, Symptom, or Wastebasket?

Alan J. Ward and
H. Allen Handford

The diagnostic classification of early infantile autism (EIA) has generated much research and treatment interest in the last two decades. Since the syndrome was originally labelled (Kanner 1943), there has been a wide spectrum of opinion as to the necessary criteria for this diagnosis.

Some theorists have felt it important to distinguish between EIA and childhood schizophrenia. Rimland (1964) points to such differences from childhood schizophrenia as: (1) the syndrome being present from the beginning of life (2) the lack of physical responsiveness (3) autistic aloneness (4) preservation of sameness (5) good physical health and motor performance (6) unusual capabilities in regards to memory, music, and mechanical performance. Reiser (1963) distinguishes "infantile psychosis" from childhood schizophrenia by the time of onset, and feels the latter term includes both those children whose disordered behavior appeared after an initial period of normal development and those where pathology becomes evident past the age of five years. Kessler (1966) feels that autism is relative rather than absolute, while Goldfarb (1961) considers childhood schizophrenia as a symptomatic classification which is subdivided according to presenting symptoms and etiology. Bender (1954) has included EIA under her classification of the pseudo-defective child; while Mahler (1954), Starr (1954), and Norman (1954) all agree on the characteristics of affective disturbance, lack of affective response, and an unstimulating and excessively diluted mother-infant relationship as being necessary for such a diagnosis. Thus, the spectrum of diagnostic criteria ranges from the very general one of affective disturbance and lack of affective response, to the twelve specific criteria listed by Kanner (1943):

1. Autistic child always aloof as opposed to a withdrawal from established contact
2. Autistic child looks normal, alert, and expressive
3. Motor coordination seems normal with quick, skillful movements
4. Avoidance of eye contact and lack of visual or auditory response to others
5. No physical reaching out from infancy
6. No imitation of gestures or sounds
7. Failure to use speech for purposes of communication
8. Marked facility with objects in contrast to response to people and language
9. Psychometric performance yielded evidence of normal or superior intelligence
10. Obsessive desire to maintain sameness
11. Rarely find bedwetting, thumbsucking, nailbiting, or masturbation
12. Rate of occurrence of less than 1% in the general population.

The wide range of diagnostic criteria listed above indicate a need for clarification in the diagnosis of EIA. It was felt that one manner of clarifying this diagnostic problem would be to intensively examine those children who had already been labelled as "autistic." Examination of a later paper by Kanner and Lesser (1958) revealed that Kanner's diagnostic criteria had been reduced in number from twelve features to two features: (1) the maintenance of sameness by "elaborately conceived rituals" and (2) autistic aloneness. It was decided that the research definition of EIA would include the following criteria:

1. Lack of object relations (autistic aloneness)
2. Maintenance of sameness via stereotypic behavior (elaborately conceived rituals)
3. The lack of the *use* of speech for communication
4. No major neurological dysfunction.

The criterion of "lack of use of speech for communication" was retained from Kanner's original list (1943) due to a feeling that it reflected an important aspect of the EIA subject's lack of object relations and reality contact. The final criterion was included as a precaution against the inclusion of subjects whose primary problem was one of mental retardation or brain damage.

METHODOLOGY

Subjects:

The subjects were fifteen male children who ranged in age from 6-1 to 13-8, and five female children who ranged in age from 10-6 to 13-8. All subjects were in residential treatment on a unit devoted to the treatment of EIA, in a hospital for the treatment of emotionally disturbed children. All were accepted as "autistic" children at the time of evaluation, in spite of the fact that they had been involved in various types of therapy for periods of time ranging from three months to five years (table 1).

TABLE 1. Subject Data

	MALE (15 children)	FEMALE (5 children)
Age range	6.1-13.6 years	10.5-13.6 years
Age mean	9.9 years	11.9 years
Mean length of treatment	12.8 months	28.6 months

Apparatus

The following criteria were sought in both clinical evaluation and examination of history:

1. Affective disturbance
2. Lack of affective response
3. Lack of object relations
4. Unstimulating mother-infant relationship
5. Lack of a period of normal development
6. The use of speech for communication
7. Maintenance of sameness via stereotypic behavior
8. No organic dysfunction.

Procedure

The birth records and developmental histories of all subjects were obtained and subjected to careful study by psychologists, psychiatrists, pediatricians, social workers, speech therapists, neurologists, and nursing personnel.

Cases which presented thorny diagnostic problems were given the appropriate diagnostic tests or given trial periods of individual therapy for periods of time ranging up to nine months.

A count was made by the experimenters (Ward & Handford) of the occurrence, in each case, of each of the eight criteria listed above. A final diagnosis was arrived at in each case, which incorporated data from the previous history, current diagnostic tests, and trial periods in therapy.

RESULTS

The findings of this study emphasize the importance of rigorous diagnostic procedures to the attainment of an adequate understanding and treatment of severe childhood psychopathology. These findings support Kanner's initial impression that EIA is a very rare phenomenon, and show that it is often confused with many more prosaic types of childhood disorders.

Diagnostic reevaluation indicated that a wide variety of childhood disorders are mistakenly viewed as EIA, and referred for treatment on this basis. This unit reserved for the treatment of EIA was found to contain not only cases of EIA (4), but also cases whose final diagnoses included:

a. Primary retardation, 7 cases
b. Secondary retardation, 2 cases
c. Developmental retardation associated with diffuse brain damage, 2 cases
d. Childhood schizophrenia, 5 cases (see table 2).

In addition, six of the eight behavioral characteristics used by many theorists for a differential diagnosis of EIA were found to be nondiscriminating, among the five diagnostic categories identified on the unit. All the subjects were found to display the characteristic of affective disturbance, while subjects from all five diagnostic categories were found to display the diagnostic characteristics of "lack of affective response," "lack of object relationships," "no use of speech for communication," and of having come from an "unstimulating mother-infant relationship" (see table 2). "Lack of a period of normal development" occurred much less frequently, but was also found to be reported in the histories of cases of EIA, secondary retardation, and childhood schizophrenia.

Only two diagnostic characteristics were found to be restricted in their occurrence among five diagnostic categories of patients on the unit. The four subjects diagnosed as cases of EIA and one case of developmental retardation were the only ones which were felt to show "no organic dysfunction." The least frequent and most exclusive diagnostic characteristic was "maintenance of sameness via stereotypic behavior," found only in those cases which had been previously diagnosed as cases of EIA (see table 2). Thus, the cases of EIA were distinguished from the other diagnostic categories by (1) their freedom from organic involvement and (2) "maintenance of sameness via stereotypic behavior." The EIA cases met all the criteria used by various theorists for diagnosis, and were found to display thirty of a possible thirty-two of these criteria (see table 2).

CONCLUSIONS AND IMPLICATIONS

These results support the view of EIA as a distinct diagnostic classification. However, this study clearly indicates the manner in which a lack of careful diagnostic evaluation can result in a ruinous dilution of the usefulness of the category of EIA. It is now obvious that many of the characteristics used for differential diagnosis of EIA tap levels of functioning that have varied etiologies. Thus, it is possible for a child to display a "lack of affective response" due to a failure to develop intellectually (primary retardation), varying types of central nervous system trauma leading to a regression to this level (secondary retardation), preoccupation with fantasy life (childhood schizophrenia), or development in a nonstimulating environment that does not draw him into contact with the world (EIA).

The above finding suggests how a brain-damaged or retarded child may display many of the characteristic incapacities usually attributed solely to cases of EIA. The EIA cases met all the criteria suggested by other theorists, but were the only subjects who met the research criterion for EIA. It was the *capacity* labelled as "maintenance of sameness via stereotypic behavior" which differentiated the cases of EIA, rather than an incapacity. Thus, whereas the subjects in the other diagnostic categories were distinguished by a deficit or loss in specific areas of functioning, the EIA subjects manifested the capacity to create a particular kind of behavior and to maintain it consistently over a period of time. The findings of this study support the view that EIA is a rare phenomenon, often

TABLE 2. Evaluation of Diagnostic Characteristics in Population of Twenty "Autistic" Children

Subject Number	Initial Diagnosis	Sex	Length of Treatment (in months)	Age (in years and months)	Criteria Sought								Final Diagnosis
					Affective Disturbance	Lack of Affective Response	Lack of Object Relations	Unstimulating Mother-Infant Relationship	No Period of Normal Development	No Speech Communication	No Organic Dysfunction	Maintenance of Sameness via Stereotypic Behavior	
1	autism	m	14	10-5	X	X	X	X	X	X	X	X	EIA
2	autism	m	12	7-8	X								childhood schizophrenia
3	autism	m	8	6-8	X	X	X	X	X	X	X		EIA
4	autism	m	14	8-2	X	X	X	X		X	X		developmental retardation/ diffuse brain damage
5	autism	m	8	12-7	X	X		X					childhood schizophrenia
6	autism	m	12	8-11	X					X			primary retardation
7	autism	f	60	13-8	X				X	X			primary retardation
8	autism	m	9	9-8	X	X	X	X		X	X	X	EIA
9	autism	m	3	6-1	X	X	X	X		X	X	X	EIA
10	autism	m	3	8-4	X	X		X		X			developmental retardation/ diffuse brain damage
11	autism	f	29	10-6	X	X	X	X		X			primary retardation
12	autism	f	10	12-0	X	X		X		X			childhood schizophrenia
13	autism	m	6	12-3	X	X	X			X			primary retardation
14	autism	f	5	11-8	X	X		X		X			primary retardation
15	autism	m	24	15-3	X	X		X					primary retardation
16	autism	m	9	6-11	X	X	X		X	X			secondary retardation
17	autism	m	26	12-6	X	X	X			X			secondary retardation
18	autism	m	15	11-10	X			X	X	X			childhood schizophrenia
19	autism	f	39	11-11	X					X			childhood schizophrenia
20	autism	m	29	12-4	X		X	X		X			primary retardation
					20	15	10	13	5	17	5	3	

easily confused with other childhood disorders, but distinguished from them by the fact that the child takes a particular, consistent, complex adaptive position toward the world, which excludes people. Thus, the syndrome of EIA appears to be a type of deviant, organized ego development, rather than a collection of unrelated peculiar handicaps. However, further understanding of this syndrome demands more attempts at understanding its adaptive function. Otherwise, a continuation of the diagnostic approach of finding groups of peculiar symptoms cannot fail to result in EIA becoming a wastebasket category for all manner of difficult diagnostic cases.

REFERENCES

BENDER, LAURETTA. *A dynamic psychopathology of childhood.* Springfield: C. C. Thomas, 1954.

GOLDFARB, W. *Childhood Schizophrenia.* Cambridge, Mass.: Harvard University Press, 1961.

KANNER, L. Autistic disturbances of affective contact. *Nervous Child,* 1943, 2: 217–240.

KANNER, L. and LESSER, L. Early infantile autism. *Pediatric Clinics of North America,* 1958, 5 (3) : 711–730.

KESSLER, JANE. *Psychopathology of childhood.* Englewood Cliffs, N.J.: Prentice-Hall, 1966.

MAHLER, MARGARET. Childhood schizophrenia. *American Journal of Orthopsychiatry,* 1954, 24: 523–526.

NORMAN, E. Reality relationships of schizophrenic children. *British Journal of Medical Psychology,* 1954, 27: 126–141.

REISER, D. Psychosis of infancy and early childhood, as manifested by children with atypical development. *New England Journal of Medicine,* 1963, pp. 790–798, 844–850.

RIMLAND, B. *Infantile autism.* New York: Appleton, 1964.

STARR, P. H. Psychoses in children: Their origin and structure. *Psychoanalytic Quarterly,* 1954, 23: 544–565.

3

An Application of Structural Therapy to the Residential Treatment of Early Infantile Autism*

The purpose of this paper is to report on the development and application of a treatment approach to the syndrome of early infantile autism (EIA). This treatment approach is based upon many of the conceptions involved in DesLauriers'[1] structural therapy, but the author assumes sole responsibility for all modifications to this approach and for the etiological conceptualizations of early infantile autism.

STRUCTURAL THERAPY: AN OVERVIEW

Structural therapy is comprised of a collection of active, intrusive techniques which have been used at various times by many different therapeutic approaches. It was originated as a specific treatment approach by DesLauriers[1] and this term was used to describe his treatment of schizophrenic adolescents at Kansas State Hospital, in association with the Menninger Foundation.

This treatment approach is based upon a diagnostic conception of the schizophrenic child as having an inadequacy and incapacity in dealing with reality; and an incapacity in dealing with people. This inadequacy and incapacity is seen as being of a structural nature. That is,

*Reprinted with permission from *Schizophrenia* 2 (1970) : 92–102.

the schizophrenic child is seen as being deficient in the development of ego and superego processes to channel his *id* impulses.

DesLauriers[1,2] describes the schizophrenic child as having very few ego mechanisms available for the purpose of structuring or realizing his impulses, and as a result he is very unskilled and inefficient in gaining his desired ends. Thus, the schizophrenic child is described as an incompetent, incomplete human being, who has only fragmented bits of behavior available to him. This behavior is not well integrated and results in what is labelled clinically as "bizarre" and "inappropriate" behavior.

Structural therapy draws its name from both the view of the schizophrenic child as having a structural deficit in ego development, as well as the therapeutic focus of an attempt to stimulate the development of these deficient ego processes.

DesLauriers[1] suggests that this deficiency of ego processes in schizophrenic children is due to their poor awareness of their body image and their lack of differentiation of themselves from the surrounding environment. These children are described as being very "fluid," and as having a very poor body image. Examples of this fluidity of ego boundaries are often seen during diagnostic evaluations. If such a child is asked to draw something, he will often not only draw on the paper, but on the table, himself and sometimes even on the examiner.

DesLauriers[1] indicated that the level of ego development of the schizophrenic child rendered inappropriate any attempts of a therapist to deal with him on solely an interpretive and/or verbal interactional level. It was suggested that these more sophisticated levels of ego functioning be largely ignored, in favor of a focus upon an earlier level of development which has been labelled variously as "body ego" (Freud[3]), "corporal feeling" (Federn[4]) and "body schemata" (Schilder[5]). These and other descriptions of this level of development define it as the first experience of the ego. This first experience of reality arises from an establishment of the actuality of body limits and boundaries. Body ego is what people mean when they refer to the child's or adult's awareness of his own body limits, of its capabilities and of how it functions in relation to the world around him.

Since the schizophrenic child's deficiency has been described as a deficiency in body ego, the structural therapist attempts to promote its development. These therapeutic efforts all emphasize the provision of an increased level of stimulation to the body of the patient. The therapist uses both verbal and physical stratagems to help the patient cathect his bodily limits. These stratagems include talking to the patient about himself—the color of his hair; his eyes; the attractiveness of his physical person; the number of hands, fingers, arms and legs. Also included are such stratagems as tickling of sensitive areas, soothing, stroking, hugging or swinging the child to give him a motoric kinesthetic experience of his whole body. Anything which the therapist can think of in a spontaneous, creative, game-like atmosphere which will aid the child in completing the differentiation of himself from the environment as a distinct and separate human being, is something which would fall under the rubric of the treatment approach labelled as structural therapy. Thus, the schizophrenic child is urged and encouraged to become more spontaneous, focus more upon his body boundaries rather than internal fantasies, and tie together the fragmented bits of body ego and higher ego processes which are available to him.

Structural therapy has shown some limited effectiveness, on a research basis, with verbal schizophrenic adolescents (DesLauriers[1,2]). However, there is no available report of the effectiveness of this treatment approach with latency age or pre-school children who have been diagnosed as being either cases of childhood schizophrenia or early infantile autism.

EARLY INFANTILE AUTISM

Numerous etiologic concepts have been put forth for the syndrome of early infantile autism. Thus, early infantile autism has been labelled as a "total psychobiological disorder" stemming from an "emotional deprivation" due to the "refrigeration" of the parents (Kanner[6,7]), a "reaction to an overwhelming inner or outer assault at a vulnerable developmental stage" (Garcia and Sarvis[8]), "the smothering, symbiotic attitude of the mother" (Green and Schecter[9]), "emotional isolation" (Lewis and Van Ferney[10]), and various malfunctions of the perceptual apparatus which may include psychogenic factors (Polan and Spencer[11]), minimal brain damage and lack of adequate definition of limits (Loomis[12]), and an "unknown basic disease" which is manifested by a breakdown of homeostatic regulation of sensory input (Ornitz and Ritvo[13]).

The child who is diagnosed as a case of early infantile autism is usually described as having manifested "autistic aloneness" or "lack of object relations" since birth (Kanner[6]), showing an "obsessive desire to maintain sameness" via stereotypic behavior, a failure to use speech for communication and displaying no neurologic dysfunction. These are the four diagnostic criteria used in this research project.

Numerous anecdotal and clinical reports indicate that the classically autistic child described by Kanner has no interest in or awareness of his physical body. Instead, the classically autistic child appears to be fixated upon one narrow area of functioning that is used to maintain sameness in the environment. Thus, the child may echolalically repeat snatches of long-past conversation, assemble or disassemble mechanical toys, go through a complex ritual of self-mutilation, perform extended feats of memory, etc. Thus, it appears that the children who fall within the syndrome of early infantile autism are completely lacking in the development of any body ego.

Behavioral Ego

The lack of body ego in early infantile autism appears to have allowed for a deviant type of ego development. The classically autistic child always manifests one area of skill which he uses to maintain sameness. Interruption of the pattern of this stereotypic behavior usually results in either a rage or withdrawal reaction that lasts until the stereotypic behavior is allowed to resume. Thus, it is obvious that the autistic child is much more concerned and involved with what happens to his pattern of stereotypic behavior than what happens to his body. Thus, a pattern of behavior has been cathected rather than a part of the body, the whole body or outer reality. I have postulated that this cathexis of a pattern of repetitive, stereotypic behavior should be labelled as a behavioral ego level of development.

The behavioral ego would be defined by the repetitive occurrence of a complex set of stereotypic behaviors which appear to exist to the exclusion of body ego or any higher ego processes. The classically autistic child appears to be fixated at a behavioral ego level of development, and to use this level of functioning to avoid the acknowledgment of outer reality. It seems as if some event or circumstance has caused the autistic child to cease developing, after having experienced only a very little of the world around him.

It is hypothesized that through the functioning of the behavioral ego, the autistic child carries on the same activities of exploration, stimulation and relaxation that occur in the infinitely larger areas of experience available to the healthier child. These behaviors are labelled as a specific type of ego development because they appear to be the means by which the child achieves his desires and experiences, and attains a limited amount of stimulation. The autistic child guards these behaviors with the same care that the more psychologically developed child guards his body. Interruption of these behavior sequences is responded to with a great deal of negative and fearful affect, whereas physical injury often elicits no observable affective response and many times appears to be completely ignored.

The behavioral ego is representative of the first possible successful unified adaptive position, whereas the schizophrenic child has no single adaptive position and usually displays a number of fragmented adaptive positions. The autistic child has been quite successful in controlling his parents, attaining his desires without learning to speak, and being the sole source of novelty and variation in his restricted environment. He has succeeded in restricting reality to dimensions which he can comfortably handle.

Importance of Stimulation

Examination of the question of the etiology of early infantile autism suggests that these children have suffered from a deficit of novelty, of variation and of patterned stimulation in the environment in their early developmental history. Numerous studies (Provence and Lipton[14]; Hess[15]; Frantz[16]; Levine[17]; Spitz[18], etc.) attest to the importance of varying stimulation in the early development of the infant. Varying etiological concepts (Kanner[6]; Ornitz and Ritvo[13]) all deal with the level of stimulation received by the child, while a large body of research literature (Solomon, et al.[19]) attests to the negative effect of sensory deprivation upon the functioning of normal adults.

A great amount of current research indicates the need of the human organism for a structured environment which allows for the occurrence of novel and varied situations. A recent study (Stechler and Latz[20]) has revealed that young infants will spend up to 15 minutes simply staring at one part of the environment. Other studies (Roffwarg, et al.[21]) indicate that there is an extremely high level (approx. 75-80%) of rapid eye movement (REM) activity in the young infant. Rapid eye movement activity is felt to be related to organizing activity within the brain. In short, the above and many other studies support the view of the infant as a strongly motivated processing instrument, rather than as a passive recipient of external stimulation. The infant is working very hard to learn how to make some sense out of the "buzzing, booming confusion" (James[22]) of the world around him.

The mothering figure has an important role to play in helping the infant to organize the world. She serves as a filter for many of the stimuli impinging upon the child, and gives him time to both organize those stimuli which do get through to him, as well as to use her own behavior as a model. Thus, the mothering figure protects from stimulation, organizes stimulation, provides stimulation and serves as a model for the organization of new and varied stimuli. If the mothering figure does not fulfill these requirements of the child, it is not unexpected that the infant would be content with any behavior which does fulfill the above requirements, even though this behavior might not be very inclusive. Thus, the fulfillment of the above requirements, in a very narrow and limited sense, seems to be the function of the stereotypic behavior of the autistic child, which has been labelled as a behavioral ego.

Etiology

There appear to be three basic sources of an early developmental history of a lack of the experience of a varied and stimulating patterned environment. This refers to the question of whether or not the infant was born into a household that set limits in a regular fashion, while encouraging responsiveness and exploration. The first source of such a history appears to lie in the birth of a child with an abnormally high stimulus barrier due to some organic problem, such as a visual or auditory deficit, or a child who is developmentally retarded. These and many other similar kinds of problems would render the child unaware of many stimuli in his environment, and result in his being thrown largely upon his own scanty resources. This situation can result in many odd and limited behaviors (Burlingham[23]). Secondly, the child may be hypersensitive to external stimuli due to some organic problem (Bergman and Escalona[24]) and attempt to withdraw from the painful impingement of external stimuli upon his faulty stimulus barrier. This situation can result in a withdrawal from the world which again leaves the child dependent upon his own scanty resources. Finally, the home environment may be so non-nurturent, unstimulating and unpatterned that the child has no recourse but to develop whatever patterns of behavior he can organize by himself. This last category appears to contain those children for whom Kanner originally labelled the syndrome of early infantile autism. The lack of stimulation may result from either the physical or psychological absence of the mother figure. The latter situation may be caused by an extended post-partum depression or psychosis, uncertainty and fearfulness as to what to do with an infant, or a rigidity of personality that does not allow the regression to take place which is necessary to be warm, spontaneous and open with an infant.

A recent study (Rothstein[25]) provides some support for the above position. This report was entitled "Stimulational and Interaction Patterns of Autistic Children and Their Parents." These parents were compared to the parents of normal children and the parents of brain damaged children, in regards to their spontaneity, their use of physical stimulation and their sensitivity to the non-verbal cues which were emitted by their children. The parents of schizophrenic and autistic children were found to rate significantly lower than the parents of the other two groups, on all of these criteria.

The above study, studies by Kanner,[6,7,26] many other studies and our own experience with parents of the children in this research project, all support the contention that these are people who are lacking in the capacity to provide a large amount of novel and variegated stimulation to their children. Our contacts with the parents of autistic children have disclosed the presence of a great deal of emotional distance, anger and rigidity. These parents are not sensitive to the feelings of their children, and in addition, they seem to be unable to express their own feelings to their children.

MODIFICATIONS: STRUCTURAL THERAPY

Structural therapy was a treatment approach designed to stimulate positive change in verbal, adolescent schizophrenic patients by means of a concentration upon the improvement of fragmented body ego and body image. The focus of this therapeutic activity was to use the intrusive pleasant activity of the therapist to stimulate the further development of body ego and higher ego processes. Thus, efforts were made to gratify any desire which the patient could be encouraged to express.

Examination of the diagnostic picture presented by the syndrome of early infantile autism suggested the need for theoretical and strategic modifications of structural therapy. Whereas the presence of fragmentary body ego made it possible for the therapist to gain direct contact rather easily with the adolescent schizophrenic, the autistic child has no body ego. Thus, the therapist must attempt to gain contact with the patient on a much earlier developmental level than that described by Des-Lauriers.[1,2] The lack of object relations and lack of the use of speech for communication rank the autistic child on the level of functioning of an infant below the age of six months. The maintenance of sameness via stereotypic behavior appears to have its roots in what Piaget[27] has described as the stages of rhythm and regulation. These two stages are described as occurring within the first weeks of life. Therefore, except for that hypertrophic ego development which I have labelled as a behavioral ego level of development, the therapist is faced with a child who is completely out of touch with reality.

Since the outstanding developmental and adaptive feature of the classically autistic child appears to be the maintenance of sameness via stereotypic behavior (Kanner[26]; Ward and Handford[29]), it seemed that the therapist must concentrate his efforts upon the behavioral ego of the patient. However, whereas DesLauriers[1,2] urged a development of the body ego for the adolescent schizophrenic, it would seem that the therapist would only use the behavioral ego as a means of affectively contacting this otherwise completely isolated child. This affective contact may usually be made by actively and physically intruding into whatever the stereotypic activity of the child may be. The therapist attempts to interrupt the stereotypic behavior in as pleasant and gamelike fashion as possible, but must insist on the interruption to the point that the child acknowledges his presence.

Treatment

Therapists have been trained in structural therapy with the following set of guidelines:

1. The therapist is trained to identify the stereotypic behavior of the child and to interrupt it. This interruption is done in a graduated and game-like way, if possible. The ineffectiveness and maladaptiveness of the stereotypic behavior for dealing with people, is demonstrated to the child by interference and by physical and verbal setting of limits to the rage or avoidance reactions which often follow the interference.

2. The anxiety and anger created by the interruption of the stereotypic behavior is used to focus the attention of the child upon part of the therapist as a meaningful part-object or object. Analytically oriented interpretations accompany the use of structural therapy. The therapist attempts to interpret the child's feeling about being interrupted, and then tries to get him to emit any verbal or physical message which is directed toward the therapist. This physical, visual or verbal message is then used to focus the attention of the child upon physical likenesses and differences between himself and the therapist. This stage often needs to be preceded by a period during which the therapist presents an alternative rhythmic behavior for the child to focus upon.

3. Development of a recognition relationship with the child is followed by presentation of a number of novel and patterned activities which draw the child's attention to his own body. These activities include counting of fingers and toes, gross movements of arms and legs, physical stimulation of body, etc.
4. The development of body ego is stimulated by the use of physical, gamelike interactions that make the child more aware of his own body, and of his differences from and similarities to his therapist.
5. As behavioral ego functioning decreases and body ego becomes more predominant, more conventional play therapy techniques are included in the treatment.

ELABORATION UPON GUIDELINES

All the above phases of treatment deal with a gradual increase in the level of physical, verbal, olfactory, kinesthetic and affective stimulation which is given the child. This increase in stimulation must be carefully modulated to avoid "overloading" the child. The non-verbal child signals his distress at being overloaded in an unmistakable manner which is easily distinguished from the diffuse, tantrum-like rage that results from the interruption of the stereotypic behavior. In addition, it should be stated that all patients are expected to show regressions in development along the major points outlined above, due to internal or external stresses.

The first task of the structural therapist is to break down the functioning of the behavioral ego and attempt to eventually promote the development of a cathexis of a significant person as a representative of reality. This development will then be followed by efforts directed toward the stimulation of body ego. Until there is some initial development of body ego, the therapist and reality have no grasp upon the child. The child is self-sufficient and unreachable until his body becomes important to him. The development of a fragmentary body ego eventually allows the therapist to shift to more conventional play therapy techniques. Thus, structural therapy may be viewed in terms of a therapy which prepares autistic children to benefit from more conventional types of psychotherapy.

The structural therapist uses techniques which are very common to the behavior of the apocryphal "good mother" playing with the normal infant. He stimulates the body boundaries via simple physical body differentiation games, teaches him how to behave, sings to him, shows him pictures and in general tries to give him many new and interesting experiences of reality. The classically autistic child is seen as being woefully deficient in varied experiences of the world, and the structural therapist is attempting to give the child enough new experiences so that he will learn that he is a human being and that reality is interesting. The child must then gain enough new experiences to be able to form schemata (Piaget[28]) which he can then use to organize reality for himself. Prior to the attainment of that level of development, the therapist provides new experiences and models free, spontaneous responses to the environment. At the same time, the therapist provides a firm structure as to acceptable behavior that the child is able to fight against, simply to assure himself that it is indeed present and reliable, even under stress. Eventually the child internalizes this structure of control.

OBSERVATIONS

Observation and treatment of the syndrome of early infantile autism have shown that these children seem to progress at a relatively rapid rate, if they can ever be engaged in therapy. Thus, some autistic children have been observed to make a significant response to the intrusive approach of structural therapy after as short a period as six weeks of treatment. Clinical experience has indicated that this amount of treatment is rarely sufficient to stimulate observable changes in schizophrenic or other severely ego disturbed children. This relatively rapid rate of progress, coupled with the mediating capacity reflected in the child's success in the development of the behavioral ego, leads to the conceptualization of the autistic child as actually being more advanced in ego development than the schizophrenic child.

It seems as if the autistic child has taken a wrong fork along the road to normal development, and that this fork has culminated in the dead end of the behavioral ego. The behavioral ego is labelled as a dead end because it does not help the child in learning how to process new experiences in the environment, even though it does consist of a set of stereotypic behaviors which have an active effect upon the outside world. Thus, the behavioral ego simply allows the autistic child to repeatedly impose the same pattern upon the outside world, rather than helping him to assimilate new experiences into an organized view of the world.

However, the autistic child does have the advantage over the schizophrenic child of having had the experience of developing one unified adaptive way of handling the environment. Thus, when a therapist is

successful in routing the autistic child from the repetitive patterns produced by the behavioral ego, the child does have the benefit of this previous successful adaptive experience when he is asked to deal with the
larger world around him. Essentially, it appears that the difference in
therapeutic responsiveness between early infantile autism and childhood
schizophrenia is based upon the difference between problems rooted in
regression and those which are problems of fixation. The structural therapist must forcefully produce a regression from a behavioral ego level
of development to a body ego level of development, and then take advantage of the coping capacity developed in the formation of the behavioral
ego to help reroute the child into the mainstream of the normal developmental pathways.

The structural therapist must focus upon the development of the
autistic child's awareness of him as a distinct and separate human being.
This emphasis must be repeated over and over again to get the child to
view the therapist as a three-dimensional human being; otherwise the
child may never develop beyond the point of viewing the therapist as
a gratifying, playful, enjoyable object whose only role is to supply his
oral demands. Many times the therapist will deliberately oppose some
of the new desires expressed by the patient.

This is directly the opposite of DesLauriers' strategy with adolescent
schizophrenic patients, and is done to emphasize the differences in feeling between people, and how they can be dealt with directly and freely.
Many times the child may enjoy some activity, while the therapist may
be exhausted or bored with lifting him, swinging him, playing body differentiation games, etc. At that point, the therapist should say "I'm tired—
I'm bored—Let's do something else"—or "I don't like this." The therapist should feel free to initiate periods of rest or movement out of the
therapy room. It is extremely important that the therapist share his feelings with the patient, as these children have usually had very little experience of truthful and direct expression of feeling. Thus, it is clear that
the use of counter-transference feelings plays a large role in this modified
version of structural therapy.

The therapist is encouraged to introduce activities and experiences
which the child has not thought of, to the end of (1) being genuine and
spontaneous; (2) varying the range of stimuli to which the patient is exposed; and (3) emphasizing that his feelings and ideas are not always
the same as those of the patient. Thus, the therapist discourages the development of a pathological symbiotic relationship of grandiose omnipo-

tent fantasies. The development of a "normal" symbiotic relationship is expected and hoped for, as an indication of positive growth on the part of the patient.

Results

The above treatment approach has been applied to the organization and functioning of a 20-bed Autistic Children's Unit devoted to research on the etiology and treatment of early infantile autism. This research project has been ongoing since October, 1966. A total of 12 autistic and schizophrenic children, ranging in age from 6-1 to 12-0, have been seen in structural therapy, on a twice a week basis, for periods ranging from two years and one month to one year and one month. Individual therapists, nursing personnel and child care staff have all been trained in the aims of structural therapy. Thus, even those children who are not seen individually, are exposed to the milieu generated by structural therapy.

At the initiation of the research project, 13 of 21 children were on medication which included Mellaril, Thorazine and Librium and ranged from dosages of 10 mgm. t.i.d. to 150 mgm. t.i.d. At the present time, only 2 of 17 children receive any tranquilizing medication. Four children have been discharged in the last two years, and other children have shown marked changes. All of the children have made improvements in the development of object relations, attention span and performance in kindergarten types of classroom tasks.

Several non-verbal children have started babbling in a manner similar to that of normal infants and have been started in speech therapy. Four of these children have developed the use of words for communication.

Further analysis of both the process and outcome of this modification of structural therapy is ongoing and will be available at a later date.

REFERENCES

1. DESLAURIERS, A. M. *The experience of reality in childhood schizophrenia.* New York: International Universities Press, 1962.
2. DESLAURIERS, A. M. The schizophrenic child. *Archives of General Psychiatry,* 1967, 16: 194–201.
3. FREUD, S. *The ego and the id.* London: Hogarth Press, 1927.
4. FEDERN, P. *Ego-psychology and the psychoses.* New York: Basic Books, 1952.
5. SCHILDER, P. *The image and appearance of the human body.* New York: Wiley & Sons, 1964.

6. KANNER, L. Autistic disturbances of affective contact. *Nervous Child*, 1943, 2: 217–240.

7. KANNER, L. & EISENBERG, L. Early infantile autism. *American Journal of Orthopsychiatry*, 1956, 26: 556–564.

8. GARCIA, B. & SARVIS, M. A. Evaluation and treatment planning for autistic children. *Archives of General Psychiatry*, 1964, 10: 530–541.

9. GREEN, M. R. & SCHECTER, D. E. Autism and symbiotic disorders in three blind children. *Psychiatric Quarterly*, 1957, 31: 628–646.

10. LEWIS, R. & VAN FERNEY, S. Early recognition of infantile autism. *Journal of Pediatrics*, 1960, 56: 510–512.

11. POLAN, C. C. & SPENCER, B. L. Check list of symptoms of autism in early life. *West Virginia Medical Journal*, 1959, 55: 198–204.

12. LOOMIS, E. A. Autistic and symbiotic syndromes in children. *Monographs of the Society for Research in Child Development*, 1960, 25: 39–48.

13. ORNITZ, E. & RITVO, E. Neurophysiologic mechanisms underlying perceptual inconstancy in schizophrenic and autistic children. *Archives of General Psychiatry*, 1968, 19: 22–27.

14. PROVENCE, S. & LIPTON, R. C. *Infants in institutions.* New York: International Universities Press, 1962.

15. HESS, E. H. Imprinting. *Science*, 1959, 130: 133–141.

16. FANTZ, R. Pattern vision in newborn infants. *Science*, 1963, 140: 296–297.

17. LEVINE, S. Stimulation in infancy. *Scientific American*, 1960, 202: 80–86.

18. SPITZ, R. *The first year of life.* New York: International Universities Press, 1965.

19. SOLOMON, P. et al. *Sensory deprivation.* Cambridge, Mass.: Harvard University Press, 1961.

20. STECHLER, G. & LATZ, E. Some observations on attention and arousal in the human infant. *Journal of the American Academy of Child Psychiatry*, 1966, 5: 517–525.

21. ROFFWARG, H. P., DEMENT, W. E. & FISHER, S. Preliminary observations of the sleepdream pattern in neonates, infants, children and adults. In Harms, E. (Ed.), *Problems in sleep and dreams of children.* New York: Pergamon Press, 1964. pp. 60–72.

22. JAMES, W. *Principles of psychology.* New York: Henry Holt & Co., 1890.

23. BURLINGHAM, D. Development considerations of the occupations of the blind. *Psychoanalytic Study of the Child*, 1967, 22, 187–198.

24. BERGMAN, P. & ESCALONA, S. K. Unusual sensitivities in very young children. *Psychoanalytic Study of the Child*, 1949, 3/4: 333–352.

25. ROTHSTEIN, R. Stimulation and interaction patterns of autistic children and their parents. *Paper presented at Eastern Psychological Association Convention*, April 1967, Boston.

26. KANNER, L. & LESSER, L. Early infantile autism. *Pediatric Clinics of North America*, 1958, 5: 711–730.
27. PIAGET, J. Les trois structures fondamentales de la vie psychique, rhythme, regulation et groupement. *Revue Suisse de Psychologie.* Pure Appliquee 1, 1942.
28. PIAGET, J. *Six psychological studies.* New York: Random House, 1967.
29. WARD, A. & HANDFORD, H. Early infantile autism: syndrome, symptom or wastebasket? *Paper presented at Mid-Western Psychological Association Convention,* May 1968, Chicago.

4

Structural Therapy: A Developmental Approach to the Treatment of Early Infantile Autism*

H. Allen Handford and Alan J. Ward

A therapeutic method involving direct structuring of the patient's words and actions, including his own responses to the therapist, was introduced by Des Lauriers (1962) for the treatment of Childhood Schizophrenia, and was further elaborated upon in 1967. The concept of Structural Therapy was based upon the inability of the schizophrenic child's Ego to bring order out of reality, thus resulting in regressive and chaotic thinking and behavior. Structural Therapy consisted of the therapist actively and directly bringing order to bear for the patient, upon which his Ego could then build. It could be compared to providing scaffolding for reconstructing a building which had partially collapsed. Etiologic considerations were secondary in the use of Structural Therapy since it was fully applicable regardless of the supposed cause or causes of Childhood Schizophrenia, providing for restructuring the weakened Ego to cope with either "organic" or "functional" disabilities, or mixtures of both.

Ward (1968), a co-worker of Des Lauriers, became interested in the

*Reprinted with permission from *Schizophrenia* 1 (1969) 243–48.

applicability of Structural Therapy to the treatment of Early Infantile Autism (Kanner, 1943), and in 1966 became Research and Treatment Director of our 20-bed Autistic Children's Unit, introducing Structural Therapy as a method of psychotherapy to be studied.

THEORETICAL BACKGROUND

Ward introduced new theoretical concepts for the work with Autistic children, on the basis that they constituted a separate, though possibly related, clinical entity from Schizophrenic children. He considered the Ego structure of the latter to be weakened and disintegrated, a fragmentary "Body Ego," an Ego which in varying degrees had lost its body boundaries. In contradistinction, he considered the Ego of the Autistic Child to have developed an abnormally tenacious structure in certain highly circumscribed functions, and to have failed to develop other functions almost entirely. Thus, he postulated that the Autistic child had developed an extremely narrow Ego which he termed a "Behavioral Ego," since it seemed rather uniformly to consist, among these children, of highly stereotyped, repetitive behaviors to the exclusion of all other activity; even encroaching upon survival functions such as eating, sleeping, and elimination. He particularly noted that these children maintained these behaviors as if they were survival functions, staunchly resisting interruptions in them, and displaying acute anxiety if they were prevented. He further maintained that the Behavioral Ego represented a successful position of adaptation if viewed from the standpoint of the child, because in his small and limited area of experience, the Autistic child "carried on the same activities of exploration, stimulation, and relaxation which occur in the infinitely larger area of experience available to the healthier child" and controlled the environment so that basic needs were met with an absolute minimum of affective, verbal, or motor response on his part. Ward's view of the adaptive function of Early Infantile Autism has subsequently been voiced by Ruttenberg (1968), who describes EIA as ". . . the lowest level that allows of long term adaptation and survival."

Ward speculated that the development of such a Behavioral Ego might occur as early as the first months of life, as the result of several possible etiologic factors. These etiologic factors were listed as organic impairment prior to, at, or subsequent to birth, in the receptive areas or receptive-integrative areas of the central nervous system; which might produce either an abnormally high or an abnormally low barrier to environmental stimuli, forcing the child either to create his own reality (as also seen in the deaf-blind child) because stimuli were not coming in, or else forcing the child to actively restrict his awareness because he found the volume of stimuli to be overwhelming. Family and, particularly, maternal overstimulation or understimulation, where they were of pathological degree, were felt to have the potential to produce essentially the same response in the developing infant, even in the absence of central nervous system impairment.

Once engaged in therapy, Ward saw the Autistic Child as progressing more rapidly in the acquisition and development of new Ego functions than the Schizophrenic Child, and accounted for this theoretically, on the basis of the greater strength already present in the Autistic Child for mediating Ego functions as they are acquired. It should be noted that rapid change is seen within the framework of Structural Therapy. Should an Autistic Child begin to acquire new Ego functions without structuring, this author (H. Allen Handford) has seen that the picture may become one of Childhood Schizophrenia with weakness in all Ego functions, as if the strength concentrated in the functions of the Behavioral Ego had been dispersed or greatly diluted.

In its approach to the individual Autistic Child, Structural Therapy is essentially developmental in nature. It follows closely the path of acquisition of Ego functions in the normal human infant and utilizes the activities, albeit to an exaggerated degree, of the normal human mother in stimulating this acquisition. The aim is to lure the child back to reality in a natural way, providing at the same time the rungs of the ladder of normal development up which he must eventually climb. The stimuli provided are predominately pleasureable, as are those from the nurturing mother, and likewise consist primarily of what the therapist can give with his own hands, voice, facial expressions, and body. In this sense Structural Therapy differs fundamentally from, for example, Behavioral Therapy which extensively uses inanimate biological rewards (food) or noxious stimuli (electric shock, slapping), and evokes responses, but without providing for further natural development.

The success of the Structural Therapist where the natural mother has failed is based on two important factors. The therapist carefully rations the amount and type of stimulation, providing the optimal amount determined by the response of the child. Thus, he may at some times be stimulating the child much less than the natural mother would, while at other times he would be stimulating the child a great deal more. In cases where the natural mother has not pathologically overstimulated or understimulated the Autistic Child as an infant, she may have been dealing with an organically impaired infant and not understood how to ration stimuli to him. Preliminary work with the mothers of Autistic Children suggests that at least some of them may be taught the optimal rationing of stimuli to their children. The other important factor is the type and degree of development and change which has usually occurred in the Autistic Child since infant days. Organically, any impairment in stimulus barrier seems to have been partially alleviated by physical development of the central nervous system. As a result the child is now able to cope with stimuli if they are structured for him, and their intensity geared to his level of receptivity.

The imparting of adequate Body Image is considered to be an essential part of Structural Therapy, since there is ample evidence from the developmental literature (Schilder, 1942) that the development of an adequate concept of one's body as an object in space, independent and apart from other objects, is basic to the formation of a strong Body Ego, which is in turn fundamental to the development of more complex Ego functions. The infant's awareness of both his mother, as a separate entity from himself, and the boundaries of his own body must precede the development of the ability to discriminate all other elements of external reality and to cope intelligently with them.

TREATMENT APPROACH

In the initial phase of Structural Therapy, the Autistic Child, devoid of speech or language, without affect, and intensely occupied with his stereotyped movements of hands or solitary objects, must be engaged in the treatment process. Similarly, immediately after birth, the newborn infant must be engaged in the nurturing process. The therapist—like the doctor, the mother, the nurse—touches the child, speaks to the child knowing that it will take many weeks of touching in many different ways and speaking in many different tones before the first social responses of sustained eye contact and smile are elicited. Babbling, laughing, and directing of attention toward the therapist as a source of pleasure, when he enters the room, are usually the next responses to occur with the Autistic Child in Structural Therapy, as they are with the infant in the course of normal development. Vowel-consonant combinations such as "da," "ba," "ma," and "ga" and then single words such as "no" begin to emerge from the infant babble, and soon may begin to refer specifically to the therapist or to certain inanimate objects. Lest the situation seem entirely analogous to that of the developing infant, it should be pointed out that the Autistic Child has usually hypertrophied development in the functions which constitute the Behavioral Ego. Motor activity involving large muscle groups is often at age level or beyond, with the exception that play skills such as ball throwing or catching lag due to social avoidance. Small muscle function may be highly developed for the production of rapid stereotyped hand and finger movements, although not for drawing with a pencil or crayon. Oral activity seems arrested and hypertrophied at about the one year level. Most small objects go directly from hand to mouth, particularly if they are unfamiliar. Soft foods are preferred and the use of utensils bypassed in eating. Many objects are sucked on. As a consequence of the hypertrophy of these functions, the Structural Therapist, unlike the normal mother, does not need to bring the child along the early oral and motor milestones. Quite to the contrary, he may directly interrupt the activities in these areas in order to foster the development of functions which have been bypassed.

Turning to more specific details of Structural Therapy, the therapist initially meets with the child alone, usually in a relatively bare playroom where toys, however, are immediately available. Since the tendency of the Autistic Child is to seize upon any inanimate object to avoid contact with another person, the task of engaging the child in therapy is simplified if the number of such objects is kept at a minimum at the outset. The therapist approaches the child very directly with his voice, his hands and his body, intruding upon his withdrawal, his rituals, gently but insistently, gradually evoking recognition of his presence and then affective response to it. The quantity of stimulation varies from child to child, being enough to engage him but not so much as to overwhelm him and produce further withdrawal. For example, the use of the voice may vary from speaking softly to singing loudly, gauged always to the response of the child (the Autistic Child very often will signify by covering his ears that the sound is becoming too loud). Very often, as with an infant, if a specific sound of the voice is accompanied by an act pleasurable to the child such as rubbing his back, the child will begin to respond with affect as soon as he hears the sound. Any positive responses on the part of the child are met with an expression of pleasure on the part of the therapist, and verbal sounds or words are picked up and imitated, much as the normal mother reacts to similar arrival at new skills in her infant. It is important to note that although the therapist may produce discomfort in the child when he actively interrupts stereotyped behavior, his interaction with him is kept as much as possible pleasure-oriented. Thus, frustration may be produced, but pain is never deliberately inflicted, even though the child may at times be sufficiently provoked by the therapist's intrusions to physically attack him. Instead, such attacks are simply modified so that no physical injury is incurred, but also the child emerges with the real feeling of having vented his anger upon another person (rather than upon himself in arm biting or face slapping as is so often seen in the autistic child).

Often the therapist must set physical, as well as verbal limits, when the EIA child becomes upset at the intrusion upon his stereotypic rituals. The child may try to bang his head, bite his arm, throw himself on the floor, or bounce his body violently from one wall to the other. Then the therapist must use his own physical presence as a limit for the child. The therapist places his hands or body between the child's head and a hard surface, goes to the floor with the child, or physically surrounds him with his own body. The child is shown that all of his actions, whether directed towards himself or the environment, only succeed in bringing him into contact with people. Thus, the development of object relations is continually fostered, whether it be during periods of pleasure, frustration, quiescence, or active and structured learning. The use of seclusion rooms has been discontinued in our Unit, due to this treatment approach. It was felt antitherapeutic to isolate a child in a bare room, when his pathology appeared to be related to an inability or unwillingness to handle stimulation from human beings.

Elements of Body Image are imparted to the child by the therapist by direct stimulation of specific body parts, particularly those parts serving for exploration of the environment; such as arms and legs, hands and feet, fingers and toes, eyes, ears, nose and mouth, and skin surfaces of the face and trunk. In the Autistic Child, anal or genital stimulation is often an hypertrophied, stereotyped function to be interrupted or frustrated rather than fostered, not on moral grounds, but so that the awareness of other body parts may be enhanced. As in the nursery, fingers and toes are touched and counted, legs and arms are moved up and down, and the body as a whole is pushed and pulled, lifted and lowered, accompanied by words designating the body parts and the directions moved. The child is encouraged to explore the same parts of the therapist's body, and the latter may spend much time sitting or lying outstretched on the playroom floor so as to be more accessible. If available, the use of a large mirror also facilitates this activity.

As the child progresses, materials used in more conventional play therapy are introduced gradually, geared to the child's apparent level of conceptualization. Paper and crayons, if used by the child to scribble or draw, provide important clues to the level of Body Image achieved as compared to normal children (Kellogg, 1967). Puppets or dolls may facilitate the expression of feelings about interpersonal relationships, and so on, running the gamut of materials familiar to us all. Once the foundation of Ego functions is laid through Structural Therapy, the Autistic Child is then capable of participating with his therapist in therapies applicable to children with border and more evenly developed Ego structures.

MILIEU

Needless to say, Structural Therapy with Autistic Children cannot be carried on successfully in a vacuum. Since the therapist sees the child for relatively brief periods (30 to 60 minutes) only two or three times a week, everything which he accomplishes with the child must be reinforced by those caring for him day by day. In our Unit of 20 male and female children, nurses and child care workers of both sexes are instructed in detail as to how to respond to the emerging Ego functions of the children in treatment, on an around-the-clock basis. This is further reinforced by a structured 5 hour Nursery School program each week day, in which workers caring for the children on the Unit serve as their teachers in class. That the Structural Therapy serves primarily as a catalyst for the growth and development of the Autistic Child is nowhere more clearly illustrated than in the ratio of clock hours of therapy in a given week to clock hours of supportive reinforcement. That it serves even as a catalyst is verified by the rate of development increasing dramatically in those children receiving Structural Therapy plus supportive reinforcement, as compared to their own progress with the elements of supportive reinforcement alone, and as compared with their Unit mates, receiving only supportive reinforcement. In this regard it should be noted that almost all the children on the Unit, whether receiving Structural Therapy or not, showed some developmental progress apparently as a result of direct, positive, often imitative stimulation by those children in therapy, another interesting indication of the strong catalytic nature of the therapy.

SUMMARY

In summary, a method of psychotherapy for the treatment of Infantile Autism termed Structural Therapy has been introduced and is being studied on the Autistic Children's Unit of a large state psychiatric hospital for children. Its theoretical assumptions have their basis in Ego Psychology and more specifically in the deviant development of the Ego of the

Autistic Child as compared to that of the normal infant. The pattern of treatment by the therapist is seen to emulate in its primary elements the nurturing process of the normal mother, with important modifications. The strong catalytic nature of the therapy and the importance of supportive reinforcement by the child's environment has been described. Data concerning the specific cases are to follow in a separate paper.

REFERENCES

DesLauriers, Austin M. *The experience of reality in childhood schizophrenia.* New York: International Universities Press, 1962.

————. The schizophrenic child. *Archives of General Psychiatry,* Vol. 16, February 1967.

Kanner, Leo. Autistic disturbances of affective contact. *Nervous Child,* 1943, 2: 217–250.

Kellogg, Rhoda, with Scott O'Dell. *The psychology of children's art.* New York: Random House, 1967.

Ruttenberg, Bertram A. A classification of the childhood psychoses. Paper presented at American Association of Psychiatric Clinics for Children Convention in New York City, November 1968.

Schilder, Paul. *Mind, perception and thought.* New York: Columbia University Press, 1942.

Ward, Alan J. An application of structural therapy to the residential treatment of early infantile autism. Paper presented at American Association of Psychiatric Clinics for Children Convention in New York City, November 1968.

DIAGNOSIS

5

Childhood Psychopathology: A Natural Experiment in Etiology*

Early Infantile Autism, Symbiotic Psychosis, and Childhood Schizophrenia are fascinating and elusive concepts which continue to elicit varied and contradictory hypotheses as to their etiology (Laufer and Gair, 1969). The gamut of etiologic hypotheses ranges from the psychogenic to the organic, to any admixture of these two positions. This paper is a report on a family whose organization and development may offer important insights into the development and prevention of severe childhood psychopathology.

THE PROBLEMS

This family was brought to the attention of the Autistic Children's Treatment, Training, and Research Service by the case of Steven, a 6-year-old Caucasian boy admitted to our service in November 1966, upon being diagnosed as a case of early infantile autism. Steven met the diagnostic criteria of early infantile autism used on this service (Ward, 1970a, 1970b): he did not relate to people, did not use speech or any other means of communication, engaged in stereotypic behavior, and was neurologically

*Reprinted with permission from *Journal of the American Academy of Child Psychiatry* 13 (1974) 153–65.

normal. Investigation revealed that Steven had two other disturbed siblings, as well as three normal siblings.

The two disturbed siblings were a 3-year-old brother, who had been diagnosed as developmentally retarded, was nonverbal, and attended a nursery school for retarded children; and a 7-year-old sister, who had initially been diagnosed as a case of early infantile autism, was nonverbal, and had been rediagnosed as childhood schizophrenia after intensive psychotherapy.

The three normal siblings were a 12-year-old brother and two sisters 11 and 9 years old. These children were reported to be progressing normally, and displaying age-appropriate behavior.

The only known features which varied for the three emotionally disturbed children, as compared to their three normal siblings, were the mental health and physical presence of the mother. The mother had had a history of five psychotic breaks and psychiatric hospitalizations following the birth of her fifth child. Thus, Steven and his closest brother and sister spent many of their vital early months of development with a mother who had been repeatedly described clinically as a paranoid schizophrenic. An attempt will be made to relate the details of this mother's severe illness and frequent absences from the home to the pathology which developed in each of the three youngest children. The effect of the frequent removal of these children from the home and their placement in various settings will also be discussed.

Thus, this paper will attempt to answer the question as to how this concentration of severe childhood psychopathology came to occur in this one family.

FAMILY OUTLINE

The P. family was made up of Mr. and Mrs. P. and six children, at their initial contact with our service. All names and historical information have been changed or disguised to avoid any possible identification of this family. The ages of all family members at that time were: Mr. P., 42; Mrs. P., 38; Jason, 12; Stephanie, 11; Nancy, 9; Jacqueline, 7; Steven, 6; Robert, 3.

The family owned their own home, and Mr. P. was an employee of moderate income, who had received an honorable discharge from the armed services. He was a man of average intelligence, whom we perceived as being quite immature, with strong dependency needs and passive strivings. Mrs. P.'s therapist thought that Mr. P. was quite resentful of the burdens placed upon him by his wife's illness. This father was described as remaining "consistently detached" from all of his children, and the question was raised as to possible competition with the children to obtain oral gratification from the mother.

Mrs. P. was a housewife of average intelligence who had not been employed during her marriage. Mrs. P. became "mentally upset" after Steven's birth in 1960, which eventually culminated in her first psychotic break and hospitalization from 11/9/61 to 1/62. This was the first of a series of six hospitalizations (the dates of which are listed in Table 4). Mrs. P. was diagnosed paranoid schizophrenic, and was reported to have no insight into her illness. She had a very tenuous hold on reality, and was described as "paranoid, suspicious of people, and suspecting them of mistreating her children." Mrs. P. had a history of having entered and terminated treatment with many therapists. She was said "to have developed a symbiotic relationship with the three youngest children," but was also described as having "alternately ignored the children and fostered their excessive dependency upon her."

The three older children developed normally, attended Catholic schools, and led apparently normal lives. These children were never placed outside of the home. Generally, they expressed warm feelings toward the three younger children, although the mother attempted to "hide the younger children from the older children to prevent their suffering" from the effects of the compounded emotional problems.

DEVELOPMENT OF PATHOLOGY

Jacqueline was born 4/15/59, and displayed a normal developmental history for the first 1½ years of life. She was a full-term infant who weighed 9 pounds and was 20 inches long at birth. There were no reported complications of either pregnancy or delivery. She crawled at 4 months, sat at 6 months, walked between 6 and 8 months, and said "dada" before 1 year of age.

However, Jacqueline is reported to have stopped saying "dada" when her brother, Steven, was born on 4/26/60. Mrs. P. is said to have become progressively more emotionally upset after Steven's birth, until her overt psychotic behavior necessitated hospitalization from November 1961 until January 1962. Jacqueline was sent to stay first with an aunt, and then a maternal grandmother during this period of her mother's first hospitalization. Shortly after this move, Jacqueline drank some household poison (washing soda) and was hospitalized for 3 weeks. The close chronological relationship of these two events suggests that Jacqueline may have drunk the washing soda as part of her reaction to the separation from her mother. Jacqueline was returned to the home upon her mother's release from the hospital in January 1962. The importance of the effect of a 2-month separation upon the development of a child who had already shown herself to be vulnerable, by her loss of speech at the birth of a sibling, is difficult to estimate. However, to the separation and loss of the mother must also be added the separation and loss of the father and three siblings for the same period of time.

Mr. and Mrs. P. first sought psychological help for Jacqueline in June 1962, 5 months after her return to the home. They complained that Jacqueline was still not talking, was not toilet-trained, made noises at her own hand as if attempting to speak to it, ate poorly, ran away, and seemed to lack fear. A psychological evaluation in 7/62 found that Jacqueline "seemed able to do what a 3-year-old can do." She did only what she wanted and could not be distracted by the outside world. Jacqueline was destructive at home, and Steven was "terrified of Jacqueline, who, when alone with him, will jump on him and push his face in the dirt." She sometimes arranged objects in perfectly straight rows. The family was then referred to a local day care program for severely disturbed children, where Jacqueline was diagnosed as "classical infantile autism, severe." Jacqueline was kept in this program from 1/17/63 to the summer when she was removed by her mother who was "in a paranoid fit." The teachers thought she had made some progress in this program, but they still saw her as functioning as an autistic child, when she was withdrawn from class. A psychological evaluation in 3/63 reported that Jacqueline's *Gross Motor Behavior* was at the 36-month level, *Adaptive Behavior* at the 30-month level, *Language Behavior* at the 30-week level, and *Personal-Social Behavior* at the 24–30-month level.

The P. family was referred for help in placing their children in 12/63. Mrs. P. had delivered her youngest child, Robert (9/63), had become seriously ill again, and was hospitalized from 12/8/63 to 4/64. Jacqueline and Steven were both placed in a nursing home for retarded children on 12/11/63. Jacqueline stayed at the nursing home until 3/29/65, when she was transferred to a foster home, "due to the occurrence of considerable regression." The foster family placement lasted from 3/65–5/69, when Jacqueline was hospitalized on the Autistic Children's Treatment, Training, and Research Service. In psychological evaluation carried out on 8/12/65 by the placement agency, the examiner found Jacqueline an "extremely autistic and psychotic child." Jacqueline attained an I.Q. of approximately 32 on the Cattell Infant Scale, was still making noises at her hand, but was reported to be making "good progress" in the foster home by the placement agency, at that time. The P. family visited Jacqueline on a fairly consistent basis until Mrs. P. was hospitalized from 1/68-3/68, at which point all visits were discontinued. By 2/27/69, Jacqueline was reported to have regressed to hyperactivity, destructiveness, tearing clothing and toys, banging head, biting self, irregular sleep, and biting and pinching others. This regression stimulated the referral for residential treatment (see Table 1).

TABLE 1.   Jacqueline: Developmental Sequence.

Date of Birth		4/15/59
Brother, Steven,		J. stopped saying "dada"
born 4/26/60		
	1961	
Mother hospitalized		J. placed with relatives
11/9/61-1/62		
	1962	
J. drank washing soda and		J. returned home with
hospitalized 3 weeks		mother 1/62
J. not talking — 6/62 made noises		
at hand and lacked fear		
	1963	
Mother became pregnant		1/63
J. began refusal of foods and fluids		5/63
Brother, Robert, born		9/63
	1964	
Mother hospitalized		12/8/63 - 4/64
J. placed in nursing home for retarded		12/11/63 - 3/29/65
and experienced "regression"		
	1965	
J. placed in foster home		3/65 - 5/69
and mother visited		
	1966	
	1967	
Mother hospitalized		1/30/67 - 3/31/67
	1968	
Mother hospitalized and		1/68 - 3/68
all visits to J. stopped		
	1969	
J. regressed to assaultiveness,		2/27/69
self-mutilation, and hyperactivity		
J. hospitalized		4/14/69

Analysis. Jacqueline's severe pathology may be viewed as resulting from both the distorted nature of the mother-child relationship and the repeated separations from both mother and family. Initially, Jacqueline lost her mother to a new sibling, then to hospitalization, then to another sibling, and finally she herself was removed from her home and mother long before she had attained the psychological individuation necessary to function independently. However, the foundation for Jacqueline's pathology appears to have been laid in her first 3 years of life which were spent with an inconsistent mother who had two overt psychotic episodes and hospitalizations during this time. It is hypothesized that it was the well-known inconsistency of the adult schizophrenic which rendered Mrs. P. incapable of providing the structure necessary to enable an infant to develop an awareness of self and the surrounding world. Jacqueline apparently attempted to develop some partial mastery of the environment via an early infantile autism adaptation, but the negative nature of her relationship to her younger sibling, suggesting a rivalry for mother's attention, would indicate that her autism was of a reactive nature rather than endogenous. Thus, the history suggests a child who attained the symbiotic position (Mahler, 1968), and then was repeatedly allowed to fuse with and then to be separated from the symbiotic object.

Steven

Steven was born on 4/26/60 from a full-term pregnancy which was free of any complications. He weighed 8 pounds at birth. Steven sat alone at 9 months, crawled at 10 months, walked with support at 11 months, and walked alone at 13 months of age. Speech development began around 2 years of age, but toilet training did not take place until he was 5 years old.

This child's first year and a half of life was unremarkable, and he was placed with relatives during Mrs. P.'s first hospitalization. Steven subsequently began displaying disturbed behavior similar to that of Jacqueline. He vocalized similar sounds, manipulated his hands, and looked at them in the same manner as his older sister. Both parents became concerned that Steven might be "autistic," and he was evaluated in 11/62 by staff members of the same day care program which had treated Jacqueline. In this evaluation, the examiners noted the presence of a great deal of separation anxiety, in marked contrast to Jacqueline. Steven strove desperately to get back to his mother, and was infantile with a great deal of mouthing and feeling of textures. He also displayed an initial fear of strangers. A diagnosis of "borderline childhood psychosis" with autistic and symbiotic features was made by the staff of the day care program. In psychological evaluation in 3/63, the examiner found Steven's *Gross and Fine Motor Behavior* to be age appropriate (DQ = 100), the typical level of his *Adaptive Behavior* was 21–24 months (DQ = 65–70), his *Development of Language* ("la," "yo") was typical of 32 weeks (DQ = 20), his *Comprehension* at the level of 56 weeks (DQ = 30), and his *Personal Social Behavior* at the 2-year level (DQ = 60–80).

Steven remained in the day care program from 1/63 to 5/63, at which time he was withdrawn at the same time as Jacqueline, when Mrs. P. experienced her "paranoid fit."

After his mother's hospitalization from 12/8/63 to 4/64, following the birth of her youngest child in 9/63, Steven and Jacqueline were placed in a nursing home for retarded children in 12/63. Mrs. P. had become severely disturbed, deliberately wrecking the family car. She was hospitalized locally, left the hospital for her mother's home, was hospitalized in a nearby state, and finally was returned to a hospital in Pennsylvania for 4 months.

Steven repeatedly tried to run away while he was in the nursing home. He was placed on Mellaril and confined in a "cagelike area" at the nursing home, but was finally returned home on 6/30/65 "due to destructiveness and hyperactivity." He was described as "out of touch" when he came home, and his head was "all banged up" from hitting it against things. Steven was very jealous of his younger brother, Robert, at this time, and often "bloodied his nose and blackened his eye." This jealous attitude is very similar to that displayed by Jacqueline toward Steven when she returned home after being placed with relatives during Mrs. P.'s first hospitalization. He displayed a great many stereotypic hand movements, a great deal of crying, and destructive behavior. The presence of considerable masturbation often caused Mrs. P. to slap Steven.

Mrs. P. again became severely disturbed, and was hospitalized from 12/27/65 to 2/18/66. A social agency then sought and gained custody because they believed the "youngest three children are unable to receive the necessary care at home, and are therefore in need of the custody of this Agency." Steven was then placed in a foster home, while awaiting placement in an institution.

A psychological examination was administered on 12/30/65. Steven was observed to be always aware of and interested in his physical surroundings, but was unwilling to be separated from either his father or his younger brother. He used the hand of the examiner to get things done. The report stated that the "outstanding aspect of Steven's behavior appeared to be his determination to do what he wanted and to be in control of the situation." He obtained a tentative Mental Age of 2 to 2.5 years, while displaying a short attention span, hyperactivity, and minimal frustration tolerance. He had great anxiety about being abandoned and seemed unable to maintain himself without the presence of the parent figure. Also, Steven seemed unable to allow Robert to be separated from the family, and seemed almost to feel as if he were leaving part of himself behind. On one occasion, Steven "grabbed Robert by the hair, and pulled him until he was close to father and heading for the door." Steven was admitted to the Autistic Children's Treatment, Training, and Research Service on 11/3/66 (see Table 2).

TABLE 2.   Steven: Developmental Sequence.

Date of Birth		4/26/60
	1961	
Mother hospitalized		11/61 - 1/62
	1962	
Mother placed S. with relatives		S. displayed "disturbed behavior"
Diagnosis of borderline childhood psychosis		11/62
	1963	
Brother, Robert, born		9/63
	1964	
Mother hospitalized		12/8/63 - 4/64
S. placed in nursing home for retarded children.		12/11/63 - 6/30/65
	1965	
S. returned home "due to destructiveness and hyperactivity"		6/30/65
	1966	
Mother hospitalized		12/27/65 - 2/18/66
S. placed in foster family		12/30/65
S. hospitalized		11/3/66

Analysis. As was true in the case of Jacqueline, Steven's severe pathology appeared to relate both to a distorted mother-child relationship and to frequent separations from home and family. Similarly, also Steven found himself deprived of his mother by her hospitalization (11/61-

1/62) as he approached 1½ years of age. His own birth had deprived Jacqueline of her mother at 1 year of age. Evidence of deviant and/or retarded ego development followed or continued after Mrs. P.'s hospitalization to suggest again the deleterious effect of an inconsistent and schizophrenic mothering figure upon early child development and individuation. However, Steven's somewhat superior development adaptively, affectively, and socially seemed to suggest that Mrs. P. was able to help him to develop more than she had been able to help Jacqueline.

Steven's superior object relations development was displayed by his awareness and responsiveness to the environment and people as well as by his attempts to control the situation around him. Whereas Jacqueline had apparently entered only the initial phases of the symbiotic adjustment, Steven appeared to have developed almost to the point of individuation from the symbiotic relationship with his mother. Thus, Steven's loss of his mother stirred him to strenuous efforts to reinstate the symbiosis, while similar loss had had much more deleterious effect upon Jacqueline's body image and object constancy. The latter is shown by Jacqueline's loss of speech, "talking" to her hand, and the primitive fusion with her mother that apparently was reflected in her refusal of food and fluids when mother's negative feelings were focused upon her.

Steven had a very negative response to placement in the nursing home, as he had developed a strong relationship with the family and struggled to return as an individual member of it, rather than as simply a part of the fused symbiotic family mass. Jacqueline's lack of ego development and differentiation enabled her to have a less violent reaction to placement in the nursing home, but also seemed to doom her to a permanent fixation at that point, whereas Steven's partial focus upon the environment gave him the chance of further growth and differentiation. Steven's behavior in the nursing home suggested the presence of an anaclitic depression (Spitz, 1965).

Robert

Robert was born on 9/25/63 of a pregnancy clear of any complications. He sat at 10 months, crawled at 13 months, and walked between 16 and 18 months. Mrs. P. was hospitalized 3 months after Robert's birth, from 12/8/63 to 4/64. Robert stayed with a cousin's family during this time, and returned home when his mother did. He smiled responsively and gave up the bottle at 1 year when the nipple was changed. He said "mama" at 2 years and 3 months. Both parents felt that Robert was displaying signs of severe disturbance, and feared that he was "autistic." Mr. P. observed that Robert held his hands as Jacqueline had done, and had also started saying "la-la" as she had done.

This child was small in size, but physically well. He was kept very dependent, and would stay in a crib without complaint at the age of 2 years, 3 months. He was cared for by his mother, except for the period from 11 weeks to 6 months of age, when she was hospitalized.

Robert clung to his mother until 10/65, when she became more "upset." She was eventually hospitalized from 12/27/65 to 2/18/66. He then took a liking to the older girls. This point also marked the first time he began to let his father come near him.

The staff of the same day care program which had been attended by Jacqueline and Steven made an emergency evaluation on 12/30/65. Robert was observed to be aware of and in contact with the external environment, but to be fearful of separation, watching his father closely. He picked up toys and then visually searched the observers for their reactions. There was a good deal of cooing and gooing, and some beginning babbling, which finally resulted in Robert saying "mama." Robert also attended to his older brother Steven, and appeared to become upset by his "tantrums" and by being pulled at by him. He manipulated his father's hand to get what he wanted or to get to the door. This little boy was able to be comforted, and did look to his father for comfort. A concurrent psychological evaluation disclosed the physical features and motor behavior of a 16-18-month-old infant, with a general level of activity of an even younger child. Robert was satisfied to be held by his father. The final impression of the psychological evaluation was of a "generalized delay in maturation, probably due to a great extent to emotional deprivation and lack of stimulation."

Robert was placed in a foster home on 1/6/66, and regular visits were allowed by the family (see Table 3).

Analysis. Robert's contact with his mother was substantially different from that of his older brother and sister. Whereas they spent at least a year with their mother prior to her hospitalizations and absences from the home, Robert's initial period of contact was 6 weeks long. He was then placed in a relative's family until 5½ months of age. Thus, it seems unlikely that any but the most tenuous bonds could have been established between Robert and Mrs. P. prior to her hospitalization of 12/28/63. This fact would suggest that the foundation of object relatedness for Robert was laid in the cousin's family rather than with his biological mother. Robert's subsequent developmental retardation and ego

TABLE 3.   Robert: Developmental Sequence.

Date of Birth		9/25/63
Mother hospitalized		12/8/63 - 4/64
	1964	
Robert placed with relatives		
	1965	
Mother hospitalized		12/27/65 - 2/18/66
	1966	
Robert placed in foster home on 1/6/66, and family visits allowed		

deviation could be related either to the removal from a minimally adequate mothering (cousin's family) situation and the consequent depression, or to the setting up of the mothering relationship with his inconsistently infantilizing or ignoring schizophrenic mother. It is well known that an extended separation from the mothering figure during the last half of the first year of life can result in the development of an anaclitic depression (Spitz, 1965). This hypothesized depression could have played a large part in Robert's often noted passivity.

The phenomenological evidence would suggest that Robert was partially successful in avoiding becoming enmeshed in the intense alternating symbiotic-autistic relationship generated by his mother. Thus, he was able to move away from his mother and use an older sister as a mother surrogate, when Mrs. P. became emotionally upset and unavailable during his 3rd year of life. This capacity was one which had been beyond both Jacqueline and Steven, as their separation from the mother had resulted in severe regression. Although Robert did display a concern about separation and abandonment after his mother's hospitalization on 12/27/65, he was able to reach and form new relationships with both his father and an older sister.

DISCUSSION

The details of this case appear to raise interesting questions both as to the development of childhood psychopathology and to its therapeutic handling. The question of therapeutic handling is focused upon the advisability or value of the removal of these children from the home, which seemed to be based upon a strictly psychogenic theory of the etiology of mental illness, with relatively little attention having been paid to an evaluation of their psychological developmental level. The differential responses to separation of Jacqueline and Steven, as opposed to Robert, certainly give support to the theoretical positions of both Spitz (1965) and Mahler (1968) in regard to separation and individuation. Examination of the relationships between dates of birth, dates of hospitalizations, and dates of separations from mother and family (see Table 4) gives support to the theory of an active and dynamic process of child

TABLE 4. Hospitalizations and Placements.

Name	Birth Dates	Mother's Hospitalizations		Placements
Jacqueline	4/15/59	(1)	11/9/61 - 1/62	11/9/61 - 1/62 (Relatives)
		(2)	9/14/62 - 9/29/62	
		(3)	12/8/63 - 4/64	12/11/63 - 3/29/65 (Nursing Home)
				3/65 - 6/69 (Foster Home)
Steven	4/26/60	(1)	11/9/61 - 1/62	11/9/61 - 1/62 (Relatives)
		(2)	9/14/62 - 9/29/62	
		(3)	12/8/63 - 4/64	12/11/63 - 6/30/65 (Nursing Home)
		(4)	12/27/65 - 2/18/66	12/30/65 - 11/3/66 (Foster Home)
Robert	9/25/63	(3)	12/8/63 - 4/64	12/63 - 4/64 (Relatives)
		(4)	12/27/65 - 2/66	1/6/66 - Present (Foster Home)
		(5)	1/30/67 - 3/31/67	
		(6)	1/26/68 - 3/18/68	

development and individuation, rather than to any time-bound stage process. That is, the children in this family give clear support to the view that specific developmental tasks must be conquered before the child is free to develop further, rather than to a view that the child passes through the phases of development automatically. Neither Steven nor Jacqueline had achieved a level of individuation which allowed them to show an adaptive response to separation at the ages of 3 years, 8 months, and 4 years, 8 months; one would usually expect this task to have been handled by the age of 2 years (Mahler, 1968). Yet, Robert was able to show an adaptive response to separation at the age of 2 years, 3 months. Thus, it is apparent that the phases of development may be both expanded and contracted within the same family. The question which must be answered is: what are the variables which cause this type of change?

The P. family demonstrates that neither time nor pathology may be viewed as constants when dealing with child development and psychopathology. Merely being raised by a mothering figure for a year was not sufficient to promote individuation in Jacqueline and Steven, apparently because of their mother's inability to assist them in their tentative moves away from her toward the environment. This inability was seen as being related to Mrs. P.'s need to have a symbiotic relationship with her children, erratically alternating with a complete cessation of involvement. This erratic alternation appeared to be dictated by Mrs. P.'s fragile paranoid schizophrenic adjustment to the world.

Alternatively, Robert was able to attain a stable foundation of object relatedness during a 4-month placement with relatives shortly after his birth. This foundation endured over the next year and 8 months that he was raised by his biological mother. Thus, Robert's case appears to demonstrate that maternal psychopathology does not necessarily cause severe disturbance in a child who has mastered the initial task of awareness of self and of the external environment. This is the beginning of what has been labeled the "hatching" process (Mahler, 1968). It appears that "hatching" can be delayed a long time if the child is not helped by the mothering figure, but that once the process has begun, it can be continued under all but the most noxious of situations. Robert was able to turn to other figures when his mother had a psychotic breakdown.

Although Robert appeared to be the least damaged of the three younger children, it is interesting to note that his developmental milestones were the most delayed (see Table 5). This finding is of particular interest when viewed in light of a study (Davids et al., 1963) which disclosed that infants of "high anxiety" mothers "tend to receive lower developmental quotients in both the mental and motor areas" (p. 998). However, some of these implications appear to be confounded by the fact that the more seriously disturbed siblings (Jacqueline and Steven) had the less delayed developmental milestones.

Finally, this family certainly appears to raise serious questions as to the advisability of removing children from their natural home, without an extremely careful assessment of their level of object relatedness and their ties to the family, regardless of the pathology of the home situation. Jacqueline and Steven were in the midst of a symbiotic relationship with their mother at the time of their removal from the home, and

TABLE 5.   Developmental Milestones.

Name	Crawling	Sitting	Walking	Speech
Jacqueline	4 months	6 months	6-8 months	1 year
Steven	10 months	9 months	11-13 months	2 years
Robert	13 months	10 months	16-18 months	2 years, 3 months

had not achieved a level of individuation that enabled them to focus upon anything else but their mother. It seems questionable whether the decision to remove them from the home saved them from any emotional damage. Indeed, the placement may have caused more psychological damage than would have occurred if the P. family had been encouraged to remain intact, and been given both physical and psychological help to deal with the problems that developed. Robert spent the largest proportion of his life in this extremely disturbed family environment, compared to his two immediate siblings, and yet was the least disturbed of the three younger children. This case demonstrates the need for further detailed information and research on early child development and individuation, and its application to clinical practice.

REFERENCES

DAVIDS, A., HOLDEN, R. H. & GRAY, G. B. Maternal anxiety during pregnancy and adequacy of mother and child adjustment eight months following childbirth. *Child Development,* 1963, 34: 993–1002.

LAUFER, M. W. & GAIR, D. S. Childhood schizophrenia. In L. Bellak & L. Loeb, (Eds.), *The schizophrenic syndrome,* New York: Grune & Stratton, 1969. Pp. 378–461.

MAHLER, M. S. *On human symbiosis and the vicissitudes of individuation.* New York: International Universities Press, 1968.

SPITZ, R. A. *The first year of life.* New York: International Universities Press, 1965.

WARD, A. J. Early infantile autism: diagnosis, etiology, and treatment. *Psychology Bulletin,* 1970, 73: 350–362. (a)

————. An application of structural therapy to the residential treatment of early infantile autism. *Schizophrenia,* 1970, 2: 92–102. (b)

6

These Are Not
Autistic Children

The diagnosis of early infantile autism (EIA) has been a matter of dispute since the publication of Kanner's (1943) initial article. Several authors (Anthony, 1958; Ornitz & Ritvo, 1968; Ward, 1970) have suggested that many children labeled as "autistic" have a history of numerous organic and/or developmental problems which render them quite different from the Kannerian autistic child. Anthony described these children as cases of "secondary autism," and saw them as displaying a "period of normal development followed by an episode of great turbulence subsiding into a withdrawn, regressed and rigid period, and finally a phase of partial recovery at a lower level of functioning" (1958, p. 213).

Ornitz and Ritvo ascribed the development of EIA to "disturbances of perception" which were manifested by early developmental failure to distinguish self and environment, to imitate, and to modulate sensory input. These authors viewed EIA and other severe childhood psychopathologies as the behavioral manifestations of various types of organic and developmental malfunctions that had been caused by a breakdown of homeostatic regulation of sensory input. This breakdown was seen as having resulted in a condition of perceptual inconstancy which caused a symptomatology "expressive of underlying pathophysiology rather than being purposeful in the intrapsychic life of the child" (1968, p. 77).

Ward (1970) suggested that many cases of EIA comprised a group of children who might be labeled as "organic autistic children," due to their histories of difficult prenatal and perinatal development which were often followed by numerous types of developmental and perceptual problems. The crucial etiologic variable of the "developmental and per-

73

ceptual problems" was seen as resting in the cessation, dilution, or distortion of the child's awareness of varying and patterned stimuli in the environment during his early development. The awareness of such stimuli was seen as being vital to the development of body ego and the higher ego functions necessary for normal object relations development.

The brief review cited above offers support of the view that there has been an overemphasis upon psychodynamic interpretations in the diagnosis of the problems of young children who display strange and difficult-to-understand behavior. These psychodynamically based diagnoses have rarely succeeded in prescribing a successful course of treatment for EIA children (Ward, 1970). This paper hypothesizes that it is indeed "a mistake to . . . think that all difficulties of children must be due to environmental defects or pressures" (Wolff, 1969, p. 148), and that such an emphasis often results in an overlooking of serious physical or developmental problems which occur either in the mother during her pregnancy, or in the child subsequent to birth.

SUBJECTS

The subjects were five children hospitalized as cases of EIA.

Case 1

K was a nonverbal, Caucasian boy who was hospitalized at 6-10 for "destructive behavior, temper tantrums, uncontrollable, bizarre behavior, smearing saliva and feces, frequent crying, and pacing the floor."

The diagnosis of EIA overlooked several important facts in K's early developmental history. K was a product of a normal pregnancy and delivery, and developed normally until 18 months of age. He talked in context at 2½ years. This normal history was marred by a diagnosis of infected tonsils and adenoids at 1 month; persistent ear problems beginning at 1 year; scarlet fever followed immediately by measles at 18 months; the development of intense inner ear pain that resulted in all-night screaming and pacing the floor for periods of five to six weeks at a stretch, accompanied by K's poking and pulling his ears. There were recurrent serious inner ear infections which were treated with antibiotics between 2 and 3 years of age, and resulted in significant hearing loss in both ears (28% and 32%) before 34 months. K was operated on at 34 months and had removed "the most severely involved tonsils and adenoids that the doctor had seen." This hospitalization lasted five days and resulted in K's losing fifteen pounds, ceasing to speak, and losing the ability to play games with toys. K also contracted a staphylococcus infection in his inner ear during this hospitalization, which eventually necessitated two bilateral myringotomies at ages 3-7 and 4-5.

K then developed a "peculiar gait," became more of a behavior problem, was diagnosed as EIA, and was finally hospitalized after numerous agency contacts. The diagnosis of EIA was made, in spite of an electroencephalogram (EEG) which was given when K was 5-10, and was found to be "Abnormal because of the presence of multiple spike discharges suggesting increased cortical irritability."

The above cited history suggested that K could more accurately be viewed as a handicapped child with significant hearing loss and minimal brain damage, which had caused a moderate amount of retardation. A therapeutic strategy, which took these features of K's history into account and focused upon the development of body ego and early levels of object relations, enabled K to be removed from heavy tranquilizing medication and saw a marked decrease in temper tantrums and destructiveness, a cessation of smearing of feces and saliva, and a development of vocalizations and warm interpersonal relationships.

Case 2

E was a nonverbal, nonrelating Negro boy who was hospitalized at 6-11 for "inability to speak, very nervous." This child was described as the product of a "normal" pregnancy and delivery, but the mother was described as "very nervous," and after birth "the infant needed some resuscitation." Subsequently, E was reported to be easily startled by noise at six weeks. Also, E was kept in his crib until eighteen months.

E's need for resuscitation at birth and his hypersensitivity to noise (Bergman and Escalona, 1949), suggested the presence of significant amounts of brain damage. Exposure to a structured treatment milieu (Handford & Ward, 1969; Ward, 1968) enabled E to become more friendly, return home and attend a sheltered workshop setting for training.

Case 3

L was an echolalic, nonrelating Caucasian boy who was hospitalized at 11-2 for extreme screaming when left alone in bed and bizarre behavior. He was born in natural childbirth after a hard labor of thirty-six hours. L was "very alert" at birth (hypersensitivity), had colic from 3 to 6 weeks, and spoke of himself in the third person. L's mother had difficulty conceiving and required medical treatment; she also had an "underdeveloped uterus."

An EEG was performed when L was 12 years old and was seen as abnormal with "asymmetric delta theta [often associated with "immature" brain development and/or organicity] occurring singly and in bursts at varying stages." L had previously been exposed to eight years of intensive psychodynamically oriented psychotherapy to no avail and was finally diagnosed as a brain damaged and retarded boy who was in need of a training program.

Case 4

S was a nonverbal Caucasian female who was hospitalized at age 9-6 due to hyperactive, bizarre, and distractible behavior. She was the product of an uneventful pregnancy and delivery, sat alone at $5\frac{1}{2}$ months, walked at 16 months, and did not start to speak until almost 3 years of age. At age $2\frac{1}{2}$ S began becoming fearful, losing vocal and play patterns, and developing stereotyped hand and finger movements.

S displayed petit mal type seizures between ages 3 and 5, poor coordination, poor small muscle strength, and perceptual impairment. Abnormal EEG patterns were found at ages 5, 9 and 13; and focal seizures involving face and arms occurred at age 14. Repeated psychological testing found S to be functioning in the severely retarded range of intelligence. After years of psychodynamically oriented psychotherapy, S was finally diagnosed as a severely retarded girl.

Case 5

Z was a nonverbal, nonrelating, and ruminating Caucasian girl who was hospitalized at 7-8. She was not toilet trained, "defiant to authority," soiled self, smeared feces, and was distractible. Z was the product of a very difficult pregnancy and was delivered by induced labor a week before the actual due date. Her mother was sick at the start of pregnancy, bled with clots, and "passed out a few times."

Z cried continually her first 10 months, sat without support at 6 months, stood alone at 14-15 months, and did not walk alone until 22 months. She was described as being very soft ("like putty") as an infant, very thin, and not a good eater.

Extensive psychodynamically oriented therapy and three years in a school for emotionally disturbed children caused only minimal change in Z. However, three years of treatment in a program focused upon the development of body ego and higher ego functioning helped Z to develop communicative speech at the age of 12—more age-appropriate behavior —and to be discharged to home and enrollment in a class for the educable retarded in the public school system. An EEG performed at 12-2 revealed "a borderline abnormal EEG containing some paroxysmal diffuse activity," while another EEG given at age 13-4 showed "continued improvement with development of faster frequencies and lower voltages. Minimal sharp activity still present." The final diagnostic impression was of "chronic brain syndrome with mental deficiency."

DISCUSSION

It is felt that the cases presented above provide some supportive evidence of the hypothesis that there is indeed a separate group of children which could be labeled as "secondary autism" (Anthony, 1958) or "organic autism" (Ward, 1970). The purpose of this paper is to point out that the above cited cases do seem to indicate that children with central or peripheral perceptual problems based upon prenatal or postnatal events can display a facade of a period of "normal" development that crumbles as the environment makes increasingly complex demands upon them. The development of these children is either fixated or caused to regress depending upon the type and severity of the damage to the perceptual integration apparatus.

REFERENCES

ANTHONY, E. J. An experimental approach to the psychopathology of childhood. *British Journal of Medical Psychology,* 1958, 31: 211–223.

BERGMAN, P. & ESCALONA, S. K. Unusual sensitivities in very young children. *Psychoanalytic Study of the Child.* New York: International University Press, 1949. Pp. 3–4, 333–352.

HANDFORD, A. H. & WARD, A. J. Structural Therapy: A developmental approach to the treatment of Early Infantile Autism. *Journal of Schizophrenia,* 1969, 1 (4) : 243–248.

KANNER, L. Autistic disturbances of affective contact. *Nervous Child,* 1943, 2: 217–240.

ORNITZ, E. M. & RITVO, E. R. Neurophysiologic mechanisms underlying perceptual inconstancy in autistic and schizophrenic children. *Archives of General Psychiatry,* 1968, 19: 22–26.

WARD, A. J. The application of structural therapy to the residential treatment of Early Infantile Autism. Paper presented at meeting of the American Association of Psychiatric Clinics for Children in New York City in November 1968.

————. Early Infantile Autism: diagnosis, etiology and treatment. *Psychological Bulletin,* 1970, 73 (5) : 350–362.

WOLFF, S. *Children under stress.* London: Penguin: 1969.

7

The Multiple Pathways to Autistic Behavior

The diagnostic labels of early infantile autism (Kanner, 1943), childhood autism, and simply autism are bandied about quite loosely in the fields of early child development, child psychology, and child psychiatry. Yet, this careless usage often fails to meet any but the most simplistic definition and function of a diagnosis. The focus of this usage of the label and concept of "autism" is usually strictly and narrowly placed upon the overt observable *behavior* of the child.

The decision to label behavior as "autistic" is usually strongly influenced by the failure of the child to develop speech or by immature behavior in the young child. Often, repetitive or hard-to-understand behavior may be labeled "autistic." However, these varied usages seem to be only a shorthand way of saying that a large group of children display grossly similar symptomatology. There is little or no attempt or recognition of the fact that these children have arrived at this similar behavior in many different ways and for several different reasons.

Thus, as a recent study (Ward & Handford, 1968) has reported, children are called autistic who have quite different problems and prognosis. The organically brain damaged, the developmentally retarded, the mentally deficient, and the childhood schizophrenic all have been accurately described as displaying "autistic behavior," but there has been little or no effort to go beyond the mere labelling of this behavior.

Autism or autistic behavior must be viewed as only an indication of an existing level of functioning, but not as a statement regarding etiology, treatment, or prognosis. This is because a large portion of the current, professional literature has taken the position that childhood autism and autistic behavior are mental diseases or disorders, and that their etiology is psychogenic. This theoretical point of view then suggests that the treatment of choice should be one of conventional psychotherapy. However, a good deal of work summarized in a recent review (Ward, 1970b) has not only disclosed that conventional psychotherapy is not the treatment of choice in dealing with autistic behavior, but often that it has no effect whatsoever.

The assumption of a psychogenic etiology for autistic behavior has resulted in ignoring many features of pregnancy, birth, and early development which are suggestive or indicative of sensory defects, central nervous system problems, or organic brain damage. The similarity in behavior of blind children, deaf children, and other handicapped children has been reported (Wing, 1969) to the extent that it is no longer possible to make broad, sweeping generalizations as to etiology. Following are examples of varied backgrounds which have resulted in behavior being labelled "autistic":

SUBJECTS

The subjects were five children hospitalized as cases of autism, who have been previously reported in another context (Chapter 6). Further evaluation of this data led to the following thoughts on the utility of the concept of the syndrome of "Autism."

Case One

E was a nonverbal Caucasian boy who was hospitalized at 6-10 for "destructive behavior, temper tantrums, uncontrollable bizarre behavior, smearing saliva and feces, frequent crying and pacing the floor."

The diagnosis of autism overlooked several important facts in K's early developmental history. K was a product of a normal pregnancy and delivery, and developed normally until 18 months of age. He talked in context at 2½ years. This normal history was marred by a diagnosis of infected tonsils and adenoids at 1 month, persistent ear problems beginning at 1 year, scarlet fever followed immediately by measles at 18 months, the development of intense inner ear pain that resulted in all-night screaming and pacing the floor for periods of 5 to 6 weeks at a stretch accompanied by K's poking and pulling at his ears. There were recurrent serious inner ear infections which were treated with antibiotics between 2 and 3 years of age, and resulted in significant hearing loss in both ears (28% + 32%) before 34 months. At 34 months, "the most severely involved tonsils and adenoids that the doctor had seen" were removed from K. This hospitalization lasted five days and resulted in K's losing 15 pounds, ceasing to speak, and losing the ability to play games with toys.

K contracted a Staphylococcus infection in his inner ear during his hospitalization, which eventually necessitated two bilateral myringotomies at ages 3-7 and 4-5.

K then developed a "peculiar gait," became more of a behavior problem, was diagnosed as Autistic, and was finally hospitalized after numerous agency contacts. The diagnosis of Autism was made in spite of an EEG which was given when K was 5-10, and was found to be "Abnormal because of the presence of multiple spike discharges suggesting increased cortical irritability."

The above cited history suggested that K could be more accurately viewed as a handicapped child with significant hearing loss and minimal brain damage, which had caused a moderate amount of retardation. A therapeutic strategy which took these features of K's history into account, and focused upon the development of Body Ego and early levels of object relations enabled K to be removed from heavy tranquilizing medication, saw a marked decrease in temper tantrums and destructiveness, a cessation of smearing feces and saliva, and a development of vocalizations and warm interpersonal relationships.

Case Two

E was a nonverbal, nonrelating Negro boy who was hospitalized at 6-11 for "inability to speak, very nervous." This child was described as the product of a "normal" pregnancy and delivery, but the mother was described as "very nervous," and after birth "the infant needed some resuscitation." Subsequently, E was reported to be easily startled by noise at 6 weeks. Also, E was kept in his crib until 18 months.

E's need for resuscitation at birth and his hypersensitivity to noise (Bergman & Escalona, 1949) suggested the presence of significant amounts of brain damage. Exposure to a structured treatment milieu (Handford & Ward, 1969; Ward, 1970) enabled E to become more friendly, return home, and attend a sheltered workshop setting for training.

Case Three

L was an echolalic, nonrelating, Caucasian boy who was hospitalized at 11-2, for extreme screaming when left alone in bed and bizarre behavior. He was born in natural childbirth after a hard labor of 36 hours. L was "very alert" at birth (hypersensitivity), had colic from 3-6 weeks, and spoke of himself in the third person. L's mother had difficulty conceiving and required medical treatment. She also had an "underdeveloped uterus."

An EEG was performed when L was 12 years old, and was seen as abnormal with "asymmetric delta theta occurring singly and in bursts at varying stages." L was finally diagnosed as a brain damaged and retarded boy who was in need of a training program. L had previously been exposed to 8 years of intensive psychodynamically oriented psychotherapy to no avail.

Case Four

S was a nonverbal Caucasian female who was hospitalized at age 9-6 due to hyperactive, bizarre and distractible behavior. She was the product of an uneventful pregnancy and delivery, who sat alone at 5½ months, walked at 16 months, and did not start to speak until almost 3 years of age. At age 2½ S began becoming fearful, losing vocal and play patterns, and developing stereotyped hand and finger movements.

S displayed petit mal type seizures between ages 3 years and 5 years, poor coordination, poor small muscle strength and perceptual impairment. Abnormal EEG patterns were found at ages 5, 9 and 13; and focal seizures involving face and arms occurred at age 14. Repeated psychological testing found S to be functioning in the severely retarded range of intelligence. S was finally diagnosed as a severely retarded girl after years of psychodynamically oriented psychotherapy.

Case Five

Z was a nonverbal, nonrelating, and ruminating Caucasian girl who was hospitalized at 7-8. She was not toilet trained, "defiant to authority," soiled self and smeared feces and distractible. Z was the product of a very difficult pregnancy and was delivered by induced labor a week before the actual due date. Her mother was sick at the start of the pregnancy, bled with clots, and "passed out a few times."

Z cried continually her first 10 months, sat without support at 6 months, stood alone at 14-15 months, and did not walk alone until 22 months. She was described as being very soft ("like putty") as an infant, very thin and not a good eater.

Extensive psychodynamically oriented therapy and three years in a school for emotionally disturbed children caused only minimal change in Z. However, three years of treatment in a program focused upon the development of Body Ego and higher ego functions helped Z to develop communicative speech at the age of 12, more age-appropriate behavior, and to be discharged to home and enrollment in a class for the educable retarded in the public school system. An EEG performed at 12-2 revealed "a borderline abnormal EEG containing some paroxysmal diffuse activity," while another EEG given at age 13-4 showed "continued improvement with development of faster frequencies and lower voltages. Minimal sharp activity still present." The final diagnostic impression was of Chronic Brain Syndrome, with Mental Deficiency.

DISCUSSION

The above cases illustrate five different types of histories which were labelled as "autistic" behavior. Yet, none of these five cases could be accurately described as being of primarily psychogenic origin. Instead, the assumption of psychogenic origin resulted in years of unsuccessful and inappropriate psychotherapy for both children and their parents.

Thus, not only was an inappropriate therapeutic approach persisted in over the years in some cases, but actual physical deficits were ignored, undiscovered, and untreated. The above illustrative cases were selected because they were felt to demonstrate the varied chronological points of pregnancy, delivery, and early child development that were vulnerable to the creation of "autistic" behavior. Thus Case 1 is felt to demonstrate the danger that is inherent in allowing infections and high fevers to persist in the young child and is a very good example of what has previously been labelled as "organic autism" (Ward, 1970) or "secondary autism" (Anthony, 1958). The use of the label of autistic behavior is extremely misleading in this case, unless there is some attempt to delineate its etiology. One example of such an attempt might be:

1. Chronic brain syndrome secondary to inner ear infection
2. Significant hearing loss in both ears
3. Autistic behavior secondary to effects of the above at an early developmental level.

Case 2 is a good example of the effects of possible anoxia at birth upon central nervous system development. This child appeared to be basically an organically brain damaged child with attendant compensatory behaviors, who might be diagnosed as:

1. Chronic brain syndrome secondary to anoxia at birth
2. Autistic behavior secondary to above.

Case 3 illustrates the damage that can be done as a result of a prolonged and arduous labor, as well as possible anomalous results of medical aid in conception. This child might be more informatively diagnosed as:

1. Chronic brain syndrome secondary to difficult labor and possible conception difficulty
2. Deviant ego development and autistic behavior secondary to above.

Case 4 is a clear example of a child who displayed evidence of central nervous system and perceptual problems that were overlooked in favor of a diagnosis of autism. A more useful diagnosis might be:

1. Mental retardation, severe—unknown etiology
2. Epileptic seizures of endogenous etiology
3. Autistic behavior secondary to above factors.

Case 5 is an illustration of the fetal damage which can result from a difficult pregnancy. A more useful and informative diagnosis than autism might be:

1. Chronic brain syndrome—fetal damage resulting from difficult pregnancy
2. Mental retardation—moderate
3. Autistic behavior secondary to above factors.

CONCLUSIONS

This paper has pointed out the many other possible causes of "autistic" behavior besides the psychogenic. The increasing knowledge of early child and fetal development is demonstrating the multitudinous vulnerable points in a child's life where illness, chance, or heredity can lead to deviant ego formation and behavior. A global usage of such a term as "autistic behavior" does not take these developmental points and knowledge into account.

Thus, this advocacy of a more detailed system of diagnosis for the severely deviant younger child asks that the focus be changed: from a complete view of "autistic" behavior as resulting from just psychological problems within the child and/or the home, to a recognition and acceptance of the role that problems during pregnancy, birth, and early life have in the etiology of neurological, developmental, and perceptual handicaps that lead to the development of autistic behavior.

REFERENCES

ANTHONY, E. J. An experimental approach to the psychopathology of childhood. *British Journal of Medical Psychology*, 1958, 31: 21–223.

BERGMAN, P. & ESCALONA, S. K. Unusual sensitivities in very young children. In *The psychoanalytic study of the child*. New York: International University Press, 1949.

HANDFORD, H. A. & WARD, A. J. Structural therapy: A development approach to the treatment of early infantile autism. *Journal of Schizophrenia*, 1969, 1 (4): 243–248.

KANNER, L. Autistic disturbances of affective contact. *Nervous Child*, 1943, 2: 217–240.

WARD, A. J. The application of structural therapy to the residential treatment of early infantile autism. *Schizophrenia*, 1970, 2 (2,3) : 92–102. (a)

————. Early infantile autism: diagnosis, etiology and treatment. *Psychological Bulletin*, 1970, 73 (5) : 350–362. (b)

WARD, A. J. & HANDFORD, H. A. Early infantile autism: syndrome, symptom or wastebasket? Paper presented at Midwest Psychological Association in Chicago, Illinois, on May 2, 1968.

WING, L. The handicaps of autistic children—A comparative study. *Journal of Child Psychiatry*, 1969, 10: 1–40.

ETIOLOGY

8

Early Infantile Autism:
An Etiological Hypothesis

Numerous etiologic hypotheses have been advanced to explain the development of the syndrome of early infantile autism (EIA). These hypotheses may be broken down into two groups, one psychogenic and the other organic in focus.

The seminal article on EIA by Kanner (1943) takes the position that the syndrome is caused by an "emotional deprivation" resulting from the "refrigeration" of meticulous and compulsive parents. This hypothesis may be placed in the group of psychogenic hypotheses, along with the etiologic concepts of Garcia and Sarvis (1964), Green and Schecter (1957), Bettelheim (1967), Lewis and Van Ferney (1960), Loomis (1960), Anthony (1958), Mahler (1952), Starr (1954), Reiser (1963) and Norman (1954). Although the majority of this group of theorists feel that the roots of the syndrome are grounded in the lack of emotional stimulation of the child by the parent, there are some (Bettelheim, Garcia & Sarvis, Green & Schecter) who felt that the syndrome stems from an "overwhelming, symbiotic attitude of the mother" which frustrates and smothers the child's need for investigation, communication, and contact with the outer world.

The other group of theorists (Gordon, 1961; Ornitz & Ritvo, 1968; Polan & Spencer, 1959; Rimland, 1964) take positions which either explicitly or implicitly ascribe the development of the syndrome of EIA to some type of organic dysfunction and/or interference related to the perceptual apparatus.

Anthony (1958) attempts to bridge the theoretical gap between these two groups by proposing the concepts of primary autism (psychogenic) and secondary autism (organic). However, he takes the position that primary autism refers to the group labelled as EIA by Kanner, and he thus remains in the psychogenic group.

The etiologic hypotheses for the development of EIA range from the initial hypotheses of the "emotional refrigeration of meticulous and compulsive parents" (Kanner, 1943), to a dysfunction of the ascending reticular formation (Rimland, 1964), to the symptoms of an "unknown basic disease" (Ornitz & Ritvo, 1968). However, none of this wide range of etiologic concepts appears adequate to deal with the characteristics of lack of body ego (Mahler, 1952; Ward, 1968) and maintenance of sameness via stereotypic behavior (Kanner & Eisenberg, 1956; Ward & Handford, 1968). The lack of body ego is often manifested through the autistic child's failure to display any sense of pain, and through an apparent inability to differentiate his body from the inanimate external environment. The maintenance of sameness via stereotypic behavior has been found to be one of the few diagnostic characteristics which differentiate EIA from other severe childhood disturbances (Kanner & Eisenberg, Ward & Handford), and has been labelled as a specific type of deviant early ego development (Ward). This deviant early ego formation has been labelled "behavioral ego" because the child appears to have cathected a complex stereotypic pattern of behavior rather than his body, and its interruption leads to either a rage or withdrawal reaction until its resumption is permitted.

It has been pointed out (Ward) that both the features of lack of body ego and presence of behavioral ego are found in the first early weeks of life, and Mahler describes the autistic child as fixated at the "normal autistic phases" (0-6 months). Thus, there is some indication that EIA may involve a problem in normal development, rather than an "unknown basic disease" (Ornitz & Ritvo) or "a type of psychotic illness heretofore undescribed" (Kanner).

THE BARRIER HYPOTHESIS

Early infantile autism has often been described as a type of "functional sensory deprivation," and this concept is intimately involved in what has been labelled as the Barrier Hypothesis (Bergman & Escalona, 1949; Freud, 1920). Anthony (1958) made great use of the Barrier Hypothesis as an explanatory concept for EIA, ascribing the problem to the failure of the child to develop a "self protective ego barrier," due to a combination of a "constitutionally 'thick' barrier" and an insensitive and unresponsive mother. Essentially, Anthony proposed that some children were born who were "hard to reach," and that if they were born into an unstimulating environment they would never gain sufficient stimulation to become aware of the outside world and form an emotional tie with a "primary object." Thus, it was felt that there were two separate types of barriers which were involved, and that the first was organic in nature while the second had to be learned or developed in some manner. Anthony indicates that he feels that the EIA child has a "thicker" barrier of the first type, which accounts for the initial lack of responsiveness to the external world which has been labelled as "lack of object relations" or "autistic aloneness."

Developmental observations led Benjamin (1965) to postulate the existence of a "passive stimulus barrier" and an "active stimulus barrier." He proposed that the passive stimulus barrier existed for the first three to four weeks of life, and was a consequence of a lack of neural maturation; while the active stimulus barrier, defined by the capacity to shut out stimuli actively, depended upon a sufficient degree of neural maturation which began to appear at 8-10 weeks, and matured rapidly thereafter. These two periods of development are seen as being separated by a period of "heightened vulnerability" and sensitivity to external and internal stimuli.

These observations parallel those of Schachtel (1959) on the development of focal awareness. He found that the first four weeks disclosed a "vacant, confused stare" as the most typical behavior, while focal attention was firmly established by ten weeks of age. Martin (1968) expresses the opinion that the development of focal attention can be regarded as one facet of the development of the ego's stimulus barrier function.

Thus, recent use of the concept of the Barrier Hypothesis seems to indicate that the syndrome of EIA involves a fixation somewhere within or before the third month of normal development. The etiological question to be answered pertains to the cause of this fixation.

SENSORY DEPRIVATION

A recent paper (Ward, 1968) suggests that the EIA child has suffered from a lack of novelty and patterned stimulation in his early developmental history, and has been left to develop independently, by insensitive and unresponsive parents. However, if this were a sufficient cause of EIA, it is surprising that more of these children have not been discovered. Ward and Handford (1968) point out that EIA children are often confused with deaf and brain damaged children, and this fact seems to lend support to the position of Ornitz and Ritvo (1968) that the major problem stems from "perceptual inconstancy" related to either the environment or the condition of the perceptual apparatus. However, numerous reports have attested to the ability of the EIA child to exclude people and external stimuli almost at will. This capacity seems to indicate that there is at least some functioning of the "active stimulus barrier." Thus, it seems questionable whether the etiologic factor of external sensory and emotional deprivation alone is sufficient to account for the behavior of the EIA child, since this would seem to produce a child permanently walled off from the world by his "passive stimulus barrier."

The reports of Kanner and Eisenberg (1956) and Ward and Handford (1968), in combination with the concept of the "behavioral ego," all suggest that something has tremendously slowed down the developmental rate of EIA children. It is hypothesized that it is the combination of a child with a slow rate of development being born into a nonnurturing and unstimulating environment which results in the development of an EIA child.

This hypothesis raises the question of what could lead to such a slow rate of development in a child. There are numerous studies which indicate that postnatal development is slowed down by restricted experience of novel and patterned stimulation. In addition, Ourth and Brown (1961) suggest that the cutaneous, vestibular, and kinesthetic senses are stimulated while the fetus is in utero, and that this stimulation accounts for the sensitivities which are present at birth. They further hypothesize that birth itself could be viewed as a type of "mild deprivation," if the kinds and amounts of stimulation which the fetus is accustomed to, are not continued. Their study verifies this hypothesis by comparing the amount of crying observed in newborns who were handled at different rates during their first four days of life. A significant difference was found in the amount of crying between the two groups, and led to the conclusion that "the results of this study are consistent with a stimulus deprivation hypothesis which states that disruption of 'familiar' stimulus patterns results in generalized tension or disturbed behavior." Thus, it has been demonstrated that clinically healthy children born of "normal" mothers may experience the fact of birth itself as sensory deprivation and react with disturbed behavior if not handled and given adequate affective stimulation during their first days of life.

Evaluation of the infants of mothers described as "high anxiety" and "low anxiety" (Davids, Holden, & Gray, 1963), indicated that at eight months of age they differed significantly in mental developmental rate. Children of "high anxiety" mothers "tended to receive lower developmental quotients in both the mental and motor areas, and in general to present a less favorable picture of emotional adjustment." The authors do not make a choice between a difference in intrauterine or postnatal environments to account for the differences in these children, although they do show a bias towards the former position, when they cite data from studies with rats (Denenberg, Ottinger, & Stevens, 1962; Hockman, 1961; Thompson, 1957) showing that the offspring of extremely anxious mothers are themselves more emotional and show more signs of maladjustment.

A recent volume examines the effects of "prenatal maternal stress" upon infant behavior, and takes the theoretical position that, " . . . external events are potentially capable of influencing the developing fetus by their effects upon the mother and the transplacental transfer of active substances to the fetus" (Joffe, 1969, p. 127). Joffe states that the "most probable route for the effects of maternal stress on the foetus is that neuro-endocrinal changes, with their effects on the chemical composition of the maternal blood, are transmitted to the foetus, in which they effect neural, endocrinal, or other structures" (p. 128). Another less likely hypothesis presented is that fetal anoxia may be produced by spasmodic contraction of the uterine arteries when the pregnant female is placed in a stress situation.

A variety of animal studies suggest that the level of postnatal activity of offspring is greatly dependent upon the time of onset of prenatal stress, and one particular effect is of a "lower level of activity"; another study concludes that prenatal stress " . . . reduced the emotionality of the offspring" (Joffe, p. 151). No studies are reported which describe the production of EIA children, although several studies (Sontag, 1944, 1966; Turner, 1956) report that fetal activity which sharply increased following a "severe emotional shock," produced children with behavior similar to those described by Bergman and Escalona (1949). The prenatal effects of chronic prenatal stress in human mothers upon infant development and behavior have yet to be carefully articulated.

ETIOLOGIC HYPOTHESIS

Thus, on the basis of the material which has been earlier cited, it is proposed that the syndrome of EIA has the following etiology. First, it is proposed that the mother of the EIA child is an extremely anxious person during pregnancy, for any reason, whether it be a reaction to a reality situation, a chronic life style, or severe mental illness. Second, it is proposed that the neurological development of the EIA child is delayed as a result of the mother's high anxiety level. Third, it is proposed that the EIA child suffers a great deal of sensory deprivation at birth, due to both his own slow rate of development and the difficulty his anxious mother has in both picking up his nonverbal cues and providing spontaneous physical stimulation (Rothstein, 1967). Fourth, the EIA child is thought to take a much longer time to amass enough experiences with the environment to become able to form conceptual schemata of the world around him. Thus, it would seem likely that by the time he has become ready to form a tie to a primary object, every likely person has become exhausted and psychologically unavailable. Finally, it is proposed that the EIA child does manage to eventually bridge the gap between his long standing "passive stimulus barrier" and an "active stimulus barrier" ego function, but that he only does it in a defensive or limited way. People have usually proven to be too fleeting for the EIA child's slow development, and this has led him to focus upon objects instead of people. Thus, the behavioral ego and the capacity to shut out stimuli seem to be as far as the EIA child has been able to progress in the development of an "active stimulus barrier."

SUMMARY

This etiologic hypothesis claims that the syndrome of EIA is indeed a "total psychobiological disorder" (Kanner & Lesser, 1958), which has its roots in the crippling anxiety of the mother during her pregnancy, and that this condition produces a child slowed in the development of his awareness and understanding of the outer world. The birth of such a child into an unstimulating and nonnurturant environment results in a massive sensory deprivation or restriction which further slows down his development. Eventually, these children move to the edge of some area of competence or way of dealing with the world. However, this miniscule contact with the world usually focuses only upon objects or self-related behaviors, and results in the maintenance of sameness via stereotypic behavior which has been found to be diagnostic of EIA (Kanner & Eisenberg, 1956; Ward & Handford, 1968).

It is felt that EIA may be viewed as a rare combination of events related to early childhood development which combine the effects of emotion upon the developing fetus with the need of the young infant for an environment which offers varying and patterned stimulation. Early infantile autism is seen as being a developmental disorder rather than a type of childhood psychosis.

REFERENCES

ANTHONY, J. An experimental approach to the psychopathology of childhood. *Brit. J. Med. Psychol.*, 31: 211–223.

BENJAMIN, J. D. Developmental biology and psychoanalysis. In N. I. Greenfield & W. C. Lewis (Eds.), *Psychoanalysis and current biological thought.* Madison: University of Wisconsin Press, 1965.

BERGMAN, P. & ESCALONA, S. K. Unusual sensitivities in very young children. In *Psychoanalytic study of the child*, Vols. 3, 4. New York: International Universities Press, 1949.

BETTELHEIM, B. *The empty fortress.* New York: The Free Press, 1967.

DAVIDS, A., HOLDEN, R. H. & GRAY, GLORIA B. Maternal anxiety during pregnancy and adequacy of mother and child adjustment eight months following childbirth. *Child Development*, 1963, 34: 993–1002.

DENENBERG, V. H., OTTINGER, D. R. & STEVENS, M. W. Effects of maternal factors upon growth and behavior of the rat. *Child Development*, 1962, 33: 65–71.

FREUD, S. Beyond the pleasure principle. In J. Strachey (Ed.), *The standard edition of the complete psychological works of Sigmund Freud.* Vol. 18. London: Hogarth, 1955. (1920)

GARCIA, B. & SARVIS, M. A. Evaluation and treatment planning for autistic children. *Archives of General Psychiatry*, 1964, 10: 530–541.

GORDON, T. F. The world of the autistic child. *Virginia Medical Monthly*, 1961, 88: 469–471.

GREEN, M. R. & SCHECTER, D. E. Autism and symbiotic disorders in three blind children. *Psychiatric Quarterly*, 1957, 31: 628–646.

HOCKMAN, C. H. Prenatal maternal stress in the rat: its effect on emotional behavior in the offspring. *Journal of Comparative and Physiological Psychology*, 1961, 54: 679–684.

JAFFE, J. M. *Prenatal determinants of behavior.* New York: Pergamon, 1969.

KANNER, L. Autistic disturbances of affective contact. *Nervous Child*, 1943, 2: 217–240.

KANNER, L. & EISENBERG, L. Early infantile autism . . . Childhood schizophrenia symposium. *American Journal of Orthopsychiatry*, 1956, 26: 556–564.

KANNER, L. & LESSER, L. Early infantile autism. *Pediatric Clinics of North America*, 1958, 5 (3) : 711–730.

LEWIS, R. & VAN FERNEY, I. Early recognition of infantile autism. *Journal of Pediatrics*, 1960, 56: 510–512.

LOOMIS, E. A. Autistic and symbiotic syndromes in children. *Monograph of the Society for Research in Child Development*, 1960, 25 (3) : 29–48.

MAHLER, MARGARET I. On child psychosis and schizophrenia: autistic and symbiotic infantile psychoses. In *Psychoanalytic Study of the Child.* Vol. 7. New York: International Universities Press, 1952.

MARTIN, R. M., The stimulus barrier and the autonomy of the ego. *Psychological Review*, 1968, 75 (6) : 478–493.

NORMAN, E. Reality relationships of schizophrenic children. *British Journal of Medical Psychology*, 1954, 27: 126–141.

ORNITZ, E. M. & RITVO, E. R. Neurophysiologic mechanisms underlying perceptual inconstancy in autistic and schizophrenic children. *Archives of General Psychiatry*, 1968, 19: 22–26.

OURTH, LYNN & BROWN, K. Inadequate mothering and disturbance in the neonatal period. *Child Development*, 1961, 32: 287–295.

POLAN, C. C. & SPENCER, B. L. Check list of symptoms of autism in early life. *West Virginia Medical Journal*, 1959, 55: 198–204.

REISER, D. Psychosis of infancy and early childhood, as manifested by children with atypical development. *New England Journal of Medicine*, 1963, pp. 790–798, 844–850.

RIMLAND, B. *Infantile autism.* New York: Appleton, 1964.

ROTHSTEIN, R. Stimulational and interaction patterns of autistic children and their parents. Paper presented at Eastern Psychological Association Convention, Boston, Mass., on April 7, 1967.

SCHACHTEL, E. G. *Metamorphosis.* New York: Basic Books, 1959.

SONTAG, L. W. Differences in modifiability of fetal behavior and physiology. *Psychosomatic Medicine*, 1944, 6: 151–154.

————. Implications of fetal behavior and environment for adult personalities. *Annals of the New York Academy of Science*, 1966, 134: 782–786.

STARR, P. H. Psychoses in children: their origin and structure. *Psychoanalytic Quarterly*, 1954, 23: 544–565.

THOMPSON, W. R. Influence of prenatal maternal anxiety on emotionality in young rats. *Science*, 1957, pp. 698–699.

TURNER, E. K. The syndrome in the infant resulting from maternal emotional tension during pregnancy. *Medical Journal of Australia*, 1956, 1: 221–222.

WARD, A. J. The application of Structural Therapy to the residential treatment of Early Infantile Autism. Paper presented in Convention of American Association of Psychiatric Clinics for Children in New York City on November 8, 1968.

WARD, A. J. & HANDFORD, H. A. Early Infantile Autism: syndrome, symptom, or wastebasket? Paper presented at Mid-western Psychological Association Convention in Chicago, Illinois on April 2, 1968.

9

The Effect of Maternal Anxiety and Difficult Pregnancies Upon the Fetal and Later Development of Autistic and Autistic-Like Children

Evaluation of the question of the etiology of early infantile autism (EIA), early childhood autism (ECA), or the loosely labelled group of children who display "autistic" behavior has led to no unitary or fruitful explanations (Ward, 1969, 1971). Instead, the old questions of psychogenicity, organicity, or any combination of these extremes continue to be raised. Close examination of any group of "autistic" children usually reveals a heterogeneous group of children with a wide spectrum of physical problems, emotional problems, and developmental problems (Ward & Handford, 1968). Little evidence has been found of any etiological commonality.

A recent article (Ward, 1969) suggested that the EIA syndrome "has its roots in the crippling anxiety of the mother during her pregnancy, and that this condition produces a child slowed in the development of his awareness and understanding of the outer world" (p. 8). This hypothesis was based upon both animal research (Denenberg, Ottinger, & Stevens, 1962; Hockmann, 1961; Thompson, 1957) and research with humans (Everett & Schechter, 1971; Jost & Sontag, 1944; Sontag, 1941; and Turner, 1956). All of these studies suggested that stress and anxiety during pregnancy tended to produce offspring with higher levels of anxiety, slower rate of development, and a higher rate of emotional disturbance. Also, another study has hypothesized the basis for the mechanism involved in this progress: "The most probable route for the effects of material stress on the foetus is that neuro-endocrinal changes, with their effects on the chemical composition of the maternal blood, are transmitted to the foetus, in which they effect neural, endocrinal or other structures" (Jaffe, 1969, p. 128).

The present paper focuses upon a retrospective evaluation of both the physical and emotional status of mothers of emotionally disturbed children during their pregnancies. It is also an evaluation of the physical condition and psychological condition of these emotionally disturbed children early in their developmental histories. All of the subjects evaluated had been referred to the Autistic Children's Treatment, Training, and Research Service (ACTTRS) for residential treatment between 1964 and 1972.

The hypotheses to be examined are:

1. There are no significant occurrences of psychological stress or emotional disturbance in the histories of the pregnancies of the mothers of these disturbed children.
2. There are no significant occurrences of physical problems in the histories of the pregnancies of the mothers of these disturbed children.
3. There are no significant reports of negative affect towards these children during pregnancy.
4. There are no significant occurrences of difficult pregnancies in the histories of the mothers of these disturbed children.
5. There are no significant occurrences of difficult deliveries in the histories of the mothers of these disturbed children.
6. There are no significant occurrences of physical problems reported immediately after the birth of these children.

7. There are no significant occurrences of jaundice and/or colic in the early developmental history of these children.

8. There are no significant occurrences of physical problems in the early developmental history of these children.

9. There are no significant occurrences of spitting or vomiting in the early developmental histories of these children.

10. There are no significant occurrences of reported negative affect toward these children early in their developmental histories.

11. There are no significant differences in the type of initial psychological problems presented by these children early in their developmental histories.

SUBJECTS

A total of 59 children, 46 boys and 13 girls, have been treated or are being treated in ACTTRS at Eastern State School and Hospital. The mean age of this group upon admission was 92 months or 7 years-8 months. There were 46 boys who had a mean age of 92 months, and 13 girls with a mean age of 88 months. The age range of the boys was 35 months through 150 months, while the age range of the girls was 41 months through 122 months (see table 1).

TABLE 1.   Biographical Data on Autistic and Autistic-Like
Children (N = 59).

Categories	Number	Mean Age	Age Range
Male	46	92 Months	35 Months - 150 Months
Female	13	87.5 Months	41 Months - 122 Months
Totals	59	91.1 Months	35 Months - 150 Months

The hospital records of all 59 subjects were examined according to a questionnaire (see figure 1). The results of this questionnaire have been collated and are reported in a series of tables.

RESULTS

Hypothesis 1: There are no significant occurrences of psychological stress or emotional disturbance in the histories of the pregnancies of the mothers of these disturbed children.

Examination of the charts of all 59 subjects revealed the following findings: Only 13 cases reported the absence of any family problems dur-

FIGURE 1.   Questionnaire: Records of Autistic and Autistic-Like Children.

Name:	Sex:
1. Date of birth:	15. State of infant at birth:
2. Date of admission:	16. Prenatal care:
3. Date of discharge:	17. Vomiting or excessive physical reaction to pregnancy:
4. Diagnosis:	
5. Age of mother at birth:	18. Physical health, newborn:
6. Number of previous pregnancies:	19. Caring (source of information) :
7. Number of previous deliveries:	20. Nurse or mother surrogate:
8. Marital status, mother:	21. Breast feeding:
9. Mother's emotional status during pregnancy:	22. Spitting up or vomiting:
	23. Jaundice or colic:
10. Family problems during pregnancy:	24. Attitude towards pregnancy during pregnancy:
11. Type of pregnancy:	25. Reaction to child after birth:
12. Type of delivery:	26. Record of excessive traveling:
13. Weight at birth:	27. Additional information:
14. Infant in hospital after mother home:	

ing the pregnancies of the subject child. Also, no relevant information was recorded for 3 other subjects. Thus, only a total of 16 out of 59 subjects (27%) were born of a pregnancy that was not complicated by some emotional and/or reality stress.

The largest group of subjects (32%) was reported to have had discord in the family during the pregnancies. Discord was a category that included such items as interference in family functioning by previous husband, feeling "insane," or frequent arguments.

The next largest group of subjects (20%) came from families where one or the other parent was experiencing severe psychiatric problems during the pregnancy. These problems included such diagnosed emotional disturbances as psychosis, schizophrenia, and nervous breakdowns.

Six subjects came from families where the parents separated during the pregnancy. Finally, there were 3 subjects each who were the result of pregnancies marked by the problem of a dominant mother-in-law and severe feelings of maternal inadequacy.

Thus, 73% of the subjects were the result of pregnancies which reported outstanding family problems, which could be hypothesized to have exerted an unusual amount of stress upon the mother (see table 2).

TABLE 2.   The Presence of Family Problems During the Pregnancies of
Mothers of Autistic and Autistic-Like Children (N = 59) .

Category	Frequency
No problems apparent	13
Discord	19
Diagnosed problems in parents*	12
Dominant mother-in-law	3
Separations of parents	6
Maternal feeling of inadequacy	3
Not recorded	3
Total	59

*Diagnosis for one or both parents include psychosis, schizophrenia, nervous
breakdowns, psychotic episode.

Hypothesis 2: There are no significant occurrences of physical problems in the histories of the pregnancies of the mothers of these disturbed
children.

Analysis of the records revealed that 41 mothers (69%) failed to report the presence of vomiting or any other excessive physical reaction during pregnancy. However, a total of 14 mothers (23%) did report excessive
physical reactions that included nausea, anemia, hypertension, and car-
diac decompensation (see table 3) . No information was available in 4
of the cases.

TABLE 3.   Presence of Vomiting and/or Excessive Reaction During Pregnancy
in Mothers of Autistic and Autistic-Like Children (N = 59) .

Category		Pregnancy
No		41
Yes — nausea (one case passed out several times)	8	
anemia (one case exhibited hypertension		
and cardiac decompensation)	3	
depression-nervous	2	
spotting	1	14
No response		4
Total		59

Hypothesis 3: There are no significant reports of negative affect directed towards the fetus during pregnancy.

Examination of the pregnancy histories of the mothers of these subjects revealed that the largest group of mothers (34%) were described as being "emotionally upset" about their pregnancies. This category included those mothers who were described as being nervous, depressed and ambivalent (see table 4).

TABLE 4.   Emotional Attitudes and Status of Mothers of Autistic and
Autistic-Like Children During Pregnancy (N = 59).

Category	Frequency
Happy—wanted baby	14
Unplanned	4
Unplanned—cause of marriage	2
Emotionally upset (nervous, depressed, ambivalent)	20
Not recorded	17
Not wanted	2
Total	59

It is important to report that the next largest group of subjects consisted of 17 cases (29%) which included no record of the mothers' attitudes towards their pregnancies. This would suggest that no strong affect was admitted or experienced in regards to the pregnancy, and that this unreported group would probably tend towards neutral or negative affect towards the fetus.

Only a total of 14 mothers (24%) were described as being happy about their pregnancies and as wanting their babies. These reports would be indicative of the strongest positive affect towards and acceptance of the fetus. Two mothers were specifically recorded as definitively not wanting the baby.

Thus, an overall summation of these cases would indicate that the majority of the cases reporting disclosed some type of significant negative affect directed towards the fetus. Inclusion of the nonreporting group would only further increase the negative bias of this sample.

Hypothesis 4: There are no significant occurrences of difficult pregnancies in the histories of the mothers of these disturbed children. The majority of mothers (53%) of these children reported a physically normal pregnancy.

A wide variety of problems characterized the pregnancies of the rest of the sample. These problems included such occurrences as rubella in-

TABLE 5.   Type of Pregnancy Experienced by Mothers of Autistic and
Autistic-Like Children (N = 59) .

Type of Pregnancy	Frequency
Normal	31
Difficult (constipation-indigestion, muscular pain, excess weight gain)	4
Bleeding	5
Rubella or other infection	2
Nausea	5
Rh problem	4
Other (anemia, congestive heart failure, appendectomy, drugs such as Preludin)	6
Not recorded	2
Total	59

fections, Rh incompatibility, spotting, appendectomy, etc. (see table 5) .
Thus, although no single problem was seen to characterize the pregnancies of these mothers, 26 cases (44%) were found to have experienced some type of physical difficulty.

Hypothesis 5: There are no significant occurrences of difficult deliveries in the histories of the mothers of these disturbed children.

Examination of the histories of the deliveries of these subjects revealed that 22 children (37%) were the result of full term, normal deliveries. However, all the other subjects were the products of deliveries which were unusual to some degree, except for the two cases which provided no information on this question. The spectrum of delivery problems included Caesarian delivery, breech delivery, excessive length of labor, and forceps delivery (see table 6) . Thus, a total of 34 cases (58%) of this sample were found to have experienced some type of difficulty at the time of delivery.

Hypothesis 6: There are no significant occurrences of physical problems reported immediately after the birth of these children.

Examination of the birth records of these disturbed children revealed that the large majority of them (68%) were normal at birth, and displayed no apparent physical problems (see table 7) . However, 7 cases (11%) were found to have had trouble breathing at birth. Also, another 7 cases were found to have had a variety of problems ranging from prematurity to infection to brain damage. Thus, a total of 14 cases (22%)

of these children gave evidence of some physical problem at birth which would have to be included in any etiological formulation of their later problems.

TABLE 6.   Nature of Delivery of Autistic and Autistic-Like Children (N = 59).

Type of Delivery	Frequency
Full term—normal	22
Full term—induced	4
Full term—Caesarian*	7
Late—more than one week	4
Early—less than one week	7
Full term—long labor, twelve hours	7
Full term—breech	2
Full term—forceps	3
No response	3
Total	59

*Several long labors terminated in Caesarian.

TABLE 7.   State of Autistic and Autistic-Like Children at Birth (N = 59).

Category	Frequency
Normal—no problems	40
Trouble breathing*	7
Brain injury indicated†	1
Treated with antibiotics	1
Cephalohematoma	2
Infection	1
Incubated—isolette‡	2
No response	5
Total	59

*One case had umbilical cord wrapped around neck—no artificial respiration used. One case was anoxia; and one case had simple infection in placenta; one case had a break in placenta.
†Abnormal deep tendon reflexes.
‡One case of rigidity.

Hypothesis 7: There are no significant occurrences of jaundice and/or colic in the early developmental histories of these children.

Examination of the early developmental histories of these disturbed children disclosed that 21 subjects (36%) had experienced either jaundice or colic (see table 8). This rate of incidence is far in excess of the usually cited incidence figure of 20% (Gustafson, 1964, p. 52).

TABLE 8.   Frequency of Reports of Jaundice and/or Colic in Early History of Autistic and Autistic-Like Children (N = 59).

Category	Frequency
Yes (one jaundice, remainder colic)	21
No	35
No response	3
Total	59

Hypothesis 8: There are no significant occurrences of physical problems in the early developmental histories of these children.

Examination of their histories disclosed a total of 37 categories and 95 incidents of physical problems for the 59 subjects in this sample (see table 9).

Hypothesis 9: There are no significant occurrences of spitting or vomiting in the early developmental histories of these children.

Examination of the records discloses a total of 21 cases (35%) which reported the presence of vomiting or spitting up (see table 10). A total of 35 cases (59%) failed to report this behavior, while 3 cases failed to report any information on this point.

Hypothesis 10: There are no significant occurrences of reported negative affect toward these children early in their developmental histories.

Examination of the records kept of the affect displayed towards these children by their mothers indicated that 14 children (24%) were regarded with "affectionate concern" (see table 11).

Another 14 cases (24%) disclosed the mothers to be very upset with the behavior of their children, with attendant guilt feelings.

Ten cases (17%) were found to have reports of "little interrelationship between mother and child"; while another 7 cases (12%) were overtly neglected, abused, and rejected.

A smaller number of cases reflected excessive contact (4 cases), denial of problems of the child (3 cases), and the mother's feeling unable to cope with the child (3 cases). No information was available from 4 cases.

TABLE 9.   Autistic and Autistic-Like Children Registering
Physical Illness or Problems (N = 59) .

Category	Frequency	Category	Frequency
Vomiting	3	Generally sickly	1
Diarrhea and/or constipation	5	Blow to head	3
Measles	6	Swallow washing soda	1
Convulsions—seizures	6	Asian Flu	1
Tonsils and adenoids removed	1	Colic	21
Scarlet Fever	1	Hernias	1
Abnormal EEG	2	Malnutrition	1
High fever	8	Surgery	1
Ear infection	3	Tranquilizers used	1
Illness	1	Deafness	1
Croup	2	Throat infection	1
Frequent colds	1	Kidney infection	1
Respiratory infection	4	Phenobarbital	1
Heavy metal ingestion	1	Broken arm	1
Rigidity	1	Roseola	1
Eye operations	2	Battered child	1
Restraints	4	Late fontanel closure	1
Chicken Pox	3	Boils	1
		Cut mouth on tooth	1
Total			95

TABLE 10.   Reports of Spitting and/or Vomiting in Early Histories of
Autistic or Autistic-Like Children (N = 59) .

Category	Frequency
Yes (includes 16 cases of colic)	21
No	35
No response	3
Total	59

Thus, a total of 38 cases (64%) may be conservatively estimated to have been the recipients of negative affect early in their developmental history. This total does not include the 3 cases of "denial of problems of child."

Hypothesis 11: There is no significant difference in the types of ini-

TABLE 11.   Affective Response of Mothers of Autistic and Autistic-Like Children to Them After Their Birth (N = 59).

Reaction to Child After Birth*	Frequency
Affectionate concern	14
Upset with behavior-guilt	14
Excessive contact	4
Neglect-abused-rejection	7
Little interrelationship—mother and child	10
Denial of problems of child	3
Mother felt unable to cope	3
No response	4
Total	59

*Recorded primarily mother's response.

tial psychological problems presented by these children early in their developmental histories.

Examination of the initial reports of psychological problems presented by these children revealed a list of 41 categories of problems with 224 separate incidents (see table 12).

The most frequent problem areas listed were feeding problems (22 subjects), slow development (19), hospitalizations (15), toilet training problems (14), regression (14), birth of a sibling (12), hyperactivity (13), no speech (11), delayed speech (11), cessation of talking (10), and rocking (10).

Thus, rather than disclosing any one pattern of problems leading to a syndrome of "autistic" behavior, examination of the emotional histories of these children reveals a total spectrum of childhood developmental and psychological problems.

DISCUSSION

A summation of the eleven proposed null hypotheses discloses that there are groups of data which would suggest that each hypothesis should be rejected. As the basic focus of this paper is upon the etiology and later development of "autistic" children, an attempt will be made to integrate the results of this study into the current understanding of these problems.

The concept of the effect of emotional stress upon foetal development is both a controversial one in science, as well as a long-standing one

TABLE 12.   Autistic and Autistic-Like Children and the Psychological Problems Registered in Early Development (N = 59).

Category		Frequency	Category	Frequency
Nightmares		3	Regressed	14
Temper tantrums		5	Poor sleeper	4
Shyness		2	Feeding problems	22
Stopped talking		10	Treats people as	
0-12 mo.	-1		objects	1
13-24 mo.	-5		Destructiveness	5
25-34 mo.	-4		No speech	11
Mother worked		1	Mother hospitalized	4
Toilet training problems		14	Delayed speech	11
Slow development		19	Placed in home	2
Short attention		1	Self-occupied—	
Birth of sibling		12	withdrawn	7
0-12 mo.	-1		Nervous	1
13-24 mo.	-8		Death in family—	
25-34 mo.	-2		grieving	1
no age given	-1		Melancholic	1
Hyperactive		13	Not affectionate	3
Undemanding		2	Loud noises upset	3
Rocking		10	Infantilized	2
Lost balance		1	Separated from parents	4
Hospitalized		15	Smearing	2
Head banger		6	Left alone—extended	
Marriage deteriorates		1	period	1
Finger play		1	Beatings	1
Lacked affect		3	Tense when held	3
Night fears		1	Contorted face	1
Total				224

in many cultures. However, little normative data is known in this area, and there is certainly a great need for such data in the area of early child development and childhood psychopathology. The lack of a control group for this study makes it impossible to definitively state that most of the findings are statistically significant. Yet, it is hoped that these findings will be found stimulating enough to lead researchers to gather both normative data in many of the suggested areas, as well as to conduct vitally needed longitudinal studies.

Although no normative figures are available as to family discord frequency during the pregnancies of normal children, the fact that the largest single group of records (32%) was characterized by family discord certainly would appear to be of significance. As this situation antedated the birth of the disturbed child, it is a clear refutation of the often stated hypothesis that it is the child's disturbance which has caused the family discord, rather than vice versa. Also, the high incidence of diagnosed psychiatric problems (20%) prior to the birth of the disturbed child certainly raises severe question as to the ability of these families to care for any child.

The fact that almost three quarters (73%) of the mothers and families of these disturbed children were undergoing some type of stress during pregnancy would seem to be a good occasion for any postulated stress effect to make itself manifest. Furthermore, the fact that 22 of 42 responding cases (52%) reported an upset or rejecting attitude towards the foetus during pregnancy indicates that any postulated negative effect upon foetal development would be compounded by a negative attitude towards the child subsequent to his birth. Finally, although the distortion of parental reports is well recognized, it is important to note that the above hypothesized negative attitude towards the neonate is supported by the results of this study. Thus, these children who are the products of significantly emotionally disturbed parents whose families are upset by all types of discord, and whose mothers have an essentially negative view towards them in utero, are born and greeted by negative affect in almost two out of three (64%) cases. Then this psychological line of development culminated in the early development of 41 different types of psychological problems, which eventually resulted in the label of "autistic" behavior and hospitalization. Thus, from an affective and psychological point of view, it seems as if these children have experienced a negative bias almost from the moment of conception.

Examination of the results of this questionnaire from a physical point of view is equally of interest. A large percentage (23%) of the mothers of these children experienced excessive or marked physical reactions to their pregnancies. Although a majority (53%) of the pregnancies were found to be normal, it is important to note the high incidence of physical problems (44%) encountered in this sample. Further attention is focused upon this area by the later finding that 58% of these mothers encountered some type of physical difficulty or anomaly at the time of delivery.

Furthermore, the report that 22% of these children displayed problems at birth ranging from difficulty in breathing to infection to brain damage continues the suggestion of a continuing line of physical difficulties in these children. Further support to the existence of such a line of development is provided by the above-the-expected incidence of colic, spitting, and vomiting reported in these children. Also, frequent complaints of slow development, high fevers, convulsions, and so forth would suggest that many of these subjects are vulnerable children and have been since conception.

In summary, the responses to this questionnaire appear to give further support to the often expressed view that "autistic behavior" is found in a wide variety of disturbed, handicapped, deviant children; and that there is no common etiology which would support the concept of a specific diagnostic category of autism or EIA. The report of frequent emotional stress, difficult pregnancies, and widespread negative affect both prior to and subsequent to birth would certainly support the possibility of an effect upon foetal development if there is such a postulated physical mechanism in operation. However, more detailed retrospective studies or longitudinal studies must be carried out to find an answer to this intriguing question.

Regardless of the final answer to the question of the effect of maternal stress upon foetal development, the findings of this study clearly demonstrate the multifactored nature of the etiology and development of those children variously labeled as atypical, autistic, and so forth. The fact that negative feelings and situations antedate the birth of these children suggests that all but the most competent of infants would have difficulty in developing in such settings. It seems quite likely that the environment is too "busy," for psychological or reality reasons, to provide the adequate growth situation for any infant who is not equipped by temperament and physiology to demand the appropriate responses.

This is not to say that autism is the fault of the parents nor that it is an organic problem. Instead, this is simply a statement that all children are different, and require a response tailored to their needs. Failure to meet these needs will result in delayed and/or deviant ego development. Thus, it would appear likely that any psychological or physical condition, on the part of the infant or the parents, which interferes with the provision of these responses to a neonate or young infant can result in slowed or deviant ego development that may eventually result in what has been labeled as "autistic behavior." However, it is important to note that the data from this study seem to indicate that there are many points of possible therapeutic intervention prior to the development of behaviors which necessitate hospitalization of the child.

REFERENCES

DENENBERG, V. H., OTTINGER, D. R. & STEVENS, M. W. Effects of maternal factors upon growth and behavior of the rat. *Child Development*, 1962, 33: 65–71.

EVERETT, R. B. & SCHECHTER, M. D. A comparative study of prenatal anxiety in the unwed mother. *Child Psychiatry and Human Development*, 1971, 2 (2) : 84–91.

GUSTAFSON, I. R. *The pediatric patient*. Philadelphia: J. B. Lippincott Co., 1964.

HOCKMANN, C. H. Prenatal maternal stress in the rat: its effect on emotional behavior in the offspring. *Journal of Comparative and Physiological Psychology*, 1961, 54: 679–684.

JAFFE, J. M. *Prenatal determinants of behavior*. London: Pergamon Press, 1969.

JOST, H. & SONTAG, L. W. The genetic factor in autonomic nervous system functions. *Psychosomatic Medicine*, 1944, 6: 308–310.

SONTAG, L. W. The significance of fetal environmental differences. *American Journal of Obstetrics and Gynecology*, 1941, 42, 996–1003.

THOMPSON, W. R. Influence of prenatal maternal anxiety on emotionality in young rats. *Science*, 1957, pp. 698–699.

TURNER, E. K. The syndrome in the infant resulting from maternal emotional tension during pregnancy. *Medical Journal of Australia*, 1956, 1: 221–222.

WARD, A. J. & HANDFORD, H. A. Early infantile autism: syndrome, symptom or wastebasket? Paper presented at Mid-western Psychological Association Convention in Chicago, Illinois on April 2, 1968.

WARD, A. J. Early infantile autism: an etiological hypothesis. Paper presented at convention of the American Association of Psychiatric Clinics for Children in Boston, Massachusetts in November 1969.

————————. The multiple pathways to autistic behavior. Presented at the convention of the American Psychological Association in Washington, D.C., on September 4, 1971.

TREATMENT

10

The Joint Treatment of an "Autistic" Child by Clinical Psychology and Speech Therapy*

Alan J. Ward and Virginia M. Leith

The purpose of this case presentation is twofold. The first is to highlight the importance of a careful differential diagnosis when dealing with severe emotional or developmental problems in very young children. The syndrome of Early Infantile Autism (Kanner, 1943) has stimulated much research and discussion in the last two decades, but relatively little data have been presented on the topic of differential diagnosis.

Many theorists view Early Infantile Autism as a distinct and separate diagnostic category (Kanner, 1943; Mahler, 1952, 1968; Reiser, 1963; Rimland, 1964), but few list specific diagnostic criteria. Kanner and Eisenberg (1956) suggest that the major diagnostic characteristics of EIA are:

1. the lack of object relations
2. the maintenance of sameness via stereotypic behavior.

*Reprinted with permission from *International Journal of Child Psychotherapy*, 1973, 2:4, 451–471.

A recent paper (Ward and Handford, 1968) reported that the only feature that differentiated EIA children was that of maintenance of sameness via stereotypic behavior. Finally, a current review of the literature (Ward, 1970b) indicates that the characteristics that differentiate EIA children are:

1. lack of object relations;
2. lack of the *use* of speech for communication;
3. maintenance of sameness via stereotypic behavior;
4. lack of any organic or neurologic dysfunction.

Many children who fail to meet the above criteria have been labeled as "autistic," hospitalized for long years (Ward and Handford, 1968), and submitted to verbal and analytically-oriented play therapy that is far above their level of conceptual functioning. Therefore, these children often do not respond to therapy, frequently regress while hospitalized, and are ultimately labeled as "hopeless" cases.

The second purpose of this case presentation is to demonstrate that the child who has regressed to early levels of emotional development (6 to 18 months), but who retains some contact with the environment, should not be labeled as a case of Early Infantile Autism and need not be hospitalized to attain significant therapeutic progress. It is also proposed that this type of child needs to be dealt with on an affective and physical level (Ward, 1970a), as opposed to the verbal interactions used in more conventional types of play therapy.

CATHY

Presenting Problems

Cathy was first referred for a diagnostic evaluation to our research project on Early Infantile Autism at the age of three years, four months, by the family pediatrician. She had previously been privately evaluated by a psychologist, who felt that Cathy had had "developmental problems since birth," which had been manifested during the first year of life in "feeding, sleep and affectional disturbances."

Cathy failed to develop speech during her second year of life, toilet training was unsuccessful, and she failed to develop age-appropriate social and play behavior patterns. This little girl was described as failing to relate to people, and she was only attentive to another person while watching television. She was described as spending "long hours" standing close to the television screen and would demand, by pointing with her finger, that her mother repeat precisely what was being shown on the television commercial; she would become very upset unless her mother said the required word. Both parents were very confused and anxious, and they could not understand what to do about the situation.

The psychological evaluation had disclosed a high degree of autistic aloneness or "imperviousness," and Cathy was described as using the toys and objects in a "sensory manner" (licking and smelling them), and arranging some of them in a "stereotyped methodical way." The patient was seen as being "severely ego-disturbed" with many "autistic-like symptoms," which it was felt required further evaluation to decide whether or not this was a case of Early Infantile Autism.

Developmental History. Cathy was the first child conceived after 13 years of marriage by parents who appeared rather settled. Her mother manifested a certain perplexity as to how to handle her daughter, and she was less spontaneous in response than was the father. Cathy weighed less than five pounds at birth after a normal, full-term pregnancy. She was considered a "premature" child, and was kept in a unit for premature children for a week after her mother had returned home. Cathy slept through the night almost immediately, and her parents took this behavior as a sign of a "good baby," and were relieved that there would not be as many "problems" such as they had anticipated. She started walking at one year and was reported using isolated words at 15 months. A sister was born when Cathy was two years old; she began to lose her speech at that same time. Cathy displayed only jargon at the time of the psychological evaluation.

Research Unit Evaluation. Cathy was a petite, auburn-haired little girl with delicate features, who was dressed in a pink dress worn over green slacks. She came willingly to the office with her parents, clung closely to them upon being approached, and explored all the objects in the office. She made little shrieking sounds on occasion and would often bounce up and down on her toes at the same time. Also, she would often seat herself on the floor and pull herself along with her hands. The parents talked of Cathy's unwillingness to draw anything except six-pointed stars from Chrysler television commercials, of her memory of the schedule on television, and of her lack of interest in toys or people. Cathy did show some interest in imitating sounds, showed feelings of loss about her parents' leaving, and failed to display any consistent stereotypic behavior. Her parents indicated that Cathy's fearfulness of people appeared to be directly related to her having had two boils lanced by her pediatrician. Subsequently, she became fearful of people, especially men. This symptom, however, began to abate at the time of evaluation.

Evaluation and Recommendations. Cathy was seen as a child:

1. whose loss of speech and atypical behavior appeared to be a situational reaction to the birth of a sibling and the traumatic incident with her pediatrician (the lancing of her boils);
2. whose low birth weight and week's stay on a unit for premature children both slowed her development of relationships with people and suggested that there were some developmental problems, with concomitant increased potential for neurological dysfunction;
3. whose mother's display of perplexity and anxiety after 13 childless years suggested a low capacity to provide the secure situation necessary for the development of basic trust and firm object relations.

Cathy was seen as an ego-disturbed child with delayed development related to her low birth weight and anxious parents.

Parental counseling, thrice weekly speech therapy, and Structural Play Therapy were recommended on an outpatient basis in December of 1967.

STRUCTURAL THERAPY: AN OVERVIEW

Structural Therapy is comprised of a collection of active, intrusive techniques that have been used at various times in many different therapeutic approaches. It was originated as a specific treatment approach by Des Lauriers (1962), and this term was used to describe his treatment of schizophrenic adolescents at Kansas State Hospital.

This treatment approach is based upon a diagnostic conception of the schizophrenic child as having an inadequacy and incapacity to deal with reality and an incapacity to relate to people. This inadequacy and incapacity is seen as being of a structural nature, that is, the schizophrenic child is seen as being deficient in the development of Ego and Superego processes to channel his Id impulses.

Des Lauriers (1962, 1967) describes the schizophrenic child as having very few ego-mechanisms available for the purpose of structuring or realizing his impulses, and as a result he is very unskilled and inefficient in gaining his desired ends. Thus, the schizophrenic child is described as an incompetent, incomplete human being who has only fragmented bits of behavior available to him. This behavior is not well integrated and results in what is labeled clinically as "bizarre" and "inappropriate" behavior.

Structural Therapy draws its name both from the view of the schizophrenic child as having a structural deficit in ego development and from the therapeutic focus of an attempt to stimulate the development of these deficient ego-processes.

Des Lauriers (1962) suggests that this deficiency of ego-processes in schizophrenic children is due to their poor awareness of their body image, and their lack of differentiation of themselves from the surrounding environment. These children are described as being very "fluid" and as having a very poor body-image. Examples of this fluidity of ego-boundaries are often seen during diagnostic evaluations. If such a child is asked to draw something, he will often draw not only on the paper, but on the table, on himself, and sometimes even on the examiner.

Des Lauriers indicated that the level of ego-development of the schizophrenic child rendered inappropriate any attempts of a therapist to deal with him on solely an interpretive and/or verbal interactional level (1962). It was suggested that these more sophisticated levels of ego-functioning be largely ignored, in favor of a focus upon an earlier level of development that has been labeled variously as "body-ego" (Freud, 1927), "corporal feeling" (Federn, 1927), and "body-schemata" (Schilder, 1964). These and other descriptions of this level of development define it as the first experience of the ego. This first experience of reality arises from an establishment of the actuality of body limits and boundaries. Body-ego is what is meant when one refers to the child's or adult's awareness of his own body limits, of its capabilities, and of how it functions in relation to the outer world.

Since the schizophrenic child's deficiency has been described as a deficiency in body-ego, the Structural Therapist attempts to promote its development. These therapeutic efforts all emphasize the provision of an increased level of stimulation to the body of the patient, using both verbal and physical stratagems to help the patient cathect his bodily limits. These stratagems include talking to the patient about himself— the color of his hair; his eyes; the attractiveness of his physical person; the number of hands, fingers, arms, and legs he has. Also included are such stratagems as tickling of sensitive areas, soothing, stroking, hugging, and swinging the child to give him a motoric kinesthetic experience of his whole body. Anything that the therapist can think of within a spontaneous, creative, game-like atmosphere that will aid the child in completing the differentiation of himself from the environment as a distinct and separate human being would fall under the rubric of the treatment approach labeled as Structural Therapy. Thus, the schizophrenic child is urged and encouraged to become more spontaneous, to focus more upon his body boundaries rather than internal fantasies, and to tie together the fragmented bits of body-ego and higher ego processes that are available to him.

Behavioral Ego

The lack of Body-Ego in Early Infantile Autism appears to have allowed for a deviant type of ego development. The classically autistic child always manifests one area of skill that he uses to maintain sameness. Interruption of the pattern of this stereotypic behavior usually results in either a rage or a withdrawal reaction that lasts until the stereotypic behavior is allowed to continue. Thus, it is obvious that the autistic child is much more concerned and involved with what happens to his pattern of stereotypic behavior than what happens to his body. A pattern of behavior has been cathected rather than a part of the body, the whole body, or outer reality. I have postulated that this cathexis of a pattern of repetitive, stereotypic behavior should be labeled as a Behavioral Ego level of development.

Behavioral Ego would therefore be defined by the repetitive occurrence of a complex set of stereotypic behaviors that appear to exist to the exclusion of Body Ego or any higher ego processes. The classically autistic child appears to be fixated at a Behavioral Ego level of development and to use this level of functioning to avoid acknowledgement of outer reality. It seems as if some event or circumstance has caused the autistic child to cease developing after having experienced only a very little of the world around him.

It is hypothesized that through the functioning of the Behavioral Ego, the autistic child carries on the same activities of exploration, stimulation, and relaxation that occur in the infinitely larger areas of experience available to the healthier child. These behaviors are labeled as a specific type of ego development because they appear to be the means by which the child achieves his desires and experiences and attains a limited amount of stimulation. The autistic child guards these behaviors with the same care that the more psychologically developed child guards his body. Interruption of these behavior sequences is responded to with a great deal of negative and fearful affect, whereas physical injury often elicits no observable affective response and many times appears to be completely ignored.

The Behavioral Ego is representative of the first possible successful unified adaptive position, whereas the schizophrenic child has no single adaptive position and usually displays a number of fragmented adaptive positions. The autistic child has been quite successful in controlling his parents, attaining his desires without learning to speak, and being the sole source of novelty and variation in his restricted environment. He has succeeded in restricting reality to dimensions which he can comfortably handle.

Treatment

Therapists have been trained in Structural Therapy with the following set of guidelines:

1. The therapist is trained to identify the stereotypic behavior of the child and to interrupt it. This interruption is done in a graduated and game-like way, if possible. The ineffectiveness and maladaptiveness of the stereotypic behavior for dealing with people is demonstrated to the child by interference, and by physical and verbal setting of limits to the rage or avoidance reactions which often follow the interference.

2. The anxiety and anger created by the interruption of the stereotypic behavior are used to focus the attention of the child upon part of the therapist as a meaningful Part Object or Object. Analytically oriented interpretations accompany the use of Structural Therapy. The therapist attempts to interpret the child's feeling about being interrupted and then tries to get him to emit any verbal or physical message that is directed toward the therapist. This physical, visual, or verbal message is then used to focus the attention of the child upon physical likenesses and differences between himself and the therapist. This stage often needs to be preceded by a period during which the therapist presents an alternative rhythmic behavior for the child to focus upon.

3. Development of a recognition relationship with the child is followed by presentation of a number of novel and patterned activities which draw the child's attention to his own body. These activities include counting of fingers and toes, gross movements of arms and legs, physical stimulation of body, etc.

4. The development of Body Ego is stimulated by the use of physical, game-like interactions that make the child more aware of his own body and of his differences from and similarities to his therapist.

5. As Behavioral Ego functioning decreases and Body Ego becomes more predominant, more conventional play therapy techniques are included in the treatment.

The first task of the Structural Therapist is to break down the functioning of the Behavioral Ego and attempt to promote eventually the development of a cathexis of a significant person as a representative of reality. This development will then be followed by efforts directed toward the stimulation of Body Ego. Until there is some initial development of Body Ego, the therapist and reality have no grasp upon the child. The child is self-sufficient and unreachable until his body becomes important to him. The development of a fragmentary Body Ego eventually allows the therapist to shift to more conventional play therapy techniques. Thus, Structural Therapy may be viewed as a therapy that prepares autistic children to benefit from more conventional types of psychotherapy.

The Structural Therapist uses techniques that are very common to the behavior of the apocryphal "good mother" playing with the normal infant. He stimulates the child's body boundaries via simple physical body differentiation games, teaches him how to behave, sings to him, shows him pictures, and in general tries to give him many new and interesting reality experiences. The classically autistic child is seen as being woefully deficient in varied experiences of the world, and the Structural Therapist attempts to give the child enough new experiences so that he will learn that he is a human being and that reality is interesting. The child must then gain enough new experiences to be able to form schemata (Piaget, 1967) which he can then use to organize reality for himself. Prior to the attainment of this level of development, the therapist provides new experiences and models free, spontaneous responses to the environment. At the same time the therapist provides a firm structure of acceptable behavior that the child may fight against, simply to assure himself that it is indeed present and reliable even under stress. Eventually the child internalizes this structure of control.

The Structural Therapist must focus upon the development of the autistic child's awareness of himself as a distinct and separate human being. This emphasis must be frequently repeated to get the child to view the therapist as a three-dimensional human being: otherwise the child may never develop beyond the point of seeing the therapist as a gratifying, playful, enjoyable object whose only role is to supply his oral demands. Often the therapist will deliberately oppose some of the new desires expressed by the patient. This is directly the opposite of Des Lauriers' strategy (1962) with adolescent schizophrenic patients, and it is done to emphasize the differences in feelings between people and how they can be dealt with directly and freely. Many times the child may enjoy some activity, and the therapist may be exhausted or bored with lifting him, swinging him, playing body differentiation games, etc. At that point, the therapist should say, "I'm tired," "I'm bored," "Let's do something else," or "I don't like this." The therapist should feel free to initiate periods of rest or movement out of the therapy room. It is extremely important that the therapist share his feelings with the patient, as these children have usually had very little experience with truthful and direct expression of feeling. Thus it is clear that the use of counter-transference feelings plays a large role in this modified version of Structural Therapy.

On the other hand, the therapist is encouraged to introduce activities and experiences that the child has not thought of, for the purpose of being genuine and spontaneous; varying the range of stimuli to which the patient is exposed; and emphasizing that his feelings and ideas are not always the same as those of the patient. The therapist therefore discourages the development of a pathological symbiotic relationship of grandiose omnipotent fantasies. The development of a "normal" symbiotic relationship is expected and hoped for, as an indication of positive growth on the part of the patient.

CATHY'S TREATMENT

The First Two Months

Speech Therapy. The patient was initially involved in speech therapy in January, 1968, following the pre-admission screening. She was three and one-half years old. The therapist who saw her at that time reported that she was not using words for communication but was using limited jargon. Cathy was hyperactive, displayed bizarre hand movements, failed to relate to people, maintained no eye contact, was not toilet trained, and was extremely fearful. During the two months of therapy, the child only cried and seemed not to respond to conventional play therapy techniques. The speech therapist moved from the area and therapy was discontinued for three weeks, at which time the second speech therapist became involved in the case.

Months Two to Six

Speech Therapy. The second speech therapist, who was affiliated with the autistic reasearch unit at Eastern State School and Hospital, was trained in play therapy based upon the Structural Therapy approach (Ward, 1968). The basic goal of the second speech therapist was to make the child affectively responsive to the therapist's presence by using extensive physical intrusiveness. During the first month of therapy, this meant a great deal of rubbing of arms and legs, tickling, swinging, clapping, and jumping. The child was never allowed to withdraw into finger play or random hyperactive behavior. The need for physical activity was channeled into interaction between the therapist and child. The therapist always stayed physically close to Cathy and had available both herself and selected objects toward which Cathy's undirected activity could be channeled. The therapist constantly approached Cathy for interaction, while at the same time trying to convey warmth and affection. Although hugging and cuddling were rejected, they were constantly imposed. The child remained unresponsive. Her face and neck were rubbed and stimulated. Any glance in the therapist's direction was affectively responded to and praised verbally.

From the therapy notes of the early sessions, this picture is conveyed of Cathy's unchanneled activity: "Cathy cried at separation from mother. Once in the office she began running and hopping around the room using bizarre hand motions. She could not sit in a chair for any period of time. She did not vocalize or seemingly relate to me. She did not look at me. When held she struggled to get free. . . ."

During the early sessions chairs were avoided. When sitting occurred it was on the floor. Cathy chose particularly to sit under the table. The therapist always sat under it with her, while stimulating her physically. While Cathy did not respond overtly, she gradually accepted more stimulation with less apparent anxiety. Her crying, also, was markedly reduced by the sixth therapy session and occurred only occasionally when the therapist was interfering with her activity. Soon after, Cathy began random vocalizing and would increase the amount of vocalization when the therapist paralleled or imitated her. The first social smile occurred during this period.

During the fourth month of therapy, a ball was introduced. It was placed in Cathy's hands. The therapist had to close her fingers around the ball. The ball was rolled and bounced with the therapist having to constantly keep her hands around Cathy's. The patient responded, after three sessions with the ball, by rolling it herself with both hands. It was not a directed roll and was not forcefully pushed. The child was hugged and verbally praised. As in every session, her actions had been verbalized for her and the object name "ball" was frequently used in short phrases. After two more sessions, Cathy was actually rolling the ball and saying "ba." At the beginning of the next session, she quickly explored the office repeating "ba" "ba." The therapist assumed she meant ball and got it out of the drawer. She smiled and carried the ball around for several minutes. Then she sat and rolled it in an undirected manner. The therapist retrieved the ball, said "ball," and then placed it in Cathy's hands. Cathy continued to respond with "ba." In this way, the first association of a sound pattern to an object was established. The pattern was repeated in many different ways, and gradually Cathy was able to select the ball upon request from other objects, find balls in pictures, and follow directions using the ball. While this one pattern was being established, the amount of interaction in vocal play increased and expanded. The child began using a variety of new sounds in imitation, and some of them were carried over into spontaneous vocal play and progressed to babbling. Cathy learned to wave "bye-bye" and began calling the therapist "Jin-Jin." However, she was still not looking at the therapist or approaching for physical comfort.

Months Six to Eight

Speech Therapy. Once the point of developmental fixation was intruded upon and structure was placed on Cathy's daily activities, the normal pattern of language development began to emerge. However, language was not used for social interaction, but rather for satisfaction of needs. Cathy became increasingly proficient at labeling and began using combinations of two words. Her play was parallel and she still remained frightened of other children. She used her mother for satisfaction of need but still did not relate to her. Toward the end of this period, Cathy became curious about her environment and wanted to be taken on "trips." These included shopping, visiting relatives' homes, and accompanying her mother on errands.

As Cathy began labeling and exploring her environment, her mother became less able to handle her new curiosity and enrolled her in a morning nursery school program. Cathy was not developmentally capable of handling this move, appeared frightened, and regressed to bed-wetting, soiling, and echolalia.

During this period, in speech therapy sessions Cathy withdrew into non-verbal behavior, was extremely anxious, and became extremely distant physically from the therapist. The next week she was home sick with diarrhea and an upset stomach. A normally slightly-built child, she became extremely thin. When she returned for speech therapy, she smiled at seeing the therapist. The next three sessions were spent re-exploring the office and redoing all the tasks and exercises she had mastered over the past three months. She was seemingly regaining control of her environment. During this time, she also stopped bed-wetting and began to communicate verbally with her mother and the therapist.

Psychological Counseling. A counseling session revealed that both parents were aware of the regression caused by Cathy's placement in the nursery school, but they had opposing ideas as to how to respond to this. Cathy's father felt that she could remain in the nursery school and that she would "adjust." Her mother was more sympathetic to the therapist's recommendation that she could not adequately cope. Finally the parents agreed to withdraw Cathy, and the mother was helped in learning how to set limits for Cathy and how to deal with her fear that this would cause her daughter to "fall apart."

At the same time, the mother reported that Cathy, for the first time, would stay in the yard when other children visited and used speech to ask her mother for books to color, or to go on a visit. Formerly, Cathy had been fearful of going out; but now she cried when she was left home. She also asked for dresses, showed a developing interest in talking toys, in anything musical, and could label all the primary colors. Cathy was described as "investigating everything," and this trait, in combination with her improved verbalization for responsiveness, led the mother to describe her as more "fun." Some of Cathy's "mystery" was dispelled when emphasis on the mother's importance as a source of information led to the discovery that the bizarre vocalization "daradio," was actually Cathy's reproduction of her mother's casual way of saying "the radio."

Months Nine to Twelve

Speech Therapy. Speech during this phase became more spontaneous. Cathy began to use three-word combinations. Her mother observed her practicing in front of a mirror at home. She now regularly referred to her therapist as "Jin-Jin," and said "hi" and "bye" while looking at her. She began to develop a reciprocal relationship with her mother. The first signs of shyness had developed, and Cathy exhibited trouble relating to two significant adults at the same time. When she saw the psychologist and speech therapist together, she covered her head with her dress. Cathy was now saying "no," though not always appropriately. She responded to direct questions, could associate objects that go together, and could answer questions about her environment and living habits. Now that Cathy was verbal enough to make needs known in a consistent manner, the mother was encouraged to begin toilet training. Toward the end of this period, Cathy approached another child and said "hi," then ran quickly away. Her play became more complex, but she still remained at the fringe of the activity, and watched the other children. Dolls and dolls' clothes began to be included in her play.

Psychological Counseling. The mother reported that Cathy was becoming more independent and at the same time more of a "discipline problem." She had become so active and curious about people that she went into other people's houses in the neighborhood. Cathy would now stay in the room when other children arrived and would engage in parallel play. She would play with her two-year-old sister but had found a four-year-old "boyfriend." Cathy and he would kiss and hug each other. Although she would say his name when she saw him at a distance, she would not call him. Her speech had become more spontaneous, and she seemed to have a larger fund of short phrases. The mother was teaching Cathy her "A, B, C's" and reported that she was still saying numbers repetitively. Cathy had shown the beginnings of feelings of shyness in the last month, and this was taken as a sign of increasing meaningfulness of human relationships. The reciprocal relationship between mother and daughter continued to improve, as the mother took Cathy on walks, to visit other children, and to different stores. Cathy now wanted and enjoyed having her mother sing to her, and counseling encouraged that she sing with the mother to emphasize the reciprocal and modeling aspects of the relationship.

A month later counseling found Cathy using three-word phrases such as "more macaroni too," and increasing the number of single-word labels for objects. For the first time, Cathy would respond verbally to a direct question as to what she had in her possession. She still showed a very concrete level of conceptualization and had to be presented with ideas singly rather than in combination; for example: "Go upstairs." and "Change your clothes," instead of "Go upstairs and change your clothes."

Cathy's improving relationships were shown by her participation in motoric games with other children and by crying and asking about "boyfriend" when he was on vacation.

Cathy had now started to use speech to ask her mother's permission to take things into her bedroom, whereas, formerly, she would just take them. Mother and daughter would go through toy catalogues together, while Cathy named all the toys. She now only manifested feelings of shyness upon seeing people she had not seen for about a month, and this usually lasted for about ten minutes.

Spontaneous verbalizations were occurring in what might be labeled "crisis situations." For example, when told that she was going to the hospital, Cathy said "no needle!" If she was being punished, she would say "Radio—Jinny—Car!" Also, she was now starting to say the words or sing a little bit when her mother was singing.

Thirteenth Month

Psychological Counseling Summary. Cathy was now able to respond appropriately to almost all verbal directions, whether single or multiple in nature. She was showing much more spontaneous use of phrases and, in addition, was singing along with the rest of the family. Parallel play continued with peers; although she would run with them she would not talk with them, but she would talk with her mother about the other children. The "boyfriend" was still of great interest to Cathy, but there was still no direct verbal communication. The mother stated that, "All they ever do is hug and kiss."

Cathy was now showing an interest in new objects, such as dolls, and was playing at feeding dolls and putting them to bed. She now asked to go out and wanted to play in the snow. Formerly, Cathy had wandered away when allowed outside, but now she showed the beginning internalization of some controls. A look from her mother stimulated Cathy to say to herself, "Cathy stay here."

Cathy now would tell her mother that she wanted to sit on her lap and be read to. Her shyness continued to have a duration of about ten minutes, with those people she had not seen for a while.

Fourteen Months

Speech Therapy. Cathy continued to learn new words and was constantly using phrases. She was beginning to talk directly to people while maintaining eye contact. Words were now being used to give directions to her mother and sister. She was calling her sister by name and had started to hug her. Also, Cathy was starting to play with a nephew and two neighborhood children. Her shyness had decreased and she was approaching other children with a good deal of curiosity, though she did not stay around them for long. She was now playing on the swings in her yard with other children and was constantly seeking out one boy whom she saw in the lobby. New experiences in her life were later acted out with her toys. Cathy was now reluctant to leave at the end of the speech therapy sessions and had become physically close to the therapist. At home she frequently asked to "go see Jin-Jin" on nonappointment days. In therapy sessions, finger songs and puppets had been introduced. Cathy could now follow two-chained commands and use "yes" and "no" appropriately. She was beginning to cut paper with scissors, using two hands. The chalkboard was being explored, and she had started scribbling with chalk in a nondirected manner. At this time, the mother expressed concern that Cathy could not throw a ball. The speech therapist had the mother present during the next session and showed her how to teach Cathy to throw a ball. Once Cathy was given a specific structure in which to organize her activity, she rapidly learned to throw the ball and, with practice, to catch it.

Fifteenth Month

Speech Therapy. Cathy was mastering the concepts of *on* and *in* and *over* and *under*. She was particularly interested in the hand puppets and used them at every opportunity. The puppets now "talked" to each other and had names. Cathy asked them the questions the therapist had asked her, as though she were the teacher and the puppets the pupil. Shyness had almost completely disappeared, and she was talking about her friends. She had been introduced to play-dough, pasting, and finger paints. Her drawing on the chalkboard was becoming more controlled. She was now drawing circles and could put in the parts of a face. During one session she spontaneously stated, "Cathy has two hands." Color names were being learned very rapidly, and her mother reported that she was practicing at home. Number concepts up to five had been mastered. Cathy was showing concern for her sister and was playing with her. She was using phrases spontaneously to ask for help at home. Recently, she had called to her mother from the bedroom, "Mommy, come, book in drawer." Cathy asked mother if she could bring toys and books to show the therapist. She was now talking about new experiences and remembered television shows she had seen. Her actions now had definite direction, and she lapsed into random hyperactive behavior only in new situations or when an existing situation suddenly became unstructured.

Psychological Counseling. Cathy continued to improve in her development and in use of her speech, as well as in her relationships with people. It was still rare for her to talk directly to people spontaneously, but she would use her speech to give need-related directions, such as "Fix toenail." Occasional snatches of echolalia persisted, with Cathy repeating the last part of what was said to her. She was using her speech with her sister in play, saying, "Mari-Lou come" or "Get up." The mother observed Cathy playing with a young nephew for the first time, and they sat on the floor and rolled a ball back and forth for five minutes.

Sixteenth Month

Cathy's continued progress in both speech development and relations with people led her parents to raise questions as to the possibility of her returning to nursery school. Also, they wondered what her intellectual potential was and what type of school, if any, would be appropriate for Cathy. It was decided that a full battery of psychological testing should be administered to Cathy to assess both her intellectual potential and her personality development. She had previously been too unrelated, hyperactive, and nonverbal to be given any type of standardized testing.

Cathy was tested in four separate sessions and showed a different reaction on each occasion. The first session found Cathy hyperactive and distractible. She was unable to draw a person, but verbally labeled her scribbles as a "man." She responded to the Bender-Gestalt test with only scribbling, and she spontaneously engaged in play with dolls and hand puppets for the rest of the session.

The second session involved the administration of the Stanford-Binet. Cathy was very curious about this test and worked diligently for about forty minutes. After this period she became fatigued, more distractible, and somewhat echolalic. She showed more difficulty in following directions and appeared to be relieved to stop, although this was denied.

Cathy was reported to have been very nervous and anxious at home following the second testing session and was observed practicing some of the items that she had failed. In addition, she was very anxious and fearful when she returned for the third session. Cathy had wanted her mother to come into the office with her for this third session, and she soon became so distractible and echolalic that it was necessary to terminate testing.

A week was allowed to elapse to let Cathy's anxiety decrease, and upon her return she led the way, running to the office. However, it was reported later that she had asked her mother about going into the office with her before the psychologist had appeared.

Analysis of the test results revealed that Cathy had obtained a Stanford-Binet IQ of 68, with a Mental Age of three years, three months. Her Chronological Age was four years, eight months. This performance placed Cathy in the Borderline Defective range of functioning (5.2%ile).

This score was seen as a minimal estimate of Cathy's potential, owing to the problems mentioned above.

Cathy obtained an IQ of 56 on the Peabody Picture Vocabulary Test. Rapport was difficult to gain with this test; Cathy resisted guessing, was taciturn and slow in responding, was distractible, and needed a great deal of praise in order to proceed. All of the previous factors listed led to the assumption that the IQ estimate was of minimum rather than maximum potential.

Finally an analysis of a Vineland Social Maturity Scale yielded a Social Quotient of 72 and an Age Equivalent score of three years, five months. The major problems were in the areas of communication, occupation of self, and socialization.

The fact that Cathy was able to participate in testing to the point of even obtaining a formal score was taken as evidence of significant therapeutic progress. The Stanford-Binet is recognized as a highly verbal test of intelligence and was chosen for that reason. Cathy showed that she had developed sufficient speech capacity to deal with this difficult test, and enough conceptual and social facility to follow the directions for standardized testing.

CONCLUSION

Cathy continued in speech therapy, and her parents continued in counseling until she was five and one-quarter-years old. A warm, reciprocal relationship had developed between mother and child, as both had learned to enjoy each other's company.

At this age a short-term placement in the public school system proved unsuccessful. Accordingly, referral was made to a private school for the brain damaged and emotionally disturbed child, and she has continued at this school on a daily basis up to the present. At the time of this report, she is seven years and ten months old. She is felt to have made excellent progress academically, and presents no behavior problems either at school or at home. Her most recent card indicates that Cathy is functioning at the second-grade level in reading and social studies, and at first-grade level in arithmetic and spelling. The most recent Stanford-Binet administered at age seven years, nine months, disclosed an IQ of 58.

We feel that Cathy demonstrates that the nonverbal, hyperactive child often mistakenly labeled as "autistic" can indeed be helped to develop appropriate speech and behavior on an outpatient basis. Structural Therapy is seen as having provided an avenue of contact with a severely regressed child, and as having helped in the stimulation of the early vo-calizations that the speech therapist must have to work with to develop speech. This case is a good demonstration of how a therapy that focuses upon the improvement of body image and human relationships stimu-lates the development of speech as well. It seems as if the development of speech is a necessary part of the development of "the human condition."

REFERENCES

DES LAURIERS, A. M. *The experience of reality in childhood schizophrenia.* New York: International Universities Press, 1962.

_____. The schizophrenic child. *Archives of General Psychiatry,* 1967, 16: 194–201.

FEDERN, P. *Ego-psychology and the psychoses.* New York: Basic Books, 1952.

FREUD, S. *The ego and the id.* London: Hogarth Press, 1927.

KANNER, L. Autistic disturbances of affective contact. *Nervous Child,* 1943, 2: 217–240.

_____. & EISENBERG, L. Early infantile autism—childhood schizophrenia sym-posium. *American Journal of Orthopsychiatry,* 1956, 26: 556–564.

MAHLER, MARGARET S. On child psychosis and schizophrenia: Autistic and sym-biotic infantile psychoses. *In Psychoanalytic Study of the Child.* New York: International Universities Press, 1952.

_____. *On human symbiosis and the vicissitudes of individuation.* Vol. 1. New York: International Universities Press, 1968.

PIAGET, J. *Six psychological studies.* New York: Random House, 1967.

REISER, D. Psychosis of infancy and early childhood as manifested by children with atypical development. *New England Journal of Medicine,* 1963, pp. 790–798, 844–850.

RIMLAND, B. *Infantile autism.* New York: Appleton-Century-Crofts, 1964.

SCHILDER, P. *The image and appearance of the human body.* New York: Wiley & Sons, 1964.

WARD, A. J. The application of structural therapy to the residential treatment of early infantile autism. *Schizophrenia,* 1970, 1 (4) : 92–102. (a)

_____. Early infantile autism: Diagnosis, etiology and treatment. *Psychologi-cal Bulletin,* 1970, 73 (5) : 350–362. (b)

_____. & HANDFORD, H. A. Early infantile autism: Syndrome, symptom or wastebasket? Paper presented at convention of Mid-Western Psychological Association in Chicago, Illinois, on May 2, 1968.

11

The Role of the Speech Therapist in the Treatment of Autistic Children

Virginia M. Leith

This paper will report on those children who have been seen in individual speech therapy. However, the program involved here goes beyond individual therapy; thus the nursing staff and child care workers are integral parts of the treatment program and provide stimulation for the children during the majority of the day. Certainly, credit for any change in the child's behavior and functioning must be shared with them.

The role of a speech therapist on a treatment team dealing with autistic children lends itself to a broad definition. One is active both as an initial therapist in breaking down the behavioral ego and as the significant person who channels random vocalizations into higher verbal functioning.

In reading about the development of verbal functioning, refer to the developmental sequence sheet illustrating the progression of verbal functioning being discussed in various cases here (see figure 1).

The children called nonverbal actually fit into the category called prespeech (some authors call this category preverbal). The children in our program have been observed to follow this general form of development (figure 1), once the point of developmental fixation was intruded upon.

FIGURE 1.   Developmental Sequence.

Prespeech
    1. Gestures without vocalization
    2. Squeals, grunts, unvoiced vowels
    3. Vowels (undifferentiated)
    4. Humming
    5. Vowel-consonants (single and repetitive)
    6. Babbles (polysyllabic)
    7. Jargon (speech melody)

Speech
    A. Conventional sequences
        8. 1, 2, 3 . . . A, B, C . . . songs
    B. Single words
        9. Noun (things)
     10. Noun (others)
     11. Noun (self)
     12. No, yes, hi, bye, okay, etc.
     13. Verbs, prepositions
     14. Pronouns
     15. Adjectives
    C. Complex phrases and sentence fragments
     16. Two-word sentences/phrases
     17. Three-word sentences/phrases
     18. Four-word sentences/phrases
     19. Five-or more word sentences/phrases
    D. Disjunctive syntax
     20. Syntax disturbance (pronoun reversal)
     21. Syntax disturbance (specified)

When we initially see a child, he is generally functioning below number three in the prespeech section. The noises which are produced in these early sessions are often used as stimulus barriers to block out the therapist's voice, since the child is not allowed to physically withdraw from the therapist. The noises are also used at times of frustration and during rage reactions. Noises, thus, have a negative quality which are used to control the environment. Through establishing pleasure-oriented associations to sounds, this negative aspect is neutralized and eventually the sounds signal a pleasurable response. In order to set up these associations the therapist makes noises and hums while physically stroking the child's back, arms, legs, and head. The child at this level of functioning is being surrounded with pleasant associations to sound. Sound takes on a signal response quality, indicating the approach of some pleasant interaction. The interaction at this level is undemanding, except for tolerance of physical contact. The therapist gives to the child completely, making the child aware of the therapist's presence in an unstressful manner. Of course, this type of interaction generally does not occur until after six or eight weeks of stressful, aggressive interaction. This course of therapeutic intervention is carried on until the child shows signs of tolerating, then accepting the therapist's presence.

In order to give a more detailed view of the type of therapy that is being done, several children will be described who are currently in treatment. The children were all initially nonverbal and are now functioning on different prespeech and speech levels.

TIMMY

Age: 9
Admitting Age: 6
Birthday: Nov. 23, 1960

Admitting Statement

History of atypical development since age one. No speech development. Mouths and smells objects, rocks, bangs head. Very destructive at home. Withdrawn, fragmentary relationships with people.

Hyperactive, non-verbal. No constructive play. Avoids eye contact. Only whines and yells.

Timmy has been seen in therapy to stimulate vocal play and various prelanguage areas since October, 1968.

At the time therapy was initiated, Timmy was doing little true vocal play. His vocal emissions consisted mainly of wavering screams. Timmy was initially unresponsive. Eye contact was extremely limited. He did not approach to be held or physically comforted. He did not grasp my hand when I held his. He constantly focused on small objects, usually of shiny metal. These objects were held in his mouth, and were only relinquished after much encouragement. He would occasionally focus upon an object that I wore, especially my ring. He did not seem to recognize me when I entered the unit, and he did not approach me or respond to my verbal commands.

While expansion and differentiation of vocal play were the main objectives of therapy, it was necessary, due to the low level of functioning, to establish a basic relationship with him using intrusive techniques. When intruded upon, Timmy would scream and cover his ears. He would occasionally throw himself on the floor. It took several months of physically intruding on Timmy's behavior before he stopped screaming and started smiling, then laughing, when being tickled.

Timmy then began using me as a part-object to satisfy his needs. My hand was used to open doors, insert keys, turn keys, and so forth. He was still resistive to physical closeness, though he seemed to tolerate it. He gradually became less fixated on small objects and began exploring the larger toys. He never played with the toys, but threw them or rolled them on the table or floor. We switched to toys that made noise: drums, xylophone, and bells. Timmy dropped them while standing on top of the table, then covered his ears. He selected the xylophone most frequently and seemed to become aware of the different ways to make noise with it (hitting, shaking, dropping). At this time, he began to make noises in meaningful protest. This was particularly evident when I said, "time to go." Generally, Timmy was beginning to make more noise both in my office and on the unit.

As Timmy responded in a more pleasurable manner to physical stimulation, he was made aware of his mouth. At this point, every sound he produced was imitated and new sounds were introduced. The sounds which were constantly presented to him were vowels in combination with the bilateral consonant. The situation was kept as playful as possible, and a good deal of physical activity took place. Timmy began incorporating the vowel sounds in his vocal play—he has progressed to the point where he now can make them in imitation. His vocal play shows the beginning of developing jargon. His use of sounds in vocabulary, while limited, is differentiated. He is now vocalizing for pleasure and amusement. He is functioning vocally at around a ten to twelve month level.

Timmy has been known to take screws out of furniture or other objects regularly over the past years. This week in my office he spontaneously replaced a screw he had removed; then repeated the process. He appeared very curious and interested in the mechanics of replacing the screw. This has progressed to putting other toys together both in my office and on the living unit.

Timmy is now responsive to me as a person. He recognizes me when I enter the unit and takes my hand or pushes me to the door. He responds to tickling, rubbing, and cuddling with pleasure. He will often seek physical comfort from me and occasionally tries to use this to get his own way.

During a year of therapy Timmy has progressed verbally from screams to using jargon both for protest and pleasure.

CHARLES

Age: 12
Admitting Age: 6 years, 9 months
Birthday: Jan. 14, 1957

Admitting Statement

Well-developed 6½ year old nonverbal child, exhibits fear when approached. Perseveres in waving toys in front of himself. Recoils from physical contact and does not relate at all. Nonresponsive to his environment. Fear reaction upon approach. Destructive of furniture and other household articles, mutilates self with head banging and slapping. Unable to relate to other children and in "another world" as far as relationships with adults.

Charlie has been in therapy to stimulate vocal play and various prelanguage areas since January, 1968. At the time therapy was initiated, Charlie was doing little true vocal play. The sounds which were produced were used in an inconsistent, noncommunicative manner.

Initially, Charlie did not relate to me or recognize me as a person. He continually held two rubber toys, one in each hand. His only form of showing frustration or anger was slapping his face. He did a good deal of finger play and eye-contact was extremely limited. No appropriate affect was noted during the first months of therapy. His level of vocal functioning was below eight months.

While expansion and differentiation of vocal play were the main objectives of therapy, it was necessary, due to the low level of functioning, to establish a basic relationship with him using intrusive techniques. After several months of developing a basic relationship, Charlie became grossly aware of my reinforcing his own limited vocal play by imitation. Charlie also began to imitate my vocal play and gradually expansion of the phonemes he was using took place. As his vocal play became differentiated, it also became more spontaneous, and some discernible signs of pleasure and frustration were made with sounds. At this point, he was able to let me hold one of his toys for a short time. This was built up until both toys were freely put on the desk until the end of the session. Then we would each take one toy and walk downstairs holding hands. My hand was also used for opening doors, turning keys, and frequently substituted for a toy when he became anxious and was about to slap. Gradually, I became a comfortable object to sit on, and occasionally he would try to crawl into my arms like a small child. On these occasions I would stimulate him physically and either talk or sing to him. Eye contact gradually developed and responsiveness to me as a person began with Charlie physically exploring my face. We started using a mirror shortly after this and began doing gross body movements in front of it. We focused on the face, then the mouth. Charlie would imitate lip and tongue movements, but it was many weeks before any sound accompanied the movements. By having him feel my throat and face and by putting his hand in front of my mouth, Charlie was encouraged to start to feel his throat for the same sensations. The mirror became an important object in our sessions. He used it while sitting next to me or on my lap when we were imitating faces and making sounds. It was also used in games like peek-a-boo and catch, and has occasionally been used to hide behind when he is angry. He now combs his hair in front of it and touches his own face freely.

Charlie's play has become more complex over the months. He is now playing meaningfully with blocks, building towers and bridges. He plays catch appropriately and has good control in throwing a ball. He does some gross actions to finger songs, but prefers clapping songs or playing the xylophone. He has in recent months included me in his play and will start new activities with me. He initiates catch and peek-a-boo. He scribbles on the board and then brings me over to see the drawing. On occasion, he hands me chalk to draw along with him.

Twice recently, Charlie has expressed his anger toward me by pinching me while looking directly at me. He had in recent months thrown objects at me to express frustration. He is generally very open and responsive in our sessions, and the appropriate expression of anger is another step forward. At the same time, he is able to accept limits with greater tolerance and does not always become anxious when told he cannot do something.

Charlie now relates to me closely as a person, as he does to Dr. Ward. Dr. Ward and I have noticed on several occasions that though Charlie relates to us individually in our sessions with him, he cannot tolerate us being together with him. He will try physically to remove one of us from the setting, or try to take one of us away. His attempts to separate us are very ambitious and he will try to move whichever one of us he can. Interestingly, I accidentally met Charlie and one of the child care workers in the lobby recently. Charlie greeted me, then pushed me onto a nearby couch. He then went and brought the child care worker over to sit next to me. Then he squeezed in between us and appeared both comfortable and pleased with himself for accomplishing the feat. This is the first time he has related to me and any other person. We played with him, pushed, tickled, and teased for almost ten minutes. He was reluctant to leave, but did so without becoming upset.

Verbal language development has been slow while other areas have reached more adequate levels. At this point, more direct pressure for words will be initiated, as Charlie's responsiveness and tolerance have increased sufficiently to handle this type of pressure. He has said several words spontaneously and in imitation, but no consistent words have been used for any real communication.

Charlie is a more difficult child to work with than Timmy. One of the reasons is the self-destructive aspects of his behavior, which the therapist must learn to handle therapeutically. Rather than just stopping Charlie from slapping, we have gradually given him a sense of being able to control his slapping. When he is anxious and slapping we allow physical contact, but then playfully move him physically away from us. This is repeated many times until he has regained control and can again function in the situation.

WILLIAM

Age: 9
Admitting Age: 6 years, 6 months
Birthday: April 26, 1960

Admitting Statement

Six-year-old Billy has not developed any intelligible speech. Behavior is destructive, impulsive, hyperactive. At home, Billy is described as being "out of touch." He is wild, prone to run away, and bangs his head so that he injures it. He is hyperactive, restless, climbs onto furniture with no fears although his balance is poor. He does not speak but makes grunting, hissing, and humming noises. He is more interested in objects than people. He can hear, but ignores even loud noises.

Bill has been seen in verbal language-oriented therapy since June, 1968. At that time, he was engaging in some spontaneous babbling and using some limited jargon. He was able to imitate, with good production, the plosive and fricative sounds. Vowel production was fair, though most of the vowels were produced nearer the neutral position, causing a lack of differentiation. His major form of communication was gestural and his orientation was predominantly visual. Inner language appeared reasonably well developed enough to concentrate on externalization of language processes.

Since Bill's orientation was mainly visual, it had to be switched so that he could focus on auditory cues before any specific verbal language development techniques could be tried. This was partially accomplished by using amplified sound to overstimulate the auditory mechanism and thus call attention to auditory phenomena. Bill responded well to this technique and would function, for gradually longer periods of time under amplified sound. He benefitted from direct sound stimulation and patterning of sounds and moved to a level where using words as labels was appropriate verbal behavior.

Bill gradually learned the names of basic objects, parts of the face, clothes, furniture, and food and with repeated practice could label objects or pictures of objects correctly. As his basic labeling vocabulary grew, words were paired in meaningful ways. At the same time, set phrases were used to establish automatic language patterns. He filled in the last word of each phrase. The phrases which were produced were used as a narrative of his actions. Phrases such as "walking up the stairs," "walking down the stairs," "opening the door," "jumping up and down," expanded his language concepts beyond basic labeling. Bill is now able to use these phrases to describe actions while continuing to increase his labeling vocabulary and action concepts.

Bill makes his wants known verbally in my office, though little of this has generalized to the unit living situation. Although Bill has never related to me closely as a person, he is gradually exploring my physical features, particularly my face, and has lately interacted in a more open, teasing manner. He recognizes me when I enter the unit, approaches, takes my hand, and leads me to the door. He occasionally resists leaving my office by pushing me back into the chair and saying "no" when I say "time to go downstairs." On occasion he will physically try to remain in the office by holding onto the chair or table or desk. If extremely agitated he will bang his head or hit me. He usually chooses a transitional object to take between my office and Level I. This is usually a scrap of paper or a colored chip.

Bill shows little interest in playing with toys. The only objects he seeks out are books. If no picture books are on the shelf, he will grab a professional jounal off of my desk and open it. He then taps the pages. He is always reluctant to give up the book; however, he can now be persuaded verbally to do so without a fight.

CATHY

Age: 5
Birthday: August 10, 1964

Cathy began therapy at 3½ years on an outpatient basis. She had been referred to our unit for inpatient treatment.

Treatment

See pages 123–30 of chapter ten for a detailed presentation of speech therapy with Cathy.

My personal feeling is that Cathy responded to therapy on a more rapid basis than the other children for two reasons. First, the length of time before initiation of treatment was relatively short. Second, we were able to keep her at home where many more experiences were available to her. She was exposed to normal children who were verbal, including her sister who was just learning to talk. Conventional play therapy techniques were not physically intrusive enough to establish a structure in which Cathy could begin to function. Thus, as a child who was overwhelmed by the environment, she could only respond with random hyperactive behavior or crying during the first attempt at therapy.

These children are all currently functioning on different communication levels, despite having been in therapy for approximately the same length of time. This can only be explained by their differences in terms of initial needs and the amount of related factors, particularly such things as self-mutilative behavior and complete lack of contact with reality. Those children who have been able to relate to people have developed the best use of verbal language skills. Since talking is a form of social interaction, the basic prerequisite for improvement seems to be the stimulation or development of the capacity to relate.

12

The Effect of Structural Therapy in the Treatment of a Self-Mutilating Autistic Child: A Case Report

This paper is a case report on the effect of three years of intensive individual and milieu therapy upon the functioning of a self-mutilating autistic child. This child was treated as part of a larger study investigating the application of structural therapy to the residential treatment of (EIA) early infantile autism (Handford & Ward, 1969; Ward, 1970b). This program was initiated in September of 1966 and is ongoing at the present time. The information presented in this case report was gathered in the time span of September, 1966, to September, 1969. This research was carried out in a twenty-bed unit devoted to the study and treatment of the syndrome of EIA.

EARLY INFANTILE AUTISM

Early infantile autism is viewed as a developmental disorder that has resulted in the fixation of children as early as the three-month level of object relations development (Ward, 1969; Ward, 1970b). The cause of this early development fixation is felt to be rooted in both a slowed development rate and a dearth of varied, patterned stimulation and novelty experience in the early developmental history (Ward, 1969). Children are diagnosed as presenting cases of EIA in this study when they meet the following criteria drawn from the seminal article by Kanner (1943):

1. Lack of object relations
2. Lack of the use of speech for communication
3. Maintenance of sameness via stereotypic behavior
4. Lack of major neurologic dysfunction.

EIA children are seen as lacking in body ego and are hypothesized to have cathected or focused upon a stereotyped pattern of behavior, which has resulted in the deviant ego formation labeled as behavioral ego (Handford & Ward, 1969; Ward, 1969; 1970a; 1970b).

STRUCTURAL THERAPY

Structural therapy has been operationally defined as, "the therapist actively and directly bringing order to bear for the patient upon which the ego could then build" (Handford & Ward, 1969). This therapeutic approach is essentially developmental in nature as it follows closely the pathways of the acquisition of ego functions in the normal human infant. The aim of this therapeutic approach is to focus the child upon reality in a natural manner, and at the same time provide stimulation adequate and appropriate for the development of higher ego functions.

The lack of object relations of the EIA child has necessitated that the initial goal of the structural therapist be the attainment of the acknowledgement of his existence. Clinical experience has indicated that the behavioral ego (Ward, 1969; 1970a; 1970b) is both the major differential diagnostic characteristic of the EIA child (Kanner & Lesser, 1958; Ward & Handford, 1968), as well as the most viable entry into a therapeutic relationship. The behavioral ego has been defined as "the repetitive occurrence of a complex set of stereotypic behaviors, which . . . exist to the exclusion of body ego or any higher ego processes" (Ward, 1970). The behavioral ego of the EIA child may be differentiated from the repetitive behavior of the retarded child by (1) the rage or withdrawal reaction to any interruption until resumption is allowed, and (2) the inability to shift to any other repetitive behavior.

Earlier papers (Ward, 1968; 1970b) have provided specific guidelines for the use of structural therapy which emphasize the interruption of the functioning of the behavioral ego as the initial strategy for developing a part-object relationship with an EIA child. The guidelines are:

(1)   The therapist is trained to identify the stereotypic behavior of the child and to interrupt it. This interruption is done in a graduated and game-like way, if possible. The ineffectiveness and maladaptiveness of the stereotypic behavior for dealing with people is demonstrated to the child by interference and by physical and verbal setting of limits to the rage or avoidance reactions which often follow the interference.

(2)   The anxiety and anger created by the interruption of the stereotypic behavior is used to focus the attention of the child upon part of the therapist as a meaningful part-object or object. Analytically oriented interpretations accompany the use of structural therapy. The therapist attempts to interpret the child's feeling about being interrupted, and then tries to get him to emit any verbal or physical message which is directed toward the therapist. This physical, visual, or verbal message is then used to focus the attention of the child upon physical likenesses and differences between himself and the therapist. This stage often needs to be preceded by a period during which the therapist presents an alternative rhythmic behavior for the child to focus upon.

(3)   Development of a recognition relationship with the child is followed by presentation of a number of novel and patterned activities which draw the child's attention to his own body. These activities include counting of fingers and toes, gross movements of arms and legs, physical stimulation of body, and so forth.

(4)   The development of body ego is stimulated by the use of physical game-like interactions that make the child more aware of his own body, and of his differences from and similarities to his therapist.

(5)   As behavioral ego functioning decreases and body ego becomes more predominant, more conventional play therapy techniques are included in the treatment.

Thus, structural therapy is a treatment approach which is both physically intrusive as well as supportive (Handford & Ward, 1969; Ward, 1968; 1969; 1970b) . This treatment approach postulates that the EIA child must be diverted from the "dead end" of his behavioral ego level of functioning, stimulated and aided in the development of body ego, and finally assisted in developing age-appropriate object-relations.

Although structural therapy and rage-reduction therapy (Zaslow, 1967) display superficial similarities, they were developed quite independently. Also, whereas Zaslow postulated that EIA is ". . . the most extreme example of the use of motoric resistance to express rage . . ." and that the therapist must gain "dominance" over the child's bodily actions to redirect his behavior towards more meaningful affective contact, structural therapy views EIA as a developmental disorder with concomitant deviant ego development, that results from a stimulation deficit and/or distortion in early infancy. The basic goal of structural therapy is to get the EIA child to focus upon another human being, and to learn that interpersonal interaction can be much more fun and interesting than the stereotypic behavior which comprises the behavioral ego. Thus, whereas rage-reduction therapy emphasized dominance and control of the EIA child, structural therapy emphasizes stimulation, curiosity, and a "priming of the pump" of the EIA child's interest in the surrounding environment.

Behavioral Ego

Previous articles (Handford & Ward, 1969; Ward, 1970a; 1970b) have presented the rationale for the development of the concept of the behavioral ego. The EIA child usually appears to manifest one area of stereotypic skill which is under his control, even though there is no apparent awareness of or concern with his physical being. Body ego (Freud, 1927) has been previously defined as the first experience of reality, based upon the actuality of body limits and boundaries.

However, the EIA child appears to be completely lacking an awareness of his own body, its sense, and its capabilities. Instead, the total interest and attention of the EIA child is focused upon a particular stereotypic behavior. This particular stereotypic behavior is used to maintain sameness in the environment, and is the only true connection that the EIA child has with reality. Interruption of this pattern of stereotypic behavior elicits either a rage reaction or a withdrawal reaction, whereas physical injury or other intrusions elicit no observable response. This type of reaction indicates that there was an even earlier experience of reality than that of the body, and that that was found in the awareness and control of a particular repetitive pattern of behavior. These patterns are seen in infants during the early weeks of life, and have been described by Piaget (1956) as a "primary circular reaction." Thus, it appears that for the EIA child, the first experience of reality lies in this pattern of behavior rather than in bodily awareness. This is the basis for the development of the concept of the "behavioral ego," which is seen as antedating the development of body ego.

Therapy is not possible unless the patient has some connection with reality, however fragmentary. This is the reason that structural therapy focuses upon the manipulation of the stereotypic behavior pattern that makes up the behavioral ego. It is the only lever that the therapist has in his attempt to deal with a child who is otherwise completely isolated from the surrounding reality, as well as from his body.

CASE REPORT

Robert is a 12-year-old, nonverbal, Caucasian boy who was hospitalized for residential treatment at 7 years of age due to his self-mutilating and destructive behavior and bizarre actions. This patient arrived at the hospital after a 5-year history of intensive examination, evaluation, and treatment by psychologists, psychiatrists, neurologists, speech therapists, audiologists, and so forth. These evaluations all agreed that Robert was an unrelating child with serviceable hearing who met the criteria for EIA.

DEVELOPMENTAL HISTORY

Robert is an illegitimate child who was born at the termination of a 7-year relationship between his single mother and married father. The pregnancy was stormy, and was marked by Robert's mother being rejected by her family, a cross-country trip to live with relatives, an appendectomy, bleeding during the last month, and a difficult delivery highlighted by a 48-hour labor. The birth was reported to have been a "month late" and then Robert was kept in the hospital for his first two months of life until his mother could find an apartment. Robert's mother visited him daily in the nursery during this time period.

The patient was described as a "good baby" who only cried when he was hungry, and "enjoyed" being cuddled until he was six months of age. Robert sat up at six months, watched himself in a mirror at eight months, and started walking at ten months. This child failed to respond to his name at six months of age and subsequently failed to respond consistently to sounds, even at a high intensity level. The only speech reported was the verbalization of "mama" at ten months of age.

At 1½ years of age Robert began to awaken screaming and refused to stay alone. From that time until 5 years of age Robert slept with his mother. At the age of 2½ years, Robert was observed to be repeatedly running into objects and injuring himself to the point that surgical stitches were required. At the age of 4, Robert began banging his head to the extent that he required stitches over his left eye. The patient then became very destructive of furniture, lamps, dishes, and so forth, and began turning on the water and flooding the house. Finally, Robert began to slap the left side of his face until it bled, tissue damage ensued, and infection set in.

Robert's hearing was first evaluated when he was 1 year of age. No hearing deficit was found and this and many subsequent evaluations led to Robert being described as "displaying autism, negativism and self-destructive behavior." The child was placed in a nursery school at 1 year of age, taken to "over 30" specialists, and spent his next 18 months in a residence for mentally retarded children. This placement was accompanied by such pathological behavior that a final evaluation resulted in the recommendation for residential treatment.

HOSPITALIZATION

Robert was hospitalized at the age of 6 years, 9 months and was described as a nonverbal, hyperactive, destructive, assaultive, and self-mutilating child. This child's hands were strapped together, at admission, to prevent him from doing serious injury to himself. Numerous medications had failed to affect Robert's self-mutilating behavior. At times, Robert would line up objects in a row and resist any interruption. The patient was not toilet trained and would not dress himself, but could feed himself.

TREATMENT

Robert had been hospitalized for 2 years and 5 months prior to the beginning of his treatment in structural therapy. The initiation of treatment found 9-year-old Robert receiving large amounts of tranquilizing medication, his hands tied twenty-four hours a day in long sleeved shirts that extended well beyond the tips of his fingers, nonverbal and non-vocal, unrelating, and displaying no eye contact. There was a large bald spot on the back of his head, from rolling back and forth on his back. The patient was now toilet trained, but otherwise had limited skills in relation to self-help. Also, the child had been placed on suicidal precaution due to his propensity for running blindly without apparent caution or fear for safety.

The patient was seen for approximately three hundred sessions on a twice-weekly basis over three years. During the initial phase of therapy, Robert displayed no eye contact, appeared to be content to rock or roll back and forth on the floor, was unresponsive to staff or other patients and appeared to be completely lacking in object relations. Whenever Robert's hands were untied, he would violently slap his face with his left hand as often as twenty or thirty times per minute. If allowed to continue, this self-punishment would go on to the point that blood was drawn and then spattered over anyone who would be nearby. This behavior was accompanied by a facial expression which seemed to reflect feelings of panic and loss of control, but not of pain. Robert violently resisted any efforts directed towards freeing his hands and would just as violently reject interference with his slapping once he had commenced. Thus, Robert would often behaviorally insist that his hands remain tied, even while sleeping. He sometimes added to this restraint by wrapping sheets around his arms so tightly that his circulation was interfered with.

Evaluation of Robert at this point suggested that he met the four criteria for EIA:

1. Lack of object relations
2. Maintenance of sameness via stereotypic behavior
3. Lack of use of speech for communication
4. Lack of any major neurologic dysfunction.

September 1966 - September 1967

The first six months of structural therapy focused upon helping Robert to become aware of and acknowledge the presence of the therapist. The following notes are drawn from an early session:

> Robert was seen in the treatment room for 45 minutes. I was unable to untie his hands as the patient insisted that they be left alone. He responded to the stimulation of bright toys, physical stimulation and playful attention. Robert seemed to get overstimulated and lose control. He attempted to control the stimulation input by turning off the lights.

These early efforts involved repeated physical intrusion, interruption, and stimulation. Robert was bodily lifted and swung into the air, tickled, and sung to by the therapist. His major body parts were repeatedly physically located, touched, tickled, kneaded and bounced, as well as verbally labeled in nursery school songs.

Robert's behavioral ego appeared to consist of his self-punitive behavior. He attempted to maintain sameness in his environment by both his slapping, as well as his insistence upon being restrained. The net result of these two foci was that Robert was fixated at an early level of functioning with no way of initiating any complex, interpersonal relationship. The hands, so important in learning about the environment, were immobilized and Robert was unable to explore and learn about his own body, let alone the external world. The history of running into objects "as if they were not there," minimal response to stitches and slapping to the point that blood spurted, all supported the view that Robert had failed to develop the body ego that is a necessary foundation for higher ego processes. Thus, Robert appeared to be existing in a world with a limited amount of stimulation which was almost completely under his own control. In many ways, Robert's lack of response to pain was reminiscent of that of Melzack's (1957) dogs who had been raised from puppies in a dark room in a state of sensory deprivation. When these animals were first brought into the external world, they were hyperactive, unable to relate socially, and ran into objects and injured themselves without any apparent awareness of pain.

As therapy continued during the first six months, Robert was gradually taken off the heavy medication of Librium and Mellaril which had been prescribed. This decrease and, eventually, cessation of tranquilizing medication had no deleterious effect upon the patient's behavior. Instead, it seemed that structural therapy was able to take the place of and improve upon the effect of medication. Continued therapy resulted in increased responsiveness from Robert. Initially, however, this responsiveness was of an avoidant nature. An excerpt from an early session provides an illustration:

> Robert started crying and tried to run away when I came to see him today. On the way to the treatment room, he broke away and ran wildly through an open door to the generator room with myself in hot pursuit. When we arrived in the treatment room, Robert first tried to get out the door until I moved a large chair in front of the door and sat in it. Robert then picked up a rod with his tied hands and wandered around the other end of the room, twiddling it in front of his face. I followed the patient around the room and repeatedly used my hand to block his view of the waving rod. Robert displayed no eye contact but attempted to push my hand away. Persistence aroused Robert further and I attempted to involve him in a pushing game. He responded initially, but then tried to get away from me. I lay on the floor with Robert and used my body to block him into a corner. He refused to have his hands untied but did make fleeting eye contact.

At the time of the above session, Robert usually responded to frustration by shrieking and screaming in a high pitched monotone that was often followed by a blind assault that could involve kicking, biting, throwing himself bodily against cement walls, and so forth. The end of the first six months of treatment found Robert displaying much more relatedness to the therapist, occasionally allowing his hands to be untied outside of the treatment room and coming to sit on the therapist's lap. Also, Robert was now displaying marked feelings of jealousy towards the therapist when other children approached.

The latter half of the first year of treatment may be characterized by an excerpt from the following therapy session:

> Robert came willingly to me and went down the hall to the T.R. [therapy room] ahead of me. He opened the door, put on the lights, and shut the door on request. He cried (without tears) when I rolled up his sleeves and took away some of his toys (which he had manipulated into his sleeves). Then he insisted on holding my hand. I permitted this for some time and played the Differentiation Game with his hands, arms, fingers, eyes, and hair. Robert began to show anticipation and participation by lifting his fingers as I counted them. Robert slapped himself occasionally, but would stop when I emphasized that my hand was available. Also, he gave me full attention with searching eye contact when I related his slapping to anger at my absence (3 week vacation).

Thus, this period of therapy was characterized by increasing reality contact and object relations. Robert started to display more curiosity about the environment, came in response to his name and started to direct his anger toward objects instead of himself. The patient was directed to use a pegboard and hammer set whenever he started to punish himself. Interestingly, the patient could always be stopped from slapping by the therapist placing his hand on the place where the slap was directed. Robert has never slapped anyone's hand in such a situation.

Initially, the therapist held Robert's hand with a hammer enclosed and guided him through the action of pounding the pegs. The patient was repeatedly told that this was the appropriate way to express his anger and that his slapping of himself was the wrong way to express his anger. It was suggested that Robert had a negative view of himself and, therefore, wanted to punish himself. It was also suggested that Robert was angry at the therapist for untying his hands. Robert was repeatedly told that he was a good boy, that his hands were good and that he had the ability to control his hands. This approach progressed to the point that a glance from the therapist was sufficient to interrupt a beginning of slapping, and to send Robert after the hammer and pegboard. Each blow from the hammer was accompanied by loud, enthusiastic shouts from the therapist of, "Yes, you're mad! That's right, that's what you do when you're mad! Hit it again!" The child was aided in gaining further control of his anger by giving the therapist an opportunity to use the hammer. The therapist would enthusiastically bang the pegs with comments about how angry Robert was. Finally, Robert was encouraged to make a game of hammering the pegs in different patterns and eventually graduated to the use of a toy xylophone. Robert was urged to cooperate and alternate with the therapist in all of these activities, to emphasize the reciprocal nature of the relationship and avoid any possibility of the development of another stereotypic behavior.

Robert was repeatedly engaged in various physical activities which led to direct contact and comparison of his body with that of the therapist. Fingers of Robert and the therapist were alternately tickled or counted, eyelids were felt, ears were tickled or gently pulled, noses were poked, arms and legs were stroked or tickled, toes and feet were tickled, and Robert was encouraged to point to identical body parts on himself and the therapist.

Paradoxically, as Robert showed increased relatedness and awareness of self, his self-mutilation changed from a slapping of the cheek to a punching of his chin. At the same time, Robert was reported to be vocalizing at night. The therapist soon heard this vocalizing in therapy sessions, and found that it was possible to add vocal interaction to the therapeutic interaction.

The course of structural therapy was rather stormy at times, as Robert did not take kindly to the interruption of his behavioral ego. The initial reactions to such interference were attempts at biting, kicking, throwing objects, or turning over furniture. The therapist had to follow Robert around the treatment room, all the time attempting to involve him in some distracting and pleasurable interaction. Oftentimes, the patient had to be physically restrained and sat upon for control in as nonpunitive a manner as possible. Robert was physically controlled and involved in physical differentiation games. The intrusive physical contact appeared to have the most success in reinstating controls after such events. Robert's defenses and ego controls appeared to collapse almost instantaneously when given too much stress and needed to be rebuilt gradually. That is, physical control had to be exerted by the therapist, then Robert would use an external device (crossed fingers, waving toy, long sleeves) to exert control, then could maintain control with help of only verbal encouragement, and finally could control his impulses enough to move away from the therapist while remaining relaxed.

September 1967 - September 1968

The second year of structural therapy with Robert was marked by his starting in speech therapy, his use of transitional objects (Winnicott, 1953), and increased interest and capacity to communicate his desires.

The speech therapist found Robert curious about her equipment, unwilling to release any of the toys he carried with him, unresponsive to verbal direction, and he turned off the light during their first session. The patient did follow several verbal directions late in this first session. This brief report is included to point out the recapitulation of the patient's defenses over a year of structural therapy, which appeared in this new and strange setting.

This second year of therapy found the patient allowing his hands to remain untied all day, but insisting that they be tied at night. Refusal of this demand resulted in slapping of self, punching of self, and finally aggressive acting out. During the day, the patient's sleeves were gradually shortened until they barely reached his fingertips. This strategy was responded to by Robert hunching his shoulders and folding his arms to have his hands more completely covered by the sleeve. Also, he usually kept at least three different toys in the bottom of each sleeve. Shirts with narrow sleeves were then constructed, which made it difficult for Robert to secret objects within them. Also, Robert was increasingly required to perform simple tasks that demanded that he use his hands. Gradually, a routine developed where Robert had to repeatedly put down six to eight objects every time he encountered a door, had to put on a jacket, eat a meal, and so forth. While this behavior was the normal routine every day, Robert usually felt free to have his hands exposed and empty during the full period of his therapy sessions.

Robert would look to the therapist and by both vocalization and gesture indicate that he wanted these tasks performed for him. These requests were refused by the therapist to demonstrate the maladaptive nature of Robert's response to the anxiety engendered by having his hands untied and partially exposed. Robert was given both verbal and physical support in dealing with this anxiety. He was allowed to stand very close to the therapist, encouraged to hand the therapist the various objects, and promised that he could have his objects returned immediately upon completion of the task at hand. The unit staff was encouraged to follow the same procedure, all to the end of demonstrating to Robert both the needlessness and maladaptive nature of his response to anxiety about having his hands untied.

Robert now had learned to use keys in locks, would use trial and error tactics to find the correct key on a ring of eleven hospital keys, followed most simple directions when he wanted to do so, and learned to play appropriately with balls, blocks, nested boxes, and stacking toys.

As Robert's sleeves became continually shorter, he found it more and more difficult to carry all his objects. The staff was instructed to ignore any objects or toys which were misplaced. This resulted in the eventual loss of all but one favored rubber Indian. Robert was then given only short-sleeved shirts to wear.

The patient responded to this change with some regression in the area of independence of functioning. Whereas before he had been able to move independently, he now tried to always hold a staff member's hand. Also, if possible, the patient would try and persuade the staff member to restrain him as his sleeves once had. Robert was taken for walks on the hospital grounds to expose him to many new and different experiences. On one occasion, the therapist took Robert to a nearby shopping mall in his car. Several weeks later, Robert indicated his wish to return to the shopping mall in the following manner:

> Robert came and greeted me with a smile when I entered the unit. He reached in my pocket for my keys and ran excitedly to the closet that contained the children's coats, instead of to the T.R. As I watched to see what he would do, Robert opened the closet door, put on his coat and cap, shut the closet door and pulled me to the door of the unit. The patient opened the unit door, led the way out into the hall, unlocked the door to the stairwell and took me down the stairs to the main floor. Then Robert took the therapist to his office, pulled his coat off of the hanger and tried to help him into it. The therapist put on his coat and Robert then pulled him out of his office, out of a hospital entrance to the parking lot where he then found the therapist's automobile. Robert then attempted to unlock the automobile door and clearly wanted to go for a ride.

The above incident was the first of many instances when Robert let the therapist know what he wanted to do by the use of gesture, pantomime, or direct action. These communicative efforts were often accompanied by a variety of vocalizations that at times took on the proportions of jargon. The patient's excellent memory is well illustrated by the above excerpt. Robert and the therapist explored many aspects of the shopping mall as he learned about escalators (he wanted to go up the down escalators or sit on them instead of stand), the toy store, the pet shop, and so forth. All of these new experiences were used to widen Robert's awareness of the environment and to keep his attention focused upon it.

The development of an attachment to a specific transitional object highlighted the last half of the second year of treatment. The rubber toy Indian became Robert's inseparable companion whether it was merely clutched in his hand, waved or twiddled in front of his face, or thrown in anger. Indeed, Robert and his Indian became so inseparable that one of the other children called him "Robert Indian."

Robert's handling of his Indian soon provided an excellent measure as to the adequacy of his object relations and ego controls. The very best days were always forecast by Robert showing that he was able to voluntarily and spontaneously put his Indian down and involve himself in some activity. These days were rare initially, but increased gradually. Much more common were the days when Robert could handle himself well, as long as he was allowed to clutch his Indian in his hand. However, it was obvious that Robert had great feelings of ambivalence about the importance of the role which his Indian played in his psychic economy. This ambivalence was most clearly shown on days when Robert's ego controls were at a low ebb and is illustrated by the following excerpt from a nursing report:

> Robert had been upset all evening and slapped occasionally after dropping his toy. Finally, he stood in the center of the room and threw his toy as far as he could. Then, Robert stood there and cried while slapping. He appeared to want his toy and at the same time appeared unable to go get it himself. He regained control of himself when his toy was retrieved for him.

On other occasions, Robert was able, with encouragement, to retrieve his Indian after he had thrown it away. Later, more serious efforts were made to dispose of the transitional object:

> Robert became angry at not getting the attention he seemed to desire. He started screaming, ran down the hall to the B.R. and attempted to flush his toys down the toilet. Then he became very upset and tried to get them back. Robert cried, screamed and slapped until maintenance man was able to get toys out of toilet.

The above excerpt clearly shows the variability of the acceptance of the transitional object by Robert. The initial rage reaction at frustration of his wishes led to an impulsive attempt to reject those with whom he had formed partial object relations, as represented by the transitional object. Actual loss of the transitional object was experienced as a loss of self that could not be tolerated. The staff was trained to interpret Robert's use of the transitional object as a barometer of the level of his object relations. Thus, fearful clinging to the transitional object was interpreted as indicative of regression, while attempts at disposal of it were viewed as progress in the development of individuation. Robert was encouraged to demonstrate and experience complete mastery in the handling of his transitional objects and to develop an analogous feeling of mastery and confidence in interpersonal relations. Thus, the child was encouraged to retrieve the transitional object from wherever he might throw it, and was given great praise whenever he was able to do so. Robert was seen as having achieved a stability of object relations and individuation when he no longer needed his transitional object. Thus, the staff was most pleased and encouraging on those days when Robert was able to leave his transitional objects and function without them.

Thus, Robert increasingly showed evidence of psychological growth as he attempted to function more independently. However, the last half of the second year of treatment still found Robert demanding to be allowed to restrain his arms with long sleeves before he would or could go to sleep.

At the same time as the patient failed to show any improvement in sleeping pattern, he was showing marked improvement in regard to his handling of materials in his therapy session. An excerpt from one of these sessions is illustrative:

> Robert went to the sink and wanted to play, but the therapist insisted that he roll up sleeves and put down toys first. The patient resisted initially in a playful manner, then put down his toys and took therapist's hand ... Robert was vocalizing intermittently while the therapist playfully imitated him ... Robert sat at the table and tried to wave objects in front of his face. These objects were taken away and Robert failed to show any resulting disturbance.

At this point, it was apparent that the patient felt comfortable enough about the formerly sensitive area of his hands and arms to make a nonverbal joke about them. Also, the "twiddling," which had formerly been used to block out the outside world, now appeared to be used in only a teasing manner.

The interaction between Robert and the therapist became very free and open at this period. This change appeared to be due to the fact that the patient's anxiety level had diminished to the point that he was able to devote much more energy to investigation of himself, the therapist, and the surrounding environment. The following excerpt should give the flavor of the therapeutic interaction:

> A brief period of body stimulation and differentiation followed, during which Robert ran his fingers up and down his arms. The therapist did the same thing in a game-like fashion and then played "disappearing finger" with a hollow tube that Robert had placed on one finger. The patient responded to this game with many smiles and occasional laughter.

Finally, this period of therapy saw Robert moving to play that was representative of increasing conceptual capacity and cognitive function. The following excerpt is illustrative:

> Robert started to examine the building blocks that were in a box on the table. He examined them from all angles, but was not too interested when the therapist tried to have him help in building a tower. Then Robert found a crayon in the play Doctor's bag and began to play with it in a desultory fashion. The therapist took the crayon from Robert, printed his name on a wooden block and told him what it was. Robert then began to show an interest in crayoning the other sides of the block. This was done to 6 blocks of varying shapes and sizes, which were then built into 3 separate towers on one large base block. Initially, the patient would only use blocks which he had crayoned. The highest tower consisted of 5 objects, including a toy wooden refrigerator. Robert showed great care and sense of balance in building his towers. Upon finding 2 plastic checkers Robert began incorporating them into his towers by putting them between blocks. . . . Next, Robert pulled the therapist up and towards the toy closet door, went into his pocket for keys, opened the door, put on the light and got down a set of checkers from the fourth shelf of the toy rack. . . . The box was opened and the board taken out and put on a chair while all the checkers were put on the table. These red and black plastic checkers now appeared to take the place of crayoning as they were centered on blocks of wood, placed between them in towers and arranged in pairs of similar or different colors on the blocks. The final construction created by Robert contained 17 blocks, 1 wooden refrigerator, 1 wooden sofa, and 18 checkers. . . . At the end of the 1½ hour session, Robert went and got the checkerboard, opened it up and placed it on the table against the wall behind the towers. Then the box top was placed next to it (checkerboard) with the colorful side facing out and a yellow microscope, blue and yellow hammer, red screwdriver, and a red ring toss

spike were placed at the base of the open checkerboard. Robert appeared quite happy with and protective of his construction, which was left intact on the table.

September 1968 - September 1969

The third year of treatment was marked by Robert giving up his transitional object, making marked progress in sleeping without having his arms wrapped and restrained in long sleeves, and the acquisition of a large fund of passive and receptive language. Self-mutilating behavior became completely extinguished except during periods of illness or in relation to the loss of an important person (missed home visit or therapist vacation).

Speech therapy. Robert displayed an ever-increasing comprehension of the words spoken to him and became capable of following verbal directions without accompanying gestures. Robert's development in speech therapy progressed from an almost completely mute stage, to random vocalizations, to the preword level of an 8- to 12-month-old child, to the changing of nonspeech sounds (i.e., "eck") into speech sounds (i.e., "baba"), to the consistent imitation of vowel sounds and the sounds "ba," "da," "la," "f," and "th," and to consistent but gross approximations for the words "ball" and "hi." The speech therapist (Leith, 1968) summarized some work with Robert:

> Once it was established that Robert could imitate basic tongue and lip movements, the basic sound combination "ba" was chosen as a beginning point. This sound was visually and auditorily related to the object, ball. Every time the ball was presented, the sound was made. Robert began using the lip pattern when asking for the ball. As phonation became more consistent, the final sound position "l" was added to form the word "ball."

> Robert has progressed to using a variety of sounds in his vocal play. The majority of these approximate back and mid-vowels. He is inconsistently phonating on labial and bilabial sounds. His imitation of lip positions is becoming more accurate. Robert is increasingly more aware of the vibrations made when producing sounds. He will place his hand on his throat, chin, or cheek as he is phonating. He will also place his hand on my face instead of my placing it there. His eye contact has improved from fleeting glances in the beginning, to looking at my face for clues.

At a later date, the speech therapist (Leith, 1970) commented:

Verbal language development has been slow while other areas have reached more adequate levels. At this point more direct pressure for words has been initiated, as his (Robert's) responsiveness and tolerance have increased sufficiently to handle this type of pressure. He has said several words in imitation and spontaneously, but no consistent words have been used for any real communication.

Robert has been the most difficult child the therapist has worked with in therapy. One of the reasons was the self-destructive aspect of his behavior, which the therapist had to learn to handle therapeutically. Rather than just stopping Robert from slapping, the therapists have gradually given him a sense of being able to control his slapping. This amounts to a long, slow process during which the therapist had to learn to handle her anxiety about seeing a child slap and refrain from grabbing his hands to make him stop. When he is anxious and slapping, the therapist allows him physical contact, but then playfully moves him away. This is repeated many times until he has gained control and can again function in the situation.

Structural therapy. The first month of the third year of therapy was marked by the changing of Robert into short-sleeved shirts for all his waking hours. This move was taken to completely remove the availability of any physical restraints. Although this change did not stimulate a return of the self-punitive behavior, Robert did show an obvious increase in anxiety level. The most obvious indicant of the increase in anxiety level was reflected in Robert's attempt to find a somatic substitute for the external feeling of control which had been provided by the longer sleeves and/or physical restraint. The somatic substitute that was arrived at was the expedient of crossed fingers. However, Robert did not cross just two fingers, but attempted and succeeded in crossing all of his fingers on each hand. This act not only gave his hands a grotesquely gnarled appearance, but also made it almost impossible for him to use his hands for any activity.

The same structural therapeutic techniques were applied to the defense of the crossed fingers, as had been applied to the tied sleeves. The therapist played finger games, tickled the patient's hands, insisted that he hold hands when walking, and always tried to make sure that Robert's attention was drawn to his hands—the many things that could be done with them and how inconvenient it was not to be able to use them. Robert initially responded in the same fearful and anxious manner as he had to the untying of his sleeves and went through the same repertoire of responses as he had in the earlier situation. However, Robert was able to work through this particular defense in approximately three months.

The above behavior change, which appeared to function as a defense against anxiety engendered by having to wear short-sleeved shirts which could not be used as restraints, was soon followed by the appearance of a new symptom. Robert was observed to have started to display sudden repetitive movements of arms, head, and upper torso. These movements did not appear to be related to any specific or restricted situation. Clinical observation suggested the need for a differential diagnosis between an organic or a psychological etiology to this new behavior. The major feature of these movements was a tic-like jerk of the head to the extreme right. A neurological evaluation resulted in the impression "... that the episodes ... seemed entirely more tic-like, complex and organized than would be possible for a seizure." Further evaluation and observation suggested that these movements were indeed psychologic in origin and they were treated as such. The staff and therapist ignored this repetitive behavior except for the rare occasions when they interfered with the child's functioning. Finally, this behavior ceased after a period of another three months.

At the same time as the above symptoms were appearing and being worked through, Robert was responding well to speech therapy as illustrated by the following excerpt:

> We focused on the face, then the mouth. Robert would imitate lip and tongue movements, but it was many weeks before any sound accompanied the movements. By having him feel my throat and face and by putting his hand in front of my mouth, he started to feel his throat for the same sensations. The mirror has become an important object in our sessions. He uses it while sitting next to me or on my lap when we are imitating faces and making sounds.

The last half of the third year of treatment saw the therapeutic focus placed upon the restraint while sleeping. Formerly, this area of functioning had been left untouched, although care was taken to avoid the restriction of circulation by the restraints used by the child. Now the pajama sleeves were gradually shortened and Robert was encouraged to try and sleep without restraint. The patient again became very upset when this aspect of his behavioral ego was attacked. There was the same pattern of initial anxiety and fearfulness, and the self-punitive behavior returned with renewed intensity. The handling of this problem resulted in many sleepless nights for both staff and patients over a period of six months. Finally, Robert reached the point that he could go to sleep while wearing short-sleeved pajamas.

The nature of Robert's relationships to people at this time is best shown by the following excerpt by the speech therapist:

> Robert now relates to me closely as a person, as he does to Dr. Ward. Dr. Ward and I have noticed on several occasions that though Robert relates to us individually in our sessions with him, he cannot tolerate us being together with him. He will try physically to remove one of us from the setting or try to take one of us away. . . . I accidentally met Robert and his careworker in the lobby recently. Robert greeted me and then pushed me onto a nearby couch. He then went and brought his careworker over to sit next to me. Then he squeezed in between us and appeared both comfortable and pleased with himself for accomplishing the feat. This is the first time he has related to me and any other person at the same time. We played with him, pushed, tickled and teased for almost 10 minutes. He was reluctant to leave, but did so without becoming upset.

The third year of treatment was most fruitful as Robert was completely freed from all physical restraints, gave up the transitional object which had been so vital to his self-control, ceased self-mutilating behavior except during periods of physical or psychological stress, directed anger in a controlled manner to the appropriate object, displayed a rapidly increasing fund of passive complex ego structures. The patient has responded well to visits to the shopping center, the school, and extensive exploration of the hospital environs.

Robert has continued to widen his interest in the external environment, and has displayed a quite remarkable memory in the process. His vocalizations are at the level of expressions of pleasure or distress, but continue to become more spontaneous in social situations. The patient also makes his needs known through gestures and actions.

Robert has developed definite likes and dislikes in the external environment. He has displayed special interest in the use of earphones for vocalization, other children at play, and curiosity about all locked doors, escalators, cars, and boats. Furthermore, the patient can and will follow sequential directions of up to three parts.

ADDITIONAL THERAPEUTIC PROGRAMS

Robert was the focus of many therapeutic programs within the residential treatment center, all of which attempted to incorporate and carry on the basic precepts of structural therapy. Although it is beyond the scope of this paper to describe these other programs in detail, a brief summary of each shall be presented:

1. Robert participated daily in a preschool educational program that emphasized the use of nursery school types of activities such as the use of finger paint, clay, crayoning, buttoning. He had been in this program for three years prior to the initiation of structural therapy.

2. In the year 1968–69, Robert spent two afternoons a week attending a community nursery school for 3- to 5-year-old normal children. This program was initiated to increase Robert's exposure to the external environment and to normal children who were functioning on the same developmental level as he. Robert soon learned to participate in this program after an initial period of hyperactivity and looked forward to his visits.

3. The childcare staff was trained in the precepts of structural therapy and urged to respond to Robert in a spontaneous and affective manner. They were also trained in the details of handling such specific developmental steps as the untying of hands, shortening of sleeves, and use of the transitional object. The nursing staff was very responsive to the need for variety and stimulation by Robert, as well as the other children on the unit, and frequently scheduled trips to parks, the zoo, the beach, or amusement parks.

FAMILY COUNSELING

Robert's mother was seen in intensive casework by the unit social worker under the close supervision of the author. The extent and detail of casework which was done far exceeds the scope of this paper and merits its own separate presentation. A close casework relationship was established after much initial difficulty. Robert's mother was seen from the beginning of his treatment, on an increasingly frequent and intensive basis. She was encouraged to take him home weekly for weekend visits. The social worker and the therapist often met with the mother to deal with specific questions and problems as they arose. Also, Robert's mother was often invited to come to the hospital for a full day to go through his treatment program with him. This gave her an opportunity to both observe the way various staff members handled her son, as well as to ask detailed questions. By September, 1969, a warm and collaborative relationship had been established between Robert's mother and the treatment team. She was usually contacted by her social worker on a weekly basis and showed striking progress from an initial position of isolated hostility, to one of a cooperative partner working for the further progress of her child.

CONCLUSIONS

The purpose of this case presentation was to show, in detail, the changes in ego structure and behavior that resulted from the application of structural therapy to a self-mutilating EIA child. The ego structures which have shown change are behavioral ego, body, and the higher ego processes necessary to the formation of human relationships. Robert started therapy with the bulk of his functioning at the behavioral ego level. He met stringent criteria for a diagnosis of EIA, and displayed behavioral ego functioning of self-mutilation. The child's lack of response to pain and injury to his body showed little if any development of body ego.

The following statements may be made about the effect of structural therapy upon Robert's psychological development and behavioral functioning after three years of treatment.

Lack of Object Relations

Robert met this criterion at the time treatment was initiated, a statement which can no longer be made. Robert has formed a very warm and close relationship with the therapist, as well as other staff members. He has also been observed to periodically, but spontaneously involve other children in play. Also, Robert awaits his mother's coming for home visits with great anticipation and is greatly disappointed should she fail to appear.

Maintenance of Sameness Via Stereotypic Behavior

Robert met this diagnostic criterion by virtue of self-mutilating behavior, as well as his "twiddling" of objects in front of his face. Both the self-mutilation and the restraint which was its obverse have ceased to present either a psychological or a behavioral problem. Robert has changed from a child who was either restrained or self-mutilating twenty-four hours per day, to a child who is free of restraints, does not injure himself, and uses his hands in a constructive manner.

The twiddling behavior is only sporadically manifested and is never of such intensity as to allow Robert to completely "tune out" the surrounding environment as it once was. Instead, the twiddling now seems to have two separate goals. The first goal appears to be the blocking out of specific stimuli which are anxiety producing in the external environment, while the second goal seems to have the effect of drawing attention to Robert when he feels he is being ignored.

Lack of Use of Speech for Communication

The initial stages of treatment disclosed a child who was both mute and without speech, and who displayed no awareness of nor interest in communicating affect or wish to another human being. Robert's verbal language development has been slow, but he has said several words both spontaneously and in imitation. Although words have not been *consistently* used for communication, Robert does display a *wish* and *intent* to communicate via word, vocalization, or gesture which clearly indicates that the lack of interest in people, which is the core of this criterion, no longer exists.

Lack of Major Neurologic Dysfunction

Robert's abnormal history during pregnancy and delivery, abnormal EEG's, and extreme sensitivity to infections all suggest the presence of some minimal brain damage. However, this minimal brain damage appears to have had little, if any, etiological significance to Robert's adjustment of EIA. The recalcitrance of speech development, in contrast to the other areas of development, suggests the minimal brain damage may have affected the speech areas in the brain.

Robert is no longer seen as functioning as a classically autistic child with an object relations level similar to that of a three- to four-month-old infant. Instead, Robert is now seen as a handicapped child suffering from developmental deviations in speech development and deviations in social development. Except for the area of speech development, Robert is seen as functioning within the developmental age range of 3½ to 5½ years. He is now felt to have reached a level of development where he would be most responsive to a special education program for the handicapped child.

Recommendations. Robert's response to three years of structural therapy led to the following recommendations:

1. An increase in contact with a varied and stimulating environment. Robert should go on trips to the zoo, camp, or nursery school, and there should be increased autonomy of functioning on the unit, with Robert being made responsible for particular tasks.
2. An exposure to more structured and complex tasks in the patient's

educational program. Robert should be given a mixture of cognitive and motor tasks which would increase his competence in the environment.

3. An increase in the frequency of home visits. The patient's mother should spend a day at the hospital observing her son in his different programs, and then be aided by the staff in learning how to stimulate the growth of particular areas of development during home visits.

IMPLICATIONS

The results of three years of application of structural therapy to this self-mutilating autistic boy have many implications. The cessation of self-mutilation and the development of at least part-object relations appear to demonstrate the validity of structural therapy as a therapeutic approach for this type of young, severely disturbed, hospitalized, and non-verbal patient.

Furthermore, the therapeutic progress shown by this patient appears to lend support to the etiologic conceptualization of EIA as a developmental disorder, which is largely based in a stimulation deficit in the child's early developmental history. It is felt that earlier conceptualizations of child psychopathology have failed to provide adequate tools to explain the functioning of the EIA child. The concept of the behavioral ego focuses upon aspects of early child development prior to the differentiation of the complex intra-psychic ego structures which are necessary for the development of such a disorder as childhood schizophrenia (Ward, 1970a). Thus, childhood schizophrenia must be viewed as a sophisticated level of psychopathology which far exceeds the capacity of the EIA child. Early infantile autism is a deviant type of ego development which exists only as behavior, while childhood schizophrenia exists by virtue of disordered intra-psychic processes. The diagnosis of EIA has been labelled as a "pre-ego psychopathology" in a recent article (Berenbaum, Mandel, Marcus & Roth, 1971), and the concept of the "behavioral ego" is an attempt to articulate this early level of child development.

Robert's prognosis for function in the outside world is still quite guarded. However, it does seem likely that he will eventually be able to function in some type of day program for handicapped and/or retarded children in the community. Robert's response to structural therapy strongly suggests that he and many children like him can be contacted therapeutically, and channeled into appropriate educational programs.

As far as the etiology of EIA is concerned, it is clear that a deficit of novel and patterned stimuli is implicated. However, the cause of such a deficit and the observed slow developmental rate in a classically autistic child such as Robert is not at all clear and demands further theoretical conceptualization, as well as careful research on the development of object relations and cognition in the child below one year of age.

References

Berenbaum, Harris L.; Mandel, Harvey P.; Marcus, Sander S.; & Roth, R. M. Early infantile autism: A pre-ego psychopathology. *Psychotherapy: Theory, Research and Practice*, 1971, 8, (2): 114–120.

Freud, S. *The ego and the id*. London: Hogarth Press, 1927.

Handford, H. A. & Ward, A. J. Structural therapy: A developmental approach to the treatment of early infantile autism. *Schizophrenia*, 1969, 1 (4) : 243–248.

Kanner, L. Autistic disturbances of affective contact. *Nervous Child*, 1943, 2: 217–240.

————— & Lesser, L. Early infantile autism. *Pediatric Clinics of North America*, 1958, 5 (3) : 711–730.

Leith, V. M. Language stimulation and development. Paper presented at Child-Adolescent Workshop at Eastern Pennsylvania Psychiatric Institute in Philadelphia, Pa. on November 9, 1970.

Melzack, R. & Scott, T. H. The effects of early experience on the response to pain. *Journal of Comparative Physiological Psychology*, 1957, 50: 155–161.

Piaget, J. *The origins of intelligence in children*. New York: International Universities Press, 1956.

Ward, A. J. The application of structural therapy to the residential treatment of early infantile autism. Paper presented at convention of American Association of Psychiatric Clinics for Children in New York City, in November 1968.

—————. Early infantile autism: An etiological hypothesis. Paper presented at convention of the American Association of Psychiatric Clinics for Children in Boston, Mass., in November, 1969.

—————. Early infantile autism: diagnosis, treatment and etiology. *Psychological Bulletin*, 1970, 73 (5) : 350–362. (a)

—————. An application of structural therapy to the residential treatment of early infantile autism. *Schizophrenia*, 1970, 2 (2,3) : 92–102. (b)

Ward, A. J. & Handford, H. A. Early infantile autism: syndrome, symptom or wastebasket? Paper presented at meeting of the Midwest Psychological Association, Chicago, May 2, 1968.

Winnicott, D. W. Transitional objects and transitional phenomena. *International Journal of Psychoanalysis*, 1953, 34: 89–97.

Zaslow, R. W. A psychogenic theory of the etiology of infantile autism and implications for treatment. Paper presented at California State Psychological Association in San Diego, Calif., in January 1967.

RESULTS OF TREATMENT

13

Early Childhood Autism and Structural Therapy: Outcome After Three Years

This paper is a preliminary report on the outcome of the application of structural therapy (Des Lauriers & Carlson, 1969; Handford & Ward, 1969; Ward, 1970a) to the residential treatment of early childhood autism (ECA). The term ECA is used to include both the classically defined rare cases of early infantile autism (EIA), as well as the much more common cases of organic autism (Ward, 1970b) and the variously handicapped and/or disturbed children who are mistakenly labeled as suffering from EIA (Ward & Handford, 1968; Ward, 1971).

Historical Background

The treatment of early infantile autism (EIA) is a topic which has usually aroused great feelings of futility (Kanner & Eisenberg, 1956; Polan & Spencer, 1959; Rimland, 1964). Reports of extended intensive therapeutic efforts, on more than an occasional individual case basis, are extremely rare in the literature. These efforts have usually involved the use of varied types of behavior modification programs, which focused upon the removal of such behavior as self-mutilation, mutism, or stereotypic behavior (Ferster & DeMyer, 1961; Gewirtz, 1961, Lovaas, 1966a, 1966b).

169

Bettelheim (1967) has provided the only detailed outcome study of extended, intensive residential treatment with "autistic" children, which has attempted to change more than isolated aspects of their behavior. Bettelheim suggested that feelings of therapeutic pessimism were unwarranted, and ascribed them to "the fact that all too few efforts at treatment were intensive enough, and . . . were sustained for the requisite number of years" (p. 405). No details are provided as to Bettelheim's diagnostic criteria.

Examination of outcome data reported by both Bettelheim and by Eisenberg (1956) revealed strongly contrasting findings. Eisenberg's follow-up evaluation was divided into the three categories of "poor," "fair," or "good" outcome. "Poor" was defined as referring to a patient who "had not emerged from autism to any extent, and whose present functioning was markedly maladaptive, characterized by apparent feeble-mindedness and/or grossly disturbed behavior, whether maintained at home or in an institution." "Fair" referred to a patient who was "able to attend regular classes in public or private school at a level commensurate with age and who has some meaningful contacts with other people, but who exhibits schizoid peculiarities of personality, sufficient to single him out as a deviant and to cause interference with function." "Good" referred to a patient who was "functioning well at an academic, social and community level and who is accepted by his peers, though he might remain a somewhat odd person."

The most intensive treatment received by any of the sixty-three children described in Eisenberg's 1956 follow-up was provided in three cases where the children were seen on an out-patient basis "once or twice weekly for not exceeding two years." The "good" or "fair" outcome for two of these three cases (66%) must be contrasted to the "good" or "fair" outcome obtained for a total of only seventeen out of the original follow-up group of sixty-three patients (27%). The majority of the group (thirty-six) were placed in private institutions, training schools, or state hospitals, and received little or no consistent or extended treatment. The final evaluation indicated that three patients had attained a "good" adjustment, fourteen had made a "fair" adjustment, and forty-six had made a "poor" adjustment. Thus, Eisenberg's outcome figures seem to demonstrate that severely disturbed young children show little improvement if they are not treated over the years.

Bettelheim (1967) has reported outcome figures on a group of forty "autistic" children and has used the same categories devised by Eisenberg

(1956). A "good" outcome is reported for seventeen children (42%), a "fair" outcome for fifteen children (38%), and a "poor" outcome for only eight patients (20%). These outcome figures are in marked contrast to those reported by Eisenberg of 5% for a "good" outcome, 22% for a "fair" outcome, and 73% for a "poor" outcome. The lack of diagnostic criteria makes a comparison of these two studies more difficult, but the figures do seem to support Bettelheim's contention of a more favorable therapeutic prognosis for the autistic-like child if extended and intensive treatment is made available.

DESCRIPTION OF PROJECT

A new therapeutic approach labelled Structural Therapy (Handford & Ward, 1969, 1972; Ward, 1970), and based upon many of the conceptualizations of Des Lauriers (1962, 1967) and Des Lauriers & Carlson (1969), has been used in the development of a treatment program for EIA children on a unit of a state hospital for emotionally disturbed children. This program has been described in detail in earlier presentations (Ward, 1971; Handford & Ward, 1972).

Diagnosis

Evaluation of the twenty-one original children in this program revealed only four children who met the research definition of EIA which was:

1. Lack of the development of object relations from birth
2. Lack of the use of speech for communication
3. Maintenance of sameness via stereotypic behavior, with a rage or withdrawal reaction upon interruption
4. No major neurological dysfunction.

The other children fell into the diagnostic categories of childhood schizophrenia (five), primary retardation (seven), secondary retardation (two), developmental retardation associated with diffuse brain damage (two). However, all of these children were found to display the behavioral characteristic of a "lack of affective response," while children from all five of the above diagnostic categories were found to display the characteristics of "lack of object relationships," "lack of the use of speech for communication," and of having come from an "unstimulating mother/infant relationship." These were characteristics which previous researchers had suggested were diagnostic of EIA. The four EIA cases were distinguished from the other disturbed children by the combination of: 1) lack of neurological dysfunction and (2) maintenance of sameness via stereotypic behavior. Thus, this early evaluation indicated both the rarity of true EIA children, as well as the relative plenitude of those variously disturbed and/or handicapped children who were mistakenly labelled as EIA cases (Ward & Handford, 1968; Ward, 1970b, 1971). This was the basis of the decision to label the children in the project as cases of ECA, rather than the use of the much more restrictive and exclusive diagnosis of EIA.

Treatment

The total research unit was organized according to the precepts of Structural Therapy (Handford & Ward, 1969; 1972). The milieu emphasized spontaneous physical and verbal stimulation applied to the children in a playful and game-like fashion. The goal of this approach was to increase the amount of varied and novel stimulation received by these children, and to use this increased stimulation to make them more aware of their external environment and to help them to progress from their positions of early developmental fixation. The physical stimulation was used to develop body image and bodily awareness, and to help provide the body ego that appears to be necessary for the development of higher ego functions. The details of this therapeutic approach have been provided in earlier presentations (Leith, 1969; Ward & Leith, 1969; Ward, 1970a, 1970c). Twelve of the twenty-one children were seen in individual therapy on a twice weekly basis, although often the children were seen on an informal basis five times a week. Selected children were seen for sessions in speech therapy on a twice weekly basis for periods ranging from three months to two years.

Family Counseling. Families were contacted on a weekly basis by the social workers. Group counseling was provided on a bi-weekly basis for all of the parents, and the majority of them had a weekly day visit, overnight visit, or weekend visit with their child. The parents were given an understanding of the developmental level of functioning of their child and were helped to find ways of continuing the therapeutic approach being used in the project. The emphasis was always upon the circumscribed problem of the child's problems in behavior and relationships, rather than how the family might have contributed to the child's pathology. This work was most valuable in changing the focus of the parents from exotic psychopathology to concrete problems of early child development. It would not have been possible to return these children to their homes and community programs without the extensive and intensive casework provided by the social work staff. Details of this work are now being organized for presentation.

RESULTS

As this group of patients was deemed severely enough disturbed to warrant hospitalization in a state hospital, it is felt that their therapeutic progress should be compared most closely with the outcome figures reported by Eisenberg (1956). The basic goal of this Structural Therapy treatment program has not been "cure," but development. EIA and ECA are viewed as severe developmental disorders of the same order as are often observed with the rubella child (Freedman, Fox, & Brown, 1970); the blind child (Burlingham, 1967); or the deaf child. The basic etiology is felt to be rooted in a deficit of novel and varied stimulation for manifold reasons. This treatment program has attempted to help these children to progress to the point where they achieve the goals of:

1. Relationships with people
2. Self-care such as toileting, feeding, and dressing
3. Communication of simple needs in a consistent manner
4. The capacity to follow simple directions.

The achievement of these goals reveals a child who is still functioning below age-appropriate level in regards to cognitive and affective behavior. The child is now at a point in development where more conventional play therapy, speech therapy, and/or special education can be used. Thus, these children should be viewed as being in the midst of their therapeutic course at the time of their discharge, which occurs because the institution is no longer able to provide the therapeutic level of stimulation. Therefore, those children who were discharged to home in the community seemed appropriate for placement in Eisenberg's category of "fair" outcome (1956). Each child was used as his own control in this research, but some comparisons will also be drawn with two other treatment units, in the same setting, which have attempted to work with "autistic" children.

The application of three years of Structural Therapy to the original group of twenty-one cases of ECA resulted in the discharge to home in the community of twelve of the original twenty-one children (57%). These children were placed in normal nursery schools, special classes for the

TABLE 1. Subject Data on Unit A (Experimental) at Beginning of Research.

Sex	Number	Age Range	Mean Age	Mean Length of Prior Hospitalization	Range
M	15	5-8 to 14	8.9 years	1.08 years	0 - 3.25 years
F	6	7-10 to 12-5	10.2 years	1.92 years	0 - 3 years

TABLE 2. Subject Data on Units B and C (Control) at Beginning of Research.

Unit	Sex	Number	Age Range	Mean Age	Mean Length of Prior Hospitalization	Range
B	M	21	4-11 to 11-10	7.2	6.5 months	0-2.92 years
C	F	25	5 to 17-14	8.9	5.9 months	0-3.16 years

TABLE 3. Number of Subjects Discharged Sept. 1966 - Sept. 1969 and Length of Stay in Units A, B, and C.

Unit	Discharge M	Discharge F	Mean Length of Hospitalization M	F	Percentage	Range
A	7	5	26.1 months	25 months	57%	9 months - 3 years
B	2		17 months		9	1 month - 17 months
C		5*		18.8 months	20	7 months - 3 years

*Two additional subjects discharged and readmitted during 1966-69.

retarded or the emotionally disturbed in public schools and private schools, and sheltered workshops run by the local association for retarded children. The families were referred to the appropriate agencies for continued counseling.

The experimental unit was labelled as Unit A, and had a population of boys and girls with a mean age of 8.9 years and 10.2 years respectively, whose mean length of prior hospitalization was 1.08 years and 1.92 years. Inspection of comparable data on the comparison Units B and C reveals little difference as to mean age, but a great difference as to length of prior hospitalization (see tables 1 and 2 here). These data suggest that the children on Unit A were more severely disturbed than those on Units B and C. The boys on Unit B had a mean age of 7.2 years and a mean length of prior hospitalization of 6.5 months, while the girls on Unit C had a mean age of 8.9 years and a mean length of prior hospitalization of 5.9 months (see table 2).

In the period September, 1966 to September, 1969 Unit A discharged twelve cases of ECA to home in the community, while Unit B discharged two boys and Unit C discharged five girls (see table 3). A comparison of the outcome figures of Eisenberg (1956) and Bettelheim (1967) vis-a-vis Units A, B, and C reveals that Unit A exceeded both Eisenberg and Bettelheim in regards to the number of children who achieved a "fair" outcome (see table 4). Unit B's outcome rate of 25% approximated the outcome rate reported by Eisenberg (22%), while Unit C's outcome figure of 9% fell markedly below that.

TABLE 4.   Comparative Outcome Figures (in Percentages).

	Good	Fair	Poor
Eisenberg	5%	22%	73%
Bettelheim	42	38	20
Unit A	—	57	43
Unit B	—	9	91
Unit C	—	25	75

DISCUSSION

The outcome figures of this preliminary report appear to support the hypothesis that Structural Therapy is capable of producing significant therapeutic change in children classified as ECA. However, it must be emphasized that this subject pool was comprised of a heterogeneous collection of severely disturbed young children, of whom only four met the research definition of EIA. It is not clear whether the children described by Eisenberg (1956) and Bettelheim (1967) would have met this research definition. None of the children on Units B or C satisfied the research definition of EIA, although all could be placed in the category of ECA on the basis of their overt clinical behavior.

The findings of this study have raised severe question as to the validity of the syndrome of EIA as a clinical entity. The small number of children who met the research definition of EIA in a residential setting for emotionally disturbed children, whose population regularly exceeds two hundred patients and serves half the population of Pennsylvania, raises this question. Either the definition is incorrect or else cases of EIA don't occur in eastern Pennsylvania, or else they just don't come to the only available residential setting for treatment.

However, regardless of the validity of the diagnosis of EIA, the results of this study do seem to support the hypothesis that a high stimulation, physically intrusive, game-like, novelty filled and developmentally oriented treatment approach is a viable treatment approach for those severely disturbed children who are often labelled as cases of EIA or ECA. These children are more accurately viewed as being part of a wide spectrum of handicapped children who have suffered resultant developmental delays and deviations. The EIA and ECA child is much more responsive to an insistent, structured, developmentally oriented treatment approach that deals with the child at his level of functioning rather than at the family's and therapist's respective levels of fantasy.

REFERENCES

BETTELHEIM, B. *The empty fortress.* New York: Free Press, 1967.

BURLINGHAM, D. Developmental considerations in the occupations of the blind. In *The psychoanalytic study of the child,* 1967, 22: 187–198.

DES LAURIERS, A. M. *The experience of reality in childhood schizophrenia.* New York: International Universities Press, 1962.

————. The schizophrenic child. *Archives of General Psychiatry,* 1967, 16: 194–201.

———— & CARLSON, F. *Your child is asleep: early infantile autism.* Homewood, Ill.: Dorsey Press, 1969.

EISENBERG, L. The autistic child in adolescence. *American Journal of Psychiatry,* 1956, 112: 607–612.

FERSTER, C. B. & DEMYER, M. K. The development of performances in autistic children in an automatically controlled environment. *Journal of Chronic Diseases,* 1961, 13: 312–345.

FREEDMAN, D. A., FOX-KOLENDA, B. J. & BROWN, I. L. A multihandicapped rubella baby: the first 18 months. *Journal of the American Academy of Child Psychiatry*, 1970, 9: 298–317.

FREUD, S. *The ego and the id.* London: Hogarth Press, 1927.

GEWIRTZ, J. L. A learning analysis of the effects of normal stimulation, privation and deprivation on the acquisition of social motivation and attachment. In B. M. Foss (ed.), *Determinants of infant behavior.* New York: Wiley, 1961.

HANDFORD, H. A. & WARD, A. J. Structural Therapy: A developmental approach to the treatment of Early Infantile Autism. *Schizophrenia*, 1969, 1 (4): 243–248.

————. "A.C.T.T.R.S., a state hospital research unit for autistic children: Five years' experience." Presented Eastern Psychiatric Research Association, Inc. in Third Annual Multi-state Interhospital Conference in New York, on April 5, 1972.

KANNER, L. & EISENBERG, L. Early infantile autism: childhood schizophrenia symposium. *American Journal of Orthopsychiatry*, 1956, 26: 556–564.

LEITH, V. M. "The role of the speech therapist with autistic children." Paper presented at Speech Symposium on Emotionally Disturbed Children with Language Disorders at Eastern State School & Hospital in Trevose, Pa., on Oct. 30, 1969.

LOVAAS, O. I. A program for the establishment of speech in psychotic children. In J. K. Wing (Ed.), *Early childhood autism.* London: Pergamon Press. 1966. (a)

————; BERBRICH, J. P.; PERLOFF, B. F.; & SCHAEFFER, B. Acquisition of imitative speech by schizophrenic children. *Science*, 1966, 151: 705–707. (b)

POLAN, C. C. & SPENCER, B. L. Check list of symptoms of autism in early life. *West Virginia Medical Journal*, 1959, 55: 198–204.

RIMLAND, B. *Infantile autism.* New York: Appleton, 1964.

WARD, A. J. The application of structural therapy to the residential treatment of early infantile autism. *Schizophrenia*, 1970, 2 (2,3): 92–102. (a)

————. "These are not autistic children." Paper presented at the International Association of Social Psychiatry in Zagreb, Yugoslavia, November 1970. (b)

————. The effect of Structural Therapy in the treatment of a self-mutilating, autistic child: A case report. Paper presented at the American Association of Psychiatric Services for Children in Philadelphia on November 6, 1970. (c)

————. A residential treatment program for autistic children. Paper presented at the International Association of Applied Psychology in Liege, Belgium, on July 29, 1971. (a)

————. The multiple pathways to autistic behavior. Paper presented at the meeting of the American Psychological Association in Washington, D.C., on September 4, 1971. (b)

WARD, A. J. & HANDFORD, H. A. Early infantile autism: Syndrome, symptom or wastebasket? Paper presented at Midwestern Psychological Association in Chicago, Illinois, on May 2, 1968.

WARD, A. J. & LEITH, V. M. Cathy: a case report of the joint treatment of an "autistic" child by clinical psychology and speech therapy. Paper presented at American Speech and Hearing Association in Chicago, Illinois on November 12, 1969.

14

Structural Therapy and Childhood Autism: A Follow-up on Thirteen Discharged Patients

This paper is a report on a follow-up of thirteen children discharged from the Autistic Children's Treatment, Training, and Research Service (ACTTRS). These children were diagnosed as cases of Childhood Autism, not Early Infantile Autism (EIA), as it was felt that only one of them met research criteria for such a diagnosis (Handford & Ward, 1969; Ward, 1970b; Ward, 1970c).

SUBJECTS

Twelve of these children were discharged to their families and eleven entered educational programs in the community in the period between September, 1966 and September, 1969. The thirteenth child was discharged to a residential program for the retarded in April, 1970. All of these children had been involved in both individual and milieu programs of structural therapy (Handford & Ward, 1969; Ward, 1970a) from nine months to three years (see table 1). Structural therapy is an aggressive, intrusive, high stimulation input type of treatment which is developmentally oriented and has its theoretical base in both neo-analytic conceptualization (Des Lauriers, 1962; Des Lauriers & Carlson, 1969; Ward, 1970, 1970a), and data derived from research on early child development (Roffwarg et al., 1964; Spitz, 1965; Stechler & Latz, 1966). This treatment approach takes the point of view that childhood autism is more

TABLE 1. Discharged Cases of Childhood Autism (Follow-Up, May, 1973)

Number	Subject	Date of Birth	Time in Treatment	Date of Admission ACTTRS	Date of Discharge	Type of Education Program	Continuance in Program	Pro-gressing at Home
1	C	11/59	12 mos.	6/66	6/67	Private day school for emotionally disturbed.	yes	yes
2	E	5/24/55	27	9/66	1/69	Sheltered workshop. Association for retarded children. Accepted for special class in public school 9/70.	Transferred to special class in public schools.	yes
3	F	11/26/58	28	11/66	3/69	Special class in public school system.	yes	yes
4	G	1/16/59	33	12/66	9/69	Day program. Association for retarded children.	Transferred to special class in 71.	yes
5	H	4/8/58	24	10/66	10/68	Special class in public school.	yes	yes
6	S	4/23/54	14	9/66	2/68	Day program. Association for retarded children.	yes	yes
7	L	6/23/57	27	9/66	12/68	None	no	no

Table 1. (continued)

Number	Subject	Date of Birth	Time in Treatment	Date of Admission ACTTRS	Date of Discharge	Type of Education Program	Continuance in Program	Progressing at Home
8	Z	12/8/55	36	9/66	9/69	Special class in public school.	yes	yes
9	M	9/6/55	27	9/66	12/68	Special class in public school.		
10	N	4/15/56	27	9/66	12/68	Day program for exceptional children.	yes	no
11	P	9/6/52	43	9/66	4/70	Residential program for retarded children.	yes	no
12	LS	2/2/56	28	9/66	1/69	Special class in parochial school. Residential program for retarded 3/70.	Transferred to residential program for retarded in 3/70.	no
13	SS	1/6/55	36	9/66	9/69	Day program. Association for retarded children	Transferred to special class in 5/73.	yes

of a developmental disorder than a type of mental illness (Ward, 1969; Ward, 1970c; Ward, 1971) and that its etiology is related much more to a stimulation deficit and/or inconsistency (Ornitz & Ritvo, 1968; Ward, 1970a; Ward, 1971) than to the mental health or illness of the family. Thus, although all of these children displayed problems of affective disturbance and speech difficulty, only one child met the research criteria established for EIA; which were: (1) lack of relationship with people from early life; (2) lack of the use of speech for communication; (3) maintenance of sameness via stereotypic behavior; and (4) lack of any major neurologic dysfunction.

FOLLOW-UP CASES

1. C is a fourteen-year-old Black boy who was originally hospitalized at ACTTRS on June 2, 1966, and was discharged on June 30, 1967, to home and a private day school for the emotionally disturbed child. Progress was good both at home and at school until two important events occurred in 1971. First, C's mother, with whom he had a quasi-symbiotic tie, separated from the family and left the city. Second, C experienced an acute febrile episode that was followed by a shaking of the extremities.

Following the above two events, C regressed rapidly at school, lost much of his verbal ability, and exhibited bizarre behavior, such as echolalia and avoidance of people. This regression resulted in C's hospitalization in September, 1971. During this hospitalization, C was involved in individual therapy and in the "talking typewriter" program. He was discharged to home and a specialized school setting again in August, 1973, after regaining his lost skills and capacities.

2. E is an eighteen-year-old Black boy who was originally admitted to ESSH on June 21, 1963, and was taken into ACTTRS in September, 1966. This boy was uncontrollable at home, hyperactive, constantly hit his siblings, cried a great deal, and would soil himself unless taken to the toilet. E had no recognizable speech nor was he able to dress or bathe himself without assistance. He also showed a complete lack of a sense of danger, inappropriate affect, and affective lability. When examined, E hit the examiner and then insisted on sitting on his lap, assumed bizarre postures, and failed to follow directions.

E was discharged to home on January 8, 1970, with a diagnosis of moderate retardation, severe to moderate, psychosis in remission, with possible brain damage. He entered a sheltered workshop run by the local society for retarded children during the same month, and was transferred to a special class in the public school system in September, 1970. During this time, E's parents reported that they felt he had made much progress and was now getting along well with his siblings at home.

The following year found E unable to continue attending special class due to the loss of his records. E was out of school for a year, and failed to make any progress during this time. He became isolated and withdrawn but continued to use his speech to ask for things and did not present any problems at home.

A follow-up in June, 1972, found that E had been returned to special class in the public school, and was reported to have resumed his educational progress. E was reported to be working on number concepts, and had developed the ability to write the numbers 1 to 12. He continued to be a loner at home, and was scheduled to participate in a work training program.

The last follow-up in May, 1973, found E continuing to show slow progress in a retarded educable class in the public school, and showing gradual improvement in socialization and communication at home.

3. F is a fifteen-year-old Caucasian girl who was admitted to ACTTRS in November, 1966, with minimal speech and "autistic, withdrawn, negativistic patterns of behavior." She exhibited "repetitive, compulsive patterns of behavior, poor peer relationships, and low frustration tolerance." Examination of the history of F revealed many diseases and infections were suffered by F's mother during her pregnancy. This was the apparent etiology of multiple congenital anomalies suffered by this child.

F was discharged to home on March 28, 1969, with a diagnosis of mental deficiency, moderate. She was enrolled in a special class in the public school and was happily reported by her parents to be doing very well in 1970 and 1971. F was reported to be verbalizing a great deal at home, but not so much at school. No unusual behavior problems were reported at home.

The 1972 follow-up found F to be continuing to attend special class in the public school. She continued to be erratic in her use of speech at school, and was learning to be more obedient, learning to write, playing the organ. Overall, it was felt that F had made continued progress in school, and had "calmed down a lot." F was reported to be talking a great deal at home, understanding directions better, sleeping better and longer, and seeming more relaxed. F's mother was considering obtaining outside musical training for her.

The 1973 follow-up found F continuing in special class in the public school. She was felt to be functioning on a first or second grade level, and reported to still be erratic in her use of her speech at school. Also, F is now showing more peer interaction, and has learned to play ball and square dance. Current plans are for F to learn to function in a sheltered workshop.

4. G is a fourteen-year-old Black boy who was admitted to ACTTRS in December, 1966, with problems of mutism, nervousness, management difficulty, many fears, seizures, and no contact with people. He followed only simple directions, jumped all day, ground his teeth, and made high-pitched noises. The admitting psychiatric diagnosis described G as severely mentally retarded with a failure of comprehension and a possibility of expressive aphasia. G was evaluated to be functioning at a 2- to 2½-year age level at the age of 6. He did seek out relationships with people, and was loving and affectionate. When G attempted to communicate he made certain high pitched sounds.

G was discharged in September, 1969, to home and a program of the local association for retarded children with a diagnosis of organic brain syndrome; mental deficiency, severe; aphasia, expressive type.

The 1970 follow-up found G continuing in his program, while displaying increasing curiosity and responsiveness both in school and at home. In 1971, G was still attending the same program, but was being prepared for a trial period in a special class in the public school. G had continued to show improved responsiveness, and was showing more peer interaction and participation in activities. The 1972 follow-up disclosed that G had succeeded in maintaining himself in the special class in the public school. He continued to be nonverbal, but communicated by and understood gestures. G had been coloring in school, but the teacher was unsure as to his ability to differentiate among colors. The 1973 follow-up found G maintaining himself in the same program, while making slow progress. He showed improved capacity to follow directions, and is able to follow double sequential directions. Although G has shown continued, if gradual progress, the school is uncertain as to G's eventual ability to function in a sheltered workshop due to the extreme weakness of his hands. It is felt that this exceedingly gentle boy will always need some kind of care.

5. H is a fifteen-year-old Black boy who was admitted to ACTTRS on October 20, 1966. On admission, H was a somewhat lonely child who did not take part in group activities, and was hyperactive and echolalic. He did a great deal of spinning and toe-walking, and did not relate to his environment.

H was discharged in October, 1968, to home, to a day program for the emotionally disturbed child run by ESSH. The discharge diagnosis was schizophrenic reaction, childhood type. The 1970 follow-up found H doing very well in this program and using more speech. The 1971 follow-up found him continuing in and doing very well in the same school program. He was now able to go and come from school by himself on public transportation, and participated well in class. Also H displayed more involvement with his family, occupied himself with activities in the home after school, and played structured games such as cards with the family. In 1972, H was reported to have made much progress in the same school program, and to be doing quite well. He had become more independent, did some things spontaneously, lived "less of a set pattern," and initiated and followed through on such things as saying he was going to the store and doing so. Also, H now had his own chores at home, which he performed. Due to the closing of the current program, the family was exploring placement in either the public school or a private day school for the emotionally disturbed child. The 1973 follow-up disclosed that H had been enrolled in a special class in the public school system and was doing very well. H continues to do very well at home, answers the telephone, and is now very close to his brothers. The family hopes that he will eventually be able to attend a vocational school.

6. S is a fifteen-year-old Caucasian girl who was first seen on an out-patient basis, on October 2, 1963. This girl was admitted to ACTTRS in September, 1966. The admitting diagnosis was childhood schizophrenia, in which organic factors and drug therapy (phenobarbital) seem to have been etiological factors. S's presenting problems consisted of unintelligible speech, lack of toys, negativism, and hyperactivity. Social quotients of thirty-eight and twenty-one were obtained at ages six and eight respectively.

S was discharged on February 1, 1968, to home, with a diagnosis of chronic brain syndrome, etiology unknown, with psychosis and severe mental deficiency. She remained at home until her enrollment February, 1970, in a program of the local association for retarded children. It was reported that S participated well, and seemed happier and more out-going now that she had something to do each day. The 1971 follow-up found S continuing in the same program, participating and cooperating more. S had become very good at home, but got upset when observing other children being loudly disciplined. The 1972 follow-up found S con-tinuing in the same program and making slow progress. The program consisted mainly of physical exercises and handicrafts. S was described as doing "pretty well," but not as "competitive" as the other children. S continued to improve in her family interactions and started to use some simple words at home, such as "mommy." Finally, the 1973 follow-up disclosed S to be doing "very well" in the same program, as well as at home. She had shown quite a bit of progress in the last six months, but there are no plans to do other than keep her at home. Although S is eligible for a public school education, her family is unwilling to remove her from her current programs to enroll her in the public schools.

7. L is a sixteen-year-old Black girl who was admitted to ESSH on June 16, 1964, with a diagnosis of schizophrenic reaction, childhood type. Her behavior was similar to that of an infant in that she was not toilet-trained, did not speak or feed herself, did not understand verbal directions, and displayed only minimal relationship to people. She had a very narrow skull. Also, she was hyperactive, destructive, hit other children, would not chew solid food, slept irregularly, walked the house all night, and had severe tantrums and crying spells. Furthermore, L assumed bizarre postures, smiled inappropriately, and seemed to respond to internal stimuli. She was admitted to ACTTRS in September, 1966.

L was discharged on December 6, 1968, to home, with a diagnosis of chronic brain syndrome of unknown etiology. The 1970 follow-up disclosed that L's family had been unable to enroll her in any educational program, and had been told that she was not trainable. She was described as being very nervous at home, and as "picking on the younger children." The 1971 report disclosed that L had recently been placed in long-term hospitalization for the retarded. Her mother had had another baby and L became very jealous. She threw the baby out of the crib and broke its leg. Prior to this unfortunate incident, L had been doing well at home, although she had still not been enrolled in any educational program. She was expected to be hospitalized "for awhile."

The 1972 report found L still hospitalized. She was involved in speech therapy, music therapy, and motor therapy. L can say words but must be encouraged, she responds to music and likes to dance, and goes to dances at night with a group from her ward. She keeps to herself, is toilet-trained, can partially dress herself, and eats well with a fork. Her parents visited her weekly. The 1973 follow-up found L still hospitalized. She continued in speech therapy, and could now say "hi" and "goodbye" appropriately. She participated in occupational therapy, continued to enjoy music, and had learned to comprehend the concepts of "up" and "down." L now displayed no interaction with other patients at the hospital, or with her siblings during home visits.

8. Z is an eighteen-year-old Caucasian girl who was admitted to ESSH on August 7, 1963, with a diagnosis of schizophrenic reaction, child-

hood type, with the presenting problems of extreme hyperactivity and destructiveness, slow speech development, rumination, and lack of relationship. She was not toilet-trained, would not feed herself, and was often "defiant to authority" and distractible. Z was admitted to ACTTRS in September, 1966.

Z was discharged to home and a special class in the public school in September, 1969, with a discharge diagnosis of mental retardation, moderate. The initial follow-up (1970) found Z doing "very well" in school, and her parents were very pleased with her behavior at home. She had started to use her speech more, and knew the names of all the streets on the way to school. The 1971 follow-up found Z continuing and progressing in the same school program. She was described as "doing well, improving, and using more speech." Her family also felt that she was doing well at home. Z continued in the same educational program in 1972; and was reported to be doing number work, developing more use of speech, and working at the blackboard. She continued to do well at home. The 1973 report found Z continuing in the same educational program, and elicited the following evaluation:

"Z has made positive progress in program. She was autistic upon entrance, and is now at the primal learning stage. She has a pleasant personality and is very likable. Z is capable of simple arithmetic; shops in stores and handles money with the teacher. She works well on a 1 to 1 personal basis; and makes her own decisions. If scolded in class, she sometimes reacts by hitting another child; however, she relates well to class; goes on all class trips. Z can read; she speaks quickly." Z continued to do well in her relationships at home, and it is felt that she may eventually be able to care for herself.

9. M is an eighteen-year-old Caucasian boy who was admitted to the ACTTRS on September 12, 1966, with a diagnosis of schizophrenic reaction of childhood, autistic type. He had functioned on a retarded level since infancy and did not walk until sixteen months of age. The presenting problems included mutism, jargon, rocking, thumbsucking, hyperactivity, and bizarre mannerisms and posturing. M tapped at everything with the backs of his fingers, seemed unaware of people, but would follow simple directions which were given firmly and clearly.

M was discharged to home on December 6, 1968, with a discharge diagnosis of mental deficiency, severe. The initial follow-up (1970) noted that M had recently been enrolled in a special class in the public school system. In 1971, M was reported to be continuing in the same educational program. He had made a little progress, and had also become a little more aggressive. M was reported to pinch or scratch his mother when frustrated, wanted to be left alone a lot, and rocked a great deal.

The 1972 follow-up found M continuing in the educational program and showing some limited progress. M was relating more in class, although he continued to be rather withdrawn at home. The 1973 report disclosed that M had calmed down a great deal and was now making sounds. He was reported to understand directions, but would bite his hand when frustrated (approximately once every two weeks). M has started to interact some with the other children in his class, fits into the situation quite well, and seems satisfied. It is hoped that M will be able to start work in a sheltered workshop in the next school year.

10. N is a seventeen-year-old Caucasian girl who was admitted to ESSH on June 9, 1966, and to ACTTRS in September, 1966. Her development had been considered normal until the age of thirteen months, at which time she reportedly lapsed into an "autistic state." Such symptoms as mutism, head banging, and hypersensitivity to noise necessitated an evaluation at age three. She had been involved in psychotherapy on an outpatient basis for approximately seven years, when her increased size and acting-out behavior necessitated hospitalization. The admitting diagnosis was schizophrenic reaction, childhood type.

N was discharged to home on December 6, 1968, with a discharge diagnosis of mental deficiency, severe—etiology unknown. The 1970 evaluation indicated that N had been enrolled in a private day program for the exceptional child since March, 1969, which included a summer camp program. N was reported to be verbalizing much more than previously, and to be relating much better. Her family felt that her behavior had been "very, very good." The 1971 follow-up found N continuing in the same program, verbalizing more, and completely toilet-trained. Her relationship with her family had continued to improve. The same type of slow, steady progress was noted in the 1972 report with some particular improvement noted in the areas of verbalization and relationship.

The 1973 follow-up disclosed that N had been transferred to a half-day sheltered workshop program, and was doing well and learning self-care. Progress continued to be slow and N was still essentially nonverbal. N is now showing good interaction with both her family and her teachers. The family envisions a group living situation for N in the distant future.

11. P is a twenty-one-year-old Caucasian male who was admitted to ESSH on July 26, 1963, with a diagnosis of chronic schizophrenia of childhood. P was admitted after an extended period of psychotherapy

and day care at another agency, which had proven relatively unsatisfactory. He was admitted to the ACTTRS in September, 1966. P was described as "extremely disturbed, hyperactive, and absorbed by his fantasies, although aware of objects around him." P was verbal, but usually spoke in phrases that were unintelligible and noncommunicative. He also showed erratic and limited awareness and relationship to peers and adults, as well as a lack of a sense of danger. This boy was also subject to uncontrollable rage attacks which included frequent episodes of screaming and shouting, as well as the throwing of food, and the smearing of food and saliva on the walls.

P was discharged on April 7, 1970, to a residential program for the retarded, with a discharge diagnosis of organic brain syndrome of unknown etiology. The initial follow-up (May 1970) closely followed P's discharge, and only disclosed that he seemed to be making a fair adjustment in his new setting. His parents reported that the agency staff seemed to be somewhat frustrated in their training efforts and P's depending needs in regards to self-care. The 1971 follow-up revealed that P had been transferred to a long-term facility for the retarded in another state in December, 1970. He was reported to have made a "tremendous adjustment" to his new setting, to be involved in an activities program, and to be helping with the gardening. P's behavior was described as "very variable," and ranging from "good to very difficult." The parents described P's last home visit as "awful." The 1972 follow-up found P continuing his hospitalization with its attendant programs. In February, 1972, P was taken to an adult state institution for the mentally ill where he remained for a three-month evaluation period. A new staff person who had been on his ward during a weekend, who did not know P, thought that his behavior was psychotic and ordered this transfer. The regular staff had felt that P's behavior was quite manageable. P was described as being cheerful and happy, and his family did not feel that his stay at the adult mental institution had caused any regression; he was usually well-behaved on his home visits. Finally, the 1973 report indicated that P continued his hospitalization and participation in the same programs. He showed slow progress in his programs, but was now "very good" during his home visits. P's family expects that his hospitalization will be "for the rest of his life."

12. LS is a seventeen-year-old Caucasian boy who was admitted to ESSH on August 20, 1963, with a diagnosis of schizophrenia, autistic-symbiotic type. The presenting problems included mutism, lack of relatedness, uncontrolled outbursts of crying and irritability, distractibil-

ity, hyperkinesis, an occasional fleeting tic-like shaking of his head, and a desire to drink copious daily amounts of water (three gallons). The latter behavior suggested a diagnosis of diabetes insipidus. LS was admitted to ACTTRS in September, 1966.

LS was discharged to home and a special class in the parochial school system on January 10, 1969, with a discharge diagnosis of chronic brain syndrome, mental deficiency, and severe aphasia. The initial follow-up (May 1970) revealed that LS had attended the special class from January, 1969 to April, 1969, while living at home. Then LS was admitted to a general hospital with a kidney complication stemming from his diabetes insipidus. He then returned to his special class from September, 1969 to March, 1970, and was reported to be "profiting" from it and enjoying it. Then LS was again admitted to the general hospital, and from there was transferred to a residential state facility for the retarded on March 10, 1970. His family reported that his physical condition was the "primary reason" that LS was accepted at the residential facility. During this time LS was attending a basic skills educational program on a half-day basis. The 1972 follow-up reported LS still to be hospitalized and continuing in the same educational program. This program focused upon the development of basic self-help skills such as toileting, dressing, brushing of teeth, and so forth. LS was reported to have made no progress in this program, and was even thought to have shown some signs of regression.

The 1973 follow-up reported the development of severe behavioral problems by LS. He had become very hyperactive in school, and insisted on taking off his clothes both in the school as well as his living area. This behavior was accompanied by a great deal of screaming and LS lost his ability to comprehend or follow the simplest of directions. This behavior made it impossible for LS to continue to attend his school program for approximately six months. It was felt that this regression was related to LS's problem of diabetes insipidus, in combination with the physical changes of adolescence.

LS has shown some improvement within the last month. He is now reported to be relating "on a primitive level," to be keeping his clothes on all day, and to be attending school all day. This boy will now work with simple puzzles and blocks, and is displaying an attention span of five to ten minutes. He is also interacting on a nonverbal basis, although there are periods when he will simply sit and stare blankly at nothing. However, LS does relate better to the staff than to his peers, and will occasionally use three to four word phrases for communication. Thus,

LS experienced an erection, and approached a female staff person and asked, "What should I do with this?" This boy is taken on home visits on an irregular basis, and his family is greatly pleased at the recent improvement in his behavior and functioning. LS is still viewed as being profoundly retarded, and it is expected that he will continue to require life-long supervision in an institution or group home setting. However, LS is felt to be capable of learning more basic self-help skills.

13. SS is an eighteen-year-old Black boy who was admitted to ESSH on June 24, 1963, with a diagnosis of schizophrenia, childhood type, associated with functional mental retardation. This boy had normal development to the age of three months, when he developed repeated and prolonged convulsions. Although motor development was normal after the convulsions, speech and language failed to develop and SS's behavior became markedly immature. The cause of the convulsions was unknown at the time, but was later thought to be related to lead intoxication. At the time of admission, SS was mute and was unable to either dress or bathe himself. He also giggled and smiled inappropriately at times, as well as exhibiting manneristic movements of the hands. SS was admitted to ACTTRS in September, 1966.

This boy was discharged to home and a program of the local association for retarded children on September 20, 1969. The discharge diagnosis was nonpsychotic organic brain syndrome due to lead intoxication; mental retardation, severe; and aphasia. The 1970 follow-up found SS continuing in the same program. Although his mother seemed reluctant to report any progress, the school program did state that SS had made some improvement in both awareness and relationships. The 1971 report found SS continuing in the same program and making progress. He had recently been placed in a training program with people older than he, whereas he had previously been placed with children younger than himself. The teacher felt that SS was "making a lot of progress," and hoped to be able to do more with him in the new program. However, SS continued to be "pretty much of a loner" both at school and at home, and did not relate much to his siblings.

The 1972 follow-up found SS making progress in the same educational program, and being prepared for participation in an "in-house" workshop program. SS was reported to be "behaving well" at home, but still not relating very much to the other children. Finally, the 1973 follow-up revealed that SS had been transferred from his previous program to a special class in the public school in May, 1973. His current class is made up of seven to eight children of his own age, who are both verbal and nonverbal. The class focuses upon the development of coordination and self-help and self-care skills. The class goes shopping and for walks in the community, and the children are taught how to count and make change. SS is described as doing "very well" in this program, although he was initially upset at the change, manifesting this by disruptive behavior that included screaming and stomping his feet in class. His family had to inform the program that this was his usual response to change, and that it would abate; which it did after two to three weeks.

SS's family feels that one result of the program has been the development of more independent behavior. He will now do more things for himself instead of passively waiting to be served, and has developed an emphasis upon completing any behavior he is involved in before following directions to stop. Also, SS's gestural communication has improved to the point that he can communicate affect and mood, although he continues to be nonverbal. This boy's relationship with family and peers is of a minimal nature, although he will occasionally cheerfully greet his mother at the door. The closest relationship is with his young sister who picks him up at school, and allows him to help her in the kitchen and around the house with the chores. SS's family hopes to see him enter a sheltered workshop in the near future.

RESULTS

Thus, examination of this follow-up data reveals that ten of the thirteen original discharges from ACTTRS continue to be maintained at home and in community programs, as much as six years after the initial date of discharge (see table 1). Furthermore, all thirteen of these discharged children showed some positive response to special educational programs which were developed for the retarded and/or handicapped child.

Examination of these children reveals that the eight boys had a mean age of 10.1 years at the time of their acceptance into the ACTTRS program of structural therapy, while the five girls had a mean age of 10.1 years. The mean age of the total group at their time of admission to ACTTRS was also 10.1 years (see table 2).

The eight boys were in the ACTTRS structural therapy treatment program for a mean period of 29.1 months, while the five girls were in the treatment program for a mean period of 26.4 months. The average length of stay for the whole group was 28.1 months (see table 3).

Twelve of the thirteen discharged patients were discharged to their homes in the community, and eleven of them were in special education programs at the time of the initial follow-up in May, 1970 (see table 1). An additional two of these children had to be hospitalized in long-term custodial settings after displaying specific medical problems (LS) and acting out in an unacceptable manner (L). At the time of the last follow-up in May, 1973, the mean length of discharge for the six boys remaining in the community and special education programs including the time of discharge of the boy who was hospitalized for medical reasons (LS), and excluding the boy who was discharged to another institution (P), was 44.6 months. The mean length of discharge of the five girls who were discharged, including the time prior to hospitalization of the patient who was hospitalized for acting-out (L) was 47.8 months (see table 4). The mean length for the discharge for the total group was 45.9 months.

TABLE 2. Age of Patient at Beginning of Treatment

Number	Subject	Age Male	Age Female	Total
1	C	79 months		79
2	E	136		136
3	F		96 months	96
4	G	95		95
5	H	102		102
6	S		149	149
7	L		111	111
8	Z		129	129
9	M	131		131
10	N		125	125
11	P	168		168
12	LS	127		127
13	SS	131		131
Total Scores		969	610	1,579
Mean Scores	$\overline{X}_1 = 10.1$ yrs.		$\overline{X}_2 = 10.1$ yrs.	$\overline{X}_3 = 10.1$ yrs.

It should also be noted that nine out of thirteen of these children either possessed some type of speech (echolalia, etc.) at admission, or else developed speech while in the program (see table 5).

Finally, in order to give some objective criteria as to the cognitive capacity of the children involved in this study, it should be reported that none of them were able to achieve a normal I.Q. on formal intelligence

TABLE 3.   Length of Time in Treatment

Number	Subject	Male	Female	Total
1	C	12 months		12
2	E	27		27
3	F		28 months	28
4	G	33		33
5	H	24		24
6	S		14	14
7	L		27	27
8	Z		36	36
9	M	27		27
10	N		27	27
11	P	43		43
12	LS	28		28
13	SS	36		36
Total Scores		233	132	365
Mean Scores	$\overline{X}_1 = 29.1$ mos.	$\overline{X}_2 = 26.4$ mos.		$\overline{X}_3 = 28.1$ mos.

testing. Four of these children were initially reported to be untestable unless some rating was obtained by the use of an observational instrument such as the Vineland Social Maturity Scale. The wide variety of intelligence tests used with these children may be viewed as a reflection of the multifaceted nature of the children who fall into the category of ECA (see table 5).

DISCUSSION

An overall examination of the results of this follow-up study would seem to support the validity and utility of the structural therapy program that was provided for these thirteen cases of ECA. The fact that ten out of twelve patients who were originally diagnosed as cases of ECA continued to be maintained in the community as long as fifty-five months after discharge, is seen as evidence against the great pessimism which has been expressed over the course of treatment of such children.

It is also important to note that all of these children were placed in special education programs which had been developed for the mentally retarded and/or handicapped child. These children had been referred to such programs due to a view of ECA as developmental disorder, rather than a mental illness. The program of structural therapy had fo-

TABLE 4.   Length of Time Discharged

Number	Subject	Male	Female	Total
1	C	51[a] months		51
2	E	51		51
3	F		50 months	50
4	G	44		44
5	H	55		55
6	S		63	63
7	L		(53) 29[b]	29
8	Z		44	44
9	M	53		53
10	N		53	53
11	P	(52) [c]		(52)
12	LS	(37) 14[d]		14
13	SS	44		44
Total Scores		312	239	551
Mean Scores	$\overline{X}_1 = 44.6$ mos.	$\overline{X}_2 = 47.8$ mos.		$\overline{X}_3 = 45.9$ mos.

a. Subsequently hospitalized and discharged after two years.
b. Hospitalized twenty-nine months after discharge.
c. Discharged directly to institution for the retarded.
d. Hospitalized in institution for retarded fourteen months after discharge.
( ) Indicates that these figures are not included in totals.

cused upon the development of body image, object relations, and many of the early aspects of cognitive development. Predictability and consistency that stimulated and allowed for the development of curiosity and spontaneity were important aspects of the structural therapy treatment program in which these children participated (Ward, 1970a; 1972). Thus, after physical intrusiveness had been used to strengthen the body images of these patients, it was felt that their most important needs were for programs which would shore up and stimulate their emotional and cognitive growth in previously deficient areas. This is the reason that these children were referred to such programs, rather than to other therapeutically oriented programs that would have focused upon hypothesized intrapsychic conflicts that were based upon a mental illness model. Thus, although structural therapy is strongly indebted to many psychoanalytic concepts, as well as developmental Piagetian concepts, it has attempted to integrate those two divergent theoretical positions into a unified treatment method.

TABLE 5. Presence of Speech and Level of Intelligence

Number	Subject	Male	Female	I.Q. Test	Date	Score
1	C	Echolalia		WISC Stanford-Binet	9/71	I.Q. = 49 I.Q. = 30
2	E	Echolalia		Leiter	1964	I.Q. = 50.4
3	F		Speech 9 Years	Leiter	3/67	I.Q. = 59
4	G	None		Leiter	11/67	I.Q. < 2 yrs.
5	H	Echolalia		Vineland Stanford-Binet	1965 11/60	S.Q. = 58 I.Q. = 31
6	S		Echolalia Speech	Vineland	9/67	S.Q. = 21
7	L		10 Years Speech	Merrill-Palmer Stanford-Binet	10/60 10/59	I.Q. = 30 I.Q. = 43
8	Z		11 Years	Stanford-Binet	2/69	I.Q. = 33
9	M	Isolated Words		Vineland	10/62	S.Q. = 27
10	N		None	Untestable		
11	P	Echolalia		Untestable		
12	LS	None		Vineland	1962	S.Q. = 61
13	SS	None		Stanford-Binet	4/67	I.Q. = 15

It is hoped that the presentation of this follow-up data will aid, however slightly, in achieving the following outcomes:

1. The view of ECA as a developmental disorder that has a multi-faceted etiology, rather than as a mental illness of purely psychogenic etiology.

2. An emphasis upon the development of treatment programs that continually attempt to integrate the most current data on early (less than two years of age) child development of both a cognitive and affective nature.

3. Encourage all parents of such children and those who work with them to set realistic goals for these children based upon the actual capacities, rather than to give up hope because of slow progress towards unrealistic goals.

REFERENCES

DES LAURIERS, A. M. *The experience of reality in childhood schizophrenia*. New York: International Universities Press, 1962.

DES LAURIERS, A. M. & CARLSON, C. F. *Your child is asleep*. Homewood, Ill.: Dorsey Press, 1969.

HANDFORD, H. A. & WARD, A. J. Structural therapy: A developmental approach to the treatment of early infantile autism. *Schizophrenia*, 1969, 1 (4) : 243–248.

ORNITZ, E. & RITVO, E. Neurophysiologic mechanisms underlying perceptual inconstancy in schizophrenic and autistic children. *Archives of General Psychiatry*, 1968, 19: 22–27.

ROFFWARG, H. P.; DEMENT, W. E.; & FISHER, S. Preliminary observations of the sleep-dream pattern in neonates, infants, children and adults. E. Harms (Ed.), *Problems in sleep and dreams of children*. New York: Pergamon Press, 1964.

SPITZ, R. *The first year of life*. New York: International Universities Press, 1965.

STECHLER, G. & LATZ, E. Some observations on attention and arousal in the human infant. *Journal of the American Academy of Child Psychiatry*, 1966, 5: 517–525.

WARD, A. J. Early infantile autism: An etiologic hypothesis. Paper presented at Meeting of American Association of Psychiatric Clinics for Children in Boston, Massachusetts, in November 1969.

————. The application of structural therapy to the residential treatment of early infantile autism. *Schizophrenia*, 1970, 2 (2,3) : 92–102. (a)

————. Early infantile autism: Diagnosis, etiology, and treatment. *Psychological Bulletin*, 1970, 73 (5) : 350–362 (b)

————. These are not autistic children. Paper presented at Meeting of Third International Congress of Social Psychiatry in Zagreb, Yugoslavia, in July 1970. (c)

————. The effect of structural therapy in the treatmeat of a self-mutilating autistic child: A case report. Paper presented at meeting of American Association of Psychiatric Services for Children in Philadelphia, Pa., in November 1970. (d)

————. The multiple pathways to autistic behavior. Paper presented at annual meeting of the American Psychological Association in Washington, D.C., on September 4, 1971.

————. The use of structural therapy in the treatment of autistic children. *Psychotherapy: Theory, Research, and Practice,* 1972, 9 (1): 46–50.

RETROSPECTIVE

15

A State Hospital
Research Unit for
Autistic Children:
Five Years' Experience

H. Allen Handford and
Alan J. Ward

The Autistic Children's Treatment, Training and Research Service (ACTTRS) is a 36-bed research unit within a 210-bed state children's psychiatric hospital. Eastern State School and Hospital (ESSH), just north of Philadelphia in Trevose, Pennsylvania, is a relatively young hospital which hired its first professional staff in July, 1962, and admitted its first patient in May, 1963.

HISTORICAL BACKGROUND

Because of the basic service mandate (as opposed to training or research objectives) to the staff of Eastern, the pragmatic reasons for the establishment of this special treatment, training, and research unit bear some historical review. As the hospital entered its third year of service to in-patients, it became evident to the directors of the various diagnostically heterogeneous units of children that within their subpopulations were an ever-increasing number of nonverbal, relatively regressed autistic and autistic-like children. Moreover, other than a nursing directed, nursery school type of activities program, there were no specific treatment programs for these patients. They were generally considered to be inaccessible to the usual psychotherapies, and drug therapy, when employed, was primarily useful for controlling severe hyperactivity. Intermingled in the living areas with functionally more adequate but nevertheless seriously emotionally disturbed boys and girls representing a broad diagnostic spectrum, the autistic children constituted an anomalous untreated population of potentially life-time custodial cases occupying an ever-increasing percentage of the total hospital beds.

In March, 1966, with the number of such children standing at fifty-nine in-patients and an additional fourteen out-patients waiting for beds, thirteen of the lowest functioning developmentally were grouped in the twenty-bed new treatment and research unit for autistic children. Our expressed objectives were to study the diagnostic entity of "autism" in greater depth through direct observation, detailed review of records, and casework with parents; and to develop and study treatment methods designed to breach the emotional barrier that seemed to set these children apart. At the same time, the balance of these children in the hospital population continued to be cared for in two other twenty-bed units where the emphasis was on behavior control through drug therapy employing common tranquilizers. Within nine months, the arrival of seven new admissions and one day-patient had increased the census of our research unit to twenty-one patients (fifteen boys and six girls).

ORGANIZATION

The staff composition of the initial research unit was essentially the same as that of the other hospital treatment units: namely a child psychiatrist director, head nurse, and child care workers covering three eight-hour tours of duty. In addition, a psychiatric social worker was responsible for working with the parents, and psychological services were provided as needed. In September, 1966, however, the unique nature of the unit was recognized administratively with the assignment of a clinical research psychologist to the staff. The pragmatically basic treatment-research nature of the unit was then fully established with the agreement to share directorship responsibilities between the child psychiatrist and clinical research psychologist collaborators.

DIAGNOSIS

Once organizational matters were resolved, the first order of business was to define our criteria for the diagnosis of early infantile autism (EIA). Our hope was to study the disease entity in pure culture. (We did not realize how elusive a goal we had set up.) To provide guidelines for our research and for the evaluation of new cases being referred we wrote at the time:

> The following criteria shall be used to select all future admissions to the unit. These children must display the following criteria to be given a diagnosis of Early Infantile Autism: Deficiencies in ego functioning dating from early infancy (before 18 months of age) as follows:
>
> 1. Inability or refusal to form human object relationships.
> 2. Repetitive primitive motor behavior and the need to maintain sameness in behavior and environment (reacting to change or interruption by rage, panic or withdrawal).
> 3. Failure to develop the ability to communicate through speech and language. Speech, if present, is imitative or echolalic.
>
> Such deficiencies are found to exist in the absence of specifically defined neurological disorders.

We came to find that not only did just one patient of our original thirteen meet these strict diagnostic points for EIA, but that by the time our beds were full and our census at twenty-one, only four patients, upon extended examination and study in depth of early medical and developmental records, met the criteria. We were gradually coming face to face with one of the most important findings of our five-year experience, namely that the entity of EIA, which was of admittedly low reliability and validity from both a clinical and research point of view, was becoming ruinously diluted as a useful category. The reason for this seemed to be that any or all of the behavioral or historical signs attributed to the syndrome could be present in children with other more specific neurological disorders and forms of mental deficiency. Indeed, EIA had quite obviously become a "wastebasket" category used for the referral of all manner of difficult diagnostic cases, primarily nonpsychological in etiology, to a state children's psychiatric hospital (Ward and Handford, 1968). Thus, in our first twenty cases there were seven children with primary retardation, two with secondary retardation, two with developmental retardation due to diffuse brain damage, and five with a higher level of childhood schizophrenia, in addition to the four with EIA.

With our beds full, the next phase of our program involved a two-pronged approach to the basic problems of mis-diagnosis and inappropriate referrals, and the development of an effective treatment method for the children who did have EIA.

TREATMENT

An intrusive and playful treatment approach labelled Structural Therapy (Des Lauriers and Carlson, 1969; Handford and Ward, 1969; Ward, 1970) was introduced for use with the children with specific EIA in order to render them more accessible to appropriate remedial education programs. This therapy, developed originally by Des Lauriers for use with catatonic schizophrenic adolescents, consisted of directly and playfully interrupting the maladaptive withdrawal and stereotyped behavior being defensively utilized by the patient to maintain sameness. The therapy was designed to impart structure to the child's behavior, comparable to that of the normally developing infant, by a very intrusive exaggerated imitation of the activities of the normal mother of a newborn. Laughing, singing, shouting, whispering, strolling, tickling, hugging, rubbing, romping, running, and wrestling, combined with a progressive delineation of body parts and the use and fostering of baby talk were used with striking success to break through the autistic barrier in the four pure EIA cases, as well as in the retarded and neurologically handicapped showing autistic features. All began to develop speech and language and sustained interest in educational tasks appropriate to their respective developmental levels. Members of all professional disciplines functioned as individual therapists, and were trained and supervised by the clinical psychologist.

A brief listing and description of the ACTTRS meeting schedule will further convey the type of structure under which the unit functioned best:

1. Monday morning—Weekend report was usually administered by one of the codirectors and was attended by the charge nurses, social workers, psychologists, and the other individual therapists. Behavior and problems of children and families over the weekend were summarized and plans and assignments made for handling them.

2. Tuesday—Therapy Seminar was directed by the clinical psychologist and provided an opportunity for therapists to present current details and problems with their individual cases. This meeting also provided opportunity for therapists to express and share their feelings of frustration, anger, and depression about the intense work and slow progress of working with these severely disturbed young children. This feeling on the part of the therapists has been labelled the "vacuum chamber-experience," as many therapists have talked of providing so much stimulation to the autistic child without seeing any immediate observable effects. Indeed, many excellent structural therapists have come to question not only their therapeutic skill, but also their effectiveness as human

beings. Thus, it was both necessary and invaluable to institute this meeting as a type of "decompression chamber" for our therapists.

3. Wednesday—A group meeting with the child care workers and the psychiatrist. The purpose of this meeting was to reinforce the overall philosophy of stuctural therapy with those staff who had the longest contact with the children during their hospitalization, and to let them know the details of the treatment approaches that were being used with the children. Also, this meeting provided an opportunity for the child care workers to raise questions about the handling of individual problems with the families or the children.

4. Thursday—Grand Rounds and Treatment Planning Conference were combined and conducted by the codirectors. This was the one meeting which all staff, including child care workers, attended. Therapeutic assignments, diagnoses, and administrative decisions and recommendations were made at this meeting.

SCREENINGS

Simultaneously, we were screening about one child monthly referred for possible admission to the research unit. Applying the same strict criteria for EIA and the same goals of normal family socialization and appropriate education in the community, we ruled out admission and actively participated in planning geared to the specific treatment and educational needs of some fifty children over the past five year period. A wide range of children, presented for screening for admission to ACTTRS, were labelled as "autistic." Not only did the great majority of these children fail to meet our research criteria for an EIA diagnosis, but they also seemed unlikely to meet any kind of consistent criteria. We were presented with a veritable potpourri of childhood psychopathology that only emphasized the current lack of knowledge and facilities for children in our society. The children that we screened ranged from an almost completely normal and verbal four-year-old boy, whose I.Q. was tested at 112 (Stanford-Binet), and who was living in a restrictive and nonstimulating environment, to an eleven-year-old severely retarded little girl whose muscle strength was so poor that she was unable to get up if placed prone on the floor. Many of these children were either severely or moderately retarded, with concomitant brain damage often resulting from birth injuries, or early fevers and infections. Also, delayed or partial speech or vocalization was often presented as a problem. The label of "hyperactive" or "hyperkinetic" was often placed upon children who were simply displaying a curiosity and exploratory drive that was appropriate to their mental age but not their chronological age. A "terrible two" who is actually six or ten years old is admittedly difficult to handle, but this does not necessarily require psychiatric hospitalization.

Thus, although several of these children were admitted to ACTTRS, the vast majority were not. Instead, the ACTTRS team functioned in a consulting capacity for the referring family and agency. We often found these children to be in need of speech therapy and exposure to the social functioning and stimulation of children functioning at their mental age. Therefore, a screening report might recommend parental counselling based on the developmental level of the child and the type of handling needed, out-patient speech therapy for the child on a once or twice a week basis, and enrollment of the child in a normal nursery school.

Concurrently, in September, 1968, we expanded our program to three twelve-bed cottages, accepting twenty-four children, sixteen of whom were loosely diagnosed cases from other units within the hospital in need of educational planning and placement, and eight of whom were new admissions.

TREATMENT SERVICES

Home Visits and Placements

To further foster socialization and early educational experience, three children were enrolled in nursery school programs for normal children outside the hospital where they were assisted in their adjustment by a familiar child care worker from the unit. In addition, every child spent weekends and holidays with either his own or volunteer family, and extensive casework was done with the parents to enable them to handle their child in ways appropriate to the developmental level attained. These efforts were all directed toward helping these severely unsocialized children to learn to behave in a more normal social environment than that of the hospital, with a view toward their ultimate return to the community and to their homes. Foster homes were considered for those whose families were unable to accept the responsibility for their care, even with support, or were completely unavailable. Such homes were difficult to find, partly due to the reluctance of placement agencies to make available their foster homes to children developmentally far below their chronological ages. In one case where placement was achieved, the child further increased his use of speech and was able to go on a school bus to a public school class for the retarded.

Social Work

The social workers have played an extremely important role in the functioning of ACTTRS. This is due to the fact that the majority of the families of the children admitted to our service are initially quite angry, depressed, and resistive to mental health professionals. The social workers deal with these feelings, tell the families the details of the treatment approach in collaboration with the individual therapist, and help the family adjust their expectations to the capacity of the child. Weekly contact is made with each family and the social workers are available by phone to help deal with problems that occur during home visits.

The other important aspect of the social workers' functioning has been work with community agencies regarding both admissions and discharges. Thus, the social workers must explain in detail the type of child that we feel we can help. Also, during the discharge process, the social workers must work with various agencies and schools that provide programs for our children, but are fearful or resistant to the idea of providing services to a child who has been in a mental hospital.

Speech Therapy

Within the clinical program, as the children became more accessible and workable, the expertise of the speech therapy department was enlisted for more specific diagnostic and therapeutic service, with the focus on the further acquisition of speech and language. Two children were determined to be congenitally deaf and were involved in a group and individual sign language program, while services for the retarded deaf were sought for them in the community. Other children with hearing deficiencies due to chronic middle ear infections received vigorous medical treatment, including myringotomies where indicated. In total, up to sixty percent of all the children in the cottages, both EIA and non-EIA, were included in individual or group speech and language stimulation.

Psychological Evaluation

Our experience has indicated the need for the use of infant tests in arriving at an adequate estimate of the intellectual capacity and cognitive deficits of autistic and autistic-like children regardless of their age. Tests which we have found to be particularly useful are:

1. Bayley Developmental Scales
2. Gesell Developmental Schedules
3. Leiter International Performance Scale

4. Merrill-Palmer Scale of Mental Tests
5. Peabody Picture Vocabulary
6. Stanford-Binet Intelligence Scale (Form L-M).

Developmental evaluations of scribbling and drawing are also often quite informative.

Educational Placement and Program

With correction of diagnoses of children already admitted, we set out to determine their levels of intellectual functioning and to actively seek more appropriate educational programs for the retarded and neurologically handicapped among them. Our goal was their return to the normal socialization experiences of family life, or to an institution specifically for the retarded when their family could not accept them. Of thirteen discharges followed up in May, 1970, eleven were living at home, ten of whom were in classes for the retarded. Two were in institutions for the retarded. One was in a class for children with emotional problems. Subsequently, one more of the children living at home required an institution for the retarded.

Finally, as the accessibility of the children to the learning process became more and more evident, attention was turned toward the intensification and refinement of the educational program, heretofore a nursing directed preschool operation focused upon the constant repetition of simple tasks. The concept of prescriptive teaching for each child was introduced for eight boys and girls to further prepare them for placement in special education classes in their communities. Emphasis was upon the teaching of basic skills across the entire spectrum of ego functions, and in the order of normal child development.

CONCLUSIONS

To conclude, research has been the handmaiden of clinical therapy in our program to study and treat EIA. We have attempted to carefully study all aspects of our endeavors since 1966, and have evolved a comprehensive multidisciplinary approach to the care, treatment, and management of this most serious childhood mental disorder. In summary, several points should be made:

1. Structural therapy is a viable treatment approach for engaging EIA cases and other severely ego-deficient children in the treatment process
2. The majority of autistic or autistic-like children are in need of

special educational programs, rather than classical psychotherapy, and thus should be dealt with on an out-patient basis rather
than hospitalized

3. A developmental and structural point of view seems to be more
useful in dealing with autistic and autistic-like children than a
strictly psychodynamic point of view

4. Autism seems to be more of a developmental disorder related to
a stimulation deficit or distortion in early life. Also, autism may
be viewed as a part of the spectrum of deviant ego development
that results from this stimulation deficit, rather than as a specific
diagnostic entity (Ward, 1971)

5. Early diagnosis and treatment can almost completely obviate the
need for the hospitalization of autistic and autistic-like children

6. Hospitalization of these children without the appropriate treatment and educational programs can lead to a deterioration that
results in life-long institutionalization

7. Hospitalization should only be used until the child has developed relationships with people; self-care such as toileting, feeding, and dressing; communication of simple needs in a consistent
manner; and the capacity to follow simple directions.

REFERENCES

DES LAURIERS, A. M. & CARLSON, C. T. *Your child is asleep: Early infantile autism.*
Homewood, Ill.: Dorsey Press, 1969.

HANDFORD, H. A. & WARD, A. J. Structural therapy: A developmental approach to
the treatment of early infantile autism. *Schizophrenia*, 1969, 1 (4) : 243–248.

WARD, A. J. & HANDFORD, H. A. Early infantile autism: Syndrome, symptom, or
wastebasket? Paper presented at the Midwestern Psychological Association
meeting in Chicago on May 2, 1968.

WARD, A. J. The application of structural therapy to the residential treatment
of early infantile autism. *Schizophrenia*, 1970, 2 (2,3) : 92–102.

—————. The multiple pathways to autistic behavior. Paper presented at the annual meeting of the American Psychological Association in Washington,
D.C., on September 4, 1971.

16

Childhood Autism: The Role of Residential Treatment

It has long been a practice to recommend extended residential treatment for children diagnosed as cases of Early Infantile Autism (EIA or Early Childhood Autism (ECA). However, six years of experience in a residential setting devoted to the treatment of these children raises severe questions as to the value of such extended separations from the family and the community. The original rationale for such recommendations had its roots in a view of the family as the source of the child's pathology, as well as the expectation that the child would be immersed in a twenty-four-hour-a-day, seven-day-a-week therapeutic program. Both of these assumptions now seem to be quite doubtful.

BACKGROUND

This paper is based upon the clinical and research experience of the thirty-six-bed Autistic Children's Treatment, Training and Research Service (ACTTRS), which was organized at our institution in 1966 (Handford & Ward, 1969; Handford & Ward, 1972; Ward, 1971; and Ward, 1972a). The initial research diagnosis of Early Infantile Autism (EIA) required the characteristics of:

1. Lack of object relations from birth
2. Lack of the use of speech for communication
3. Maintenance of sameness via stereotypic behavior
4. Lack of neurologic or developmental dysfunction.

211

However, application of these diagnostic criteria supported earlier state-ments as to the rarity of EIA (Kanner, 1949; Wing, 1966), and demon-strated that many children have been mistakenly diagnosed as cases of EIA (Ward & Handford, 1968). Thus, our population included many chil-dren who failed to meet the fourth diagnostic criterion of a "lack of neu-rological or developmental dysfunction," as well as some cases of child-hood schizophrenia. However, most of these children did meet the first two criteria of disturbed object relations and verbal communication. Re-flection upon the above facts, combined with extensive individual in-tensive structural therapy (Handford & Ward, 1969; Ward, 1972a), led to the decision to regard these children as cases of ECA (Ward, 1972b), defined as a developmental disorder rather than a type of childhood schizophrenia, and found to be responsive to a developmentally oriented type of treatment that used many of the concepts of both psychoanalytic theory as well as the writings of Piaget.

Children have been referred to ACTTRS who have presented a tre-mendous range and variety of problems including mutism, echolalia, hy-peractivity, assaultiveness, self-mutilation, isolation, stereotypic behavior, slow development, deafness, seizure activity, and so forth. All of these chil-dren were found to be responsive to structural therapy (Ward, 1972a), of which the treatment goals at ACTTRS have been:

1. Development of a stable relationship with another human being
2. Understandable communication of needs to another human being
3. The development of self-care skills such as dressing, feeding, and toileting
4. The ability to follow simple one- or two-part directions.

An individual therapist had to be assigned to see the child on at least a twice a week basis to attain the above goals. Experience has shown that most newly admitted cases of ECA can reach these goals within a period of six months or less. However, children who have been institutionalized for an extended period of time may take up to two years to attain the same goals. This seemed to be due to the fact that these children had gained extensive practice in their maladaptive behavior, because of their lack of involvement in an appropriate treatment program.

The attainment of these treatment goals disclosed children who functioned at a wide variety of developmental levels, regardless of their chronological ages. The observed styles of relating of these children ranged from analogues of the "stranger anxiety" of the eight-month-old infant, to the symbiotic behavior of the one- to two-year-old child, to the aggressive negativism of the "terrible two." A major result of structural therapy was the development of, or rekindling of, the exploratory drive that is so prominent in the behavior of young infants and children. This was seen as being the result of a determined effort to make the surrounding environment attractive, interesting, and rewarding. Thus, rather than focusing upon one aspect of behavior such as speech, food or behavior; the child was encouraged to learn to examine all aspects of the environment from leaves, ice cream cones, and escalators to faces and riding bicycles and playing ball. All efforts were made to stimulate the child's interest in the environment so that he would spontaneously try to deal with it himself and find the activity itself reinforcing, rather than having to rely upon an external reinforcer. Although all efforts were made to support this behavior, it soon became obvious that a residential setting was inappropriate to children who had attained this level of functioning. The situation was analogous to trying to raise thirty-six infants and young children at various stages of development and handicap in a setting that could be only minimally responsive to them for eight hours a day on a five-day-a-week basis.

EFFECTS UPON FAMILY

Residential placement of an ECA child has often been described as being the last resort, but the experience of ACTTRS is that it is often sought as the first source of treatment. The child may have been seen in many settings for diagnostic evaluations, but it is rare that any attempt at extended treatment of any type is made on an out-patient basis prior to hospitalization. This process may take up to five years, during which time the family is quite often told that they are psychologically responsible for their child's condition and the child gets no treatment at all. Thus, as the years go by, the family's guilt and depression increases while the child's behavior deteriorates. This deterioration of the child's behavior usually makes him the focus of all the frustrated rage in the family, and hospitalization quite often plays into an acting out of the family's psychological rejection of the child. In other cases, hospitalization of the ECA child fixates one or more family members at whatever stage of depression they were enduring at the time of admission. Another situation which often occurs is based upon the open expression of rage at mental health professionals. This occurs in those families who have been given multitudinous explanations for their child's behavior that all completely ignore whatever information the family has to give. These families will often directly say that the agency should completely cure the child before they will take the child back into the home.

One of the major effects of the above situations is to make the family unavailable to the child. This is a basic error that often results in lifetime institutionalization of ECA children. This is due to the fact that successful attainment of the goals of structural therapy discloses a young child who needs the attention and support of a family to raise him. Before the family can once again be made available for the ECA child, a great deal of counseling must be done to eradicate the feelings of rejection, depression, and rage. Thus, except for those children who are truly assaultive or self-mutilating, the staff of ACTTRS has found few ECA children who could not be treated on an out-patient basis. Oftentimes, those ECA children who are thought to have a pathological symbiotic relationship with a parent are later found to have some subtle neurologic dysfunction that has retarded their development and necessitated extra help from that parent. All attempts should be made to keep an ECA child in the family; to provide help to the family in caretaking; and to locate the appropriate out-patient treatment, speech therapy, and special education programs.

RESIDENTIAL TREATMENT

When the ECA children have reached the four goals set by structural therapy, experience has indicated that their needs for increasing varied stimulation cannot be met within a residential treatment setting. These children need to physically and visually explore their environment, to experiment with vocalization and speech and auditory stimuli, to be exposed to and interact with children functioning on their own and on a somewhat higher developmental level, and to develop more extensive relationships with their parents or selected parent-surrogates. However, this developmental progress means that these children become much more in need of personalized attention than they were when much more isolated. Failure to provide the above experiences on a full-time basis has resulted in a deterioration and gradual loss of previously attained skills. Thus, children who had developed speech would gradually stop speaking, those who became calmer and more manageable became hyperactive, those who had become toilet trained became more erratic, and so forth.

It seemed as if once a child had been taught to focus upon the ex-

ternal environment, that he soon exhausted the experiences available
to him in a residential setting, and required the type of total program
and attention that could only be provided in a family or a foster home.
Failure to remove the child from the residential setting after the attainment of treatment goals seemed to result in a type of sensory deprivation
that rather quickly called forth aspects of the maladaptive behavior which
had caused the initial hospitalization.

DISCUSSION

The overall result of the experience of ACTTRS is one that questions the large scale referrals for residential treatment for children diagnosed as cases of ECA. This is due to the fact that many families are often
made to suffer unnecessary guilt and anxiety or else are encouraged to
act out their fantasies of child rejection by the hospitalization of their
child. Clinical experience indicates that successful therapy with ECA children reveals children functioning on varied developmental levels, who
are in need of special education programs and the familial care and affection appropriate to a much younger child. Many aspects of most successful treatment programs can be carried on on an out-patient basis without
separating the child from his family.

Placement in a residential treatment setting is appropriate for those
assaultive or self-mutilative children who cannot safely be maintained
in the community, but should only be continued until the basic presenting problem has been dealt with, and the goals of improvement in object
relations, self-care, and communication have been met. Then all efforts
should be made to provide a therapeutic program in the community
which would allow the child to be returned to his family. Community
resources such as day nurseries, sheltered workshops, community mental
health centers, day programs for retarded children, special classes in the
public schools, and homemaker services should be explored. This recommendation is based upon the observed inadequacy of many residential
settings in dealing with large numbers of ECA children.

The inability of many residential settings to deal with large numbers
of ECA children after they have reached the above described level of development seems to be due to a strict financial and emotional problem.
The improved ECA child requires more attention on a one-to-one basis
over a longer period of time in many varied areas than he did prior to
this change. Thus, whereas three or four staff might have been adequate
to work with twelve ECA children at their admission, the demands stimu-

lated by therapeutic improvement in these children might only be capable of being met by a staff of six to eight people. Most agencies are unable to provide such an increase in staff, and this results in an inability to meet the needs of the child. This inability usually has a negative effect upon the attitude of the staff, and often lessens their ability to continue doing their excellent job in more restricted areas. Anxiety, anger, and feelings of inadequacy are stirred up in staff who can see that the children need more attention and special programming, but are realistically unable to provide it. This is the time that these children should be returned to their families and the community.

RECOMMENDATIONS

Residential treatment should only be used for cases of ECA to remove the barrier of autistic isolation when it is combined with assaultive or self-injurious behavior. Otherwise, these children should be treated on an out-patient basis to avoid the neutralization of the family as a major therapeutic agent and the sensory deprivation aspects of hospitalization.

ECA children should be referred for special educational programs as soon as their condition is diagnosed. This would encourage the involvement of special education personnel from the beginning, which is vital, as almost all of these children have shown a need for such programs subsequent to a positive response to treatment.

Families should be helped to view the problems of their ECA children from a developmental and educational point of view, as this usually enables them to focus their energies upon helping their child rather than upon their own guilt.

All agencies and legislators should be encouraged to view residential treatment of ECA children as only a relatively brief phase of programming, that then needs to be changed for a wide variety of out-patient programs. Thus, these children should be viewed as needing a complete spectrum of services that will *never* completely exclude the family or the community. Exclusion of either of these subjects ECA children to the danger of unnecessary lifetime institutionalization. Thus, residential treatment for ECA children must be viewed as only one of a number of therapeutic options. Furthermore, all such referrals should include a parallel referral for special educational services in the community. As these children progress, it becomes impossible for even a very good agency to match the job of child rearing that can be done by what is viewed as a very bad family when it is given help from the community.

REFERENCES

HANDFORD, H. A. & WARD, A. J. Structural therapy: A developmental approach to the treatment of early infantile autism. *Schizophrenia,* 1969, 1 (4): 243–248.

————. ACTTRS, A state hospital research unit for autistic children: Five years' experience. Paper presented at Eastern Psychiatric Research Association, Inc., in New York City on April 5, 1972.

KANNER, L. Problems of nosology and psychodynamics of early infantile autism. *American Journal of Orthopsychiatry,* 1956, 26: 556–564.

WARD, A. J. & HANDFORD, H. A. Infantile autism: Syndrome, symptom or wastebasket? Paper presented at Mid-Western Psychological Association in Chicago, Ill., on May 2, 1968.

WARD, A. J. Early childhood autism and structural therapy: Outcome after three years. Paper presented at a meeting of the Eastern Psychological Association in Boston, Mass., on April 27, 1972. (a)

————. The use of structural therapy in the treatment of autistic children. *Psychotherapy: Theory, Research and Practice,* 1972, 9 (1): 46–50. (b)

WING, J. K. *Early childhood autism: Clinical, educational and social aspects.* New York: Pergamon Press, 1966.

Author Index

219

Subject Index

About the Author

Alan J. Ward was co-director of the Autistic Children's Treatment, Training and Research Service of Eastern State School and Hospital, outside Philadelphia, from 1966 to 1974. His experiences at the center provided the basis for this book.

He also was director of psychological services at the institution as well as an instructor at the medical college of Thomas Jefferson University, Pennsylvania, and Temple universities. He currently is director of Henry Horner Children's Center in Chicago, a state facility for the treatment of emotionally disturbed children and adolescents.

After earning undergraduate degrees from Brandeis and Temple, he received his Ph.D. from the State University of New York at Buffalo. He undertook the study of autistic children during a two-year U.S. Public Health Service postdoctoral fellowship at Michael Reese Hospital's Psychosomatic and Psychiatric Institute in Chicago. It was here that he was exposed to the ideas and clinical skills of Austin Des Laurier, an early worker in the field.

He holds a certificate in clinical psychology from the American Board of Professional Psychologists (ABPP), has carried on the private practice treatment of severely disturbed adults and children over the last decade, and continues to be involved in the training of clinical psychologists, child psychiatrists, psychiatric social workers, and other mental health professionals. Dr. Ward is a member of the American Psychological Association, American Orthopsychiatric Association and National Society for Autistic Children, as well as many other professional societies and associations. He is also a Fellow of the Society of Personality Assessment, Inc.

Dr. Ward was a member of the executive board of the Philadelphia Society of Clinical Psychologists and a vice-president of the Philadelphia Society of Clinical Hypnosis.

He has contributed articles to the *Journal of Projective Techniques and Personality Assessment, Psychological Bulletin, Journal of the American Academy of Child Psychiatry,* and *Psychotherapy.*